This book is a must-read if...

- you want to read inspirational stories by others

- you like to read short stories you can dip in and out of as you choose

- you wish to immerse yourself in personal journeys of discovery

- you are looking to connect with like-minded female leaders who have experienced what you have

- you want to be inspired by others who are daring to raise their voice and change the world

- you want to be a change-maker and make a difference to the world around you

- you want to be inspired by people from different walks of life all over the world

"From building bridges to having one another's back, the stories contained herein showcase the effortless ways women solve problems.

It's my prayer that leadership of the future always includes more rich female perspectives which produce natural and speedy growth. Your anthology is another step on the right direction, helping women realise they've had the power all along.

Loved this from your contributor, Caroline Purvey: 'Reflecting now comes the realisation I had been leading all along without labelling myself as a leader.'"

Jeanne M Stafford

Leadership Advisor | Collaboration Specialist | Speaker
Creator of 'The Devotion Factor, Winning the War on Distraction'

"Too many stories have ignored women's voices, so this book is an important step in righting that imbalance. Eve's story — as someone who had little control over her early life — is particularly powerful and shows how women can escape to tell their own stories on their own terms."

Suzanne Heywood

Internationally Bestselling Author

"My grandmother was just 16 when the war splitting India into India and Pakistan erupted, forcing her to navigate harrowing choices interfacing her homelessness, her faith, and an arranged marriage. However, when probed, she'd attest that her toughest struggle wasn't the war, but her gender.

She'd whisper, 'A woman must first become the neck, not the crown, for a neck turns the head in the direction it desires.' Her advice carries a timeless wisdom. I find *Voices of Women* is built on this spirit. Each narrative offers the neck's subtle capacity to flex, extend, and rotate – read it and become the neck that guides your life."

Dr Ruby Kapadia D.O. M.S.

Executive Physician and Chief Medical Officer
Balance Medical Care LLC

"*Voices of Women* contributor Lyndsay Dowd is the real deal – and one of the most gracious connectors I know. You can trust her podcasts, speaking and writing to focus on inspiring, innovative ways we can be a better manager, communicator and person. As she says, 'Leadership doesn't have to be hard, it does have to be human.'

Be sure to have your pen or highlighter handy as you read. You're sure to discover 'I can use that today' insights you can use on and off the job to be a rising-tide force for good."

Sam Horn

CEO of The Intrigue Agency

"This book will help when you find professional and personal inspiration and advice."

Kim Mansfield

Family Law Associate, Pinney Talfourd Solicitors

"A book about remarkable women would always be a MUST READ, quite simply because it reminds you, that ordinary people, contain extra-ordinary within them if they have the courage to take the plunge.

I haven't yet come across all of those in this book but those that I have are an amazing example of self-belief in the face of adversity, courage and a YES, WE CAN attitude. Caroline Purvey has developed an amazing self-healing practice that I would not be without and her book *Feel It to Heal It* is also on that MUST READ list, as it will show you that almost any adversity can be surmounted.

This book is an amazing journey through the lives, experiences, challenges, highs and lows of so many amazing individuals BUT here's the thing, THEY ARE YOU! Reading this book will hopefully be the start of your new incredible life!"

Jane Martin

Business Introducer and Connector | Hospitality Consultant | Federation of Small Businesses Advisor

"As an international leader in awareness for the Voice of Women, it has been an integral role to review this book, especially for the women that have been included. Every voice has a right to be heard, one which must not bring hatred but one that gives hope.

This book includes women who are also passionate about how they reflect to the world: their voice has a message and also offers a gift to understand who they are by revealing themselves and their purpose. Many of these ladies come with high academic credentials alongside human knowledge and experience on a personal level.

Brenda Dempsey demonstrates her skills as a professional publisher and showcases each individual to stand out from the bookshelf with their unique skills, personalities and in-depth knowledge. This allows the reader the enjoyment of understanding from the onset of a great book that will make you feel like there is hope and you can achieve after understanding the background of each female voice.

Caroline Purvey, for example, has demonstrated in her voice how we can become free of trauma. A highly academic leader shows her strength through her writing capabilities to explain what she can do to help eliminate pain we hold from years of suffering trauma that we may believe we have dealt with, but actually haven't. Caroline's passion is deeply reflected in her chapter, but embedded in how she leads.

Leading with compassion, confidence and control of the voice is demonstrated by every female in the book."

Dr Lady Kendal Jaggar

Journalist | Radio Presenter | Critic | Author | Speaker

"This book offers testimony from a diverse range of inspiring women, who have stepped into leadership with strength and power. It is a welcome and timely addition to urgent debates about how women can find their voices, motivate and lead themselves and others to a better world. Eve's story, particularly, shows how women can overcome the most difficult of circumstances in order to forge their own paths and to write their own stories."

Dr Sarah Dustagheer

Reader in Early Modern Literature at the University of Kent

"From the very first moment you meet Amanda, you are instantly reeled in by her infectious positive energy. Blessed with a special gift for engaging little ones, Amanda exudes a natural, effortless and sparkling style of leadership drawing directly from her innate desire to champion those around her.

With a client list of dreams, Amanda's innovative approach to making development fun at all ages, her children's and independent business events alike shine a light on her ability to bring out the best in people. Truly, there is no one quite like Amanda."

Tracy Stone, Cl.Hyp, CPPD, ARTT, GHR (Reg.)

Founder of The CEO Whisperer and Limitless Potential

"Lyndsay Dowd, Chief Heartbeat Officer at Heartbeat for Hire, is a remarkable force in the realm of leadership. With years of hands-on leadership experience, Lyndsay possesses an acute understanding of the challenges modern leaders encounter. Her comprehensive insight into these issues sets her apart as an expert who not only comprehends, but also effectively addresses the complexities of leadership today.

Through her podcast, book, writing, coaching and speaking engagements, Lyndsay empowers leaders to inspire their teams to achieve excellence. Her approach is both innovative and deeply practical, offering tangible strategies that drive real results. Lyndsay puts her heart and soul into everything she does and cares deeply about everyone she has the opportunity to help.

Lyndsay's ability to connect with her audience and provide actionable advice is unparalleled. Her passion for fostering strong, cohesive teams is evident in every facet of her work.

Lyndsay Dowd is more than a coach or a speaker; she is a true catalyst for change, helping leaders elevate their performance and lead with heart. It is an honour to endorse her exceptional contributions to the field of leadership."

Siri Lindley

World Champion Triathlete | One of Tony Robbins' favourite speakers

Other Anthologies by Brenda Dempsey

Voices of Courage, 2019

Voices of Hope, 2019

Resilient Voices, 2021

Voices of Strength, 2023

VOICES OF WOMEN

COMPILED BY

BRENDA DEMPSEY

First published in Great Britain in 2024
by Book Brilliance Publishing
265A Fir Tree Road, Epsom, Surrey, KT17 3LF
+44 (0)20 8641 5090
www.bookbrilliancepublishing.com
admin@bookbrilliancepublishing.com

Editing by Olivia Eisinger
Typesetting, design and proofreading by Zara Thatcher

A CIP catalogue record for this book is available
at the British Library.

ISBN 978-1-913770-87-7

Typeset in Garamond.

Articles correct at time of submission.

To all the trailblazing female leaders
who have shattered glass ceilings, defied expectations,
and paved the way for future generations.

Your courage, resilience, and unwavering commitment
to excellence inspire us all.

This book is dedicated to you,
the fearless women who continue to lead with grace,
strength, and determination.

May your stories empower and uplift others
on their own journey towards leadership and equality.

Thank you for being the guiding lights in a world
that is brighter because of your presence.

Contents

Foreword

Female leadership is about embracing femininity, strength, and authenticity. It is about staying true to ourselves and not being afraid to have a voice. It is important we don't get lost in the masculinity of the world. The power of femininity should never be ignored, nor suppressed.

For when one realises her own potential, listens to the soul within, and takes action from a place of intuition, faith and alignment, they become unstoppable.

From the stories within *Voices of Women*, it is clear to see that the women are unstoppable as they stride ahead with their missions to promote female leadership, encouraging and empowering other women to do the same.

We have a responsibility and duty of care to be role models and mentors, paving the way for future generations of talent.

In her chapter *You Can't Be What You Can't See*, Lyndsay Dowd exemplifies this concept by discussing a time when her boss asked her the question, "What's your story?" From her boss showing interest in Lyndsay's story, this prompted Lyndsay to use the same tactic with her team members. It is an excellent example of role modelling in leadership.

My corporate days in the early 2000s right up to 2017 were toxic cultures, created by men for men. Having a voice, speaking up and going against the grain was never favoured.

I've been bullied, fired, spoken over in meetings, and left out of the "boy's club". If you have made it to leadership, I guarantee you have too.

I always spoke up. It cost me jobs, my mental health and, in most instances, my confidence.

Upon reflection, I'm proud of always speaking up; I stayed true to who I am and my values. My favourite quote is:

> *"Each time a woman stands up for herself,*
> *she stands up for ALL women."*

> Maya Angelou

I particularly like the idea of each woman in *Voices of Women* giving their own quote at the start of each chapter. This illustrates what they are passionate about, and passion fuels commitment to achieve what you believe in, not only for yourself but others.

Since finding my WILD in 2018, I have been able to use my voice as a force for good. I speak, I act and I am a voice for the voiceless, a pioneer for reform and a trailblazer of gender equality.

In *Voices of Women*, there are many diverse voices, but they are all connected to a desire to support and empower others to be their best version and use their voice for good.

The WILD Woman is aligned to the voice of women, demonstrating courage, embracing authenticity, speaking up, and speaking out.

She is a role model, a beacon of hope, and a shining example of an embodied female leader. She is me. She is all of us.

Emma Burdett

Founder & CEO of WILD: Women in Leadership Deliver
www.wildwomenlead.com
www.linkedin.com/in/emma-burdett-4a16a617

Introduction

*"Every woman's success should
be an inspiration to another.
We're strongest when we cheer each other on."*

Serena Williams
American former professional tennis player

This powerful quote by tennis sensation Serena Williams encapsulates the essence of solidarity and empowerment among women. It reminds us that by celebrating each other's victories and supporting one another, we not only uplift individual spirits, but collectively strengthen the fabric of our communities. Let these words be a rallying cry for unity and encouragement, as together, we forge a future where every woman thrives.

Welcome to *Voices of Women*, an anthology of female leaders from the UK, USA, Barbados, the UAE, the Middle East, India, and Africa. This collection brings together the wisdom, experience, and insights of extraordinary women shaping the future across four diverse and interconnected regions.

From the vibrant landscapes of Africa to the bustling cities of the USA, UK and Dubai, these leaders represent a tapestry of strength, resilience, and innovation. Their stories, rooted in their unique cultural backgrounds, share a common thread of unwavering determination and a commitment to inspire change locally and globally.

Join us on a journey that transcends borders and celebrates the Voices of Women from diverse corners of the world, united in their mission to empower, uplift, and create change.

In the United Kingdom, we encounter leaders who blend tradition with modernity. These women are at the forefront of cultural and economic transformation, driving progress while honouring their heritage. Their journeys illustrate the delicate balance between embracing change and preserving core values. Through their narratives, we learn the importance of adaptability and the strength found in unity and diversity.

Across the Atlantic, in the United States and Barbados, we find trailblazers redefining industries and breaking glass ceilings. These women embody the spirit of innovation and resilience, navigating complex landscapes with grace and tenacity. Their stories are a testament to the power of determination and the impact of visionary leadership. They show us that with courage and conviction, anything is possible.

Oman and Dubai are synonymous with rapid growth and futuristic ambition in the Arabic region, which is rich, diverse, and welcoming. We meet pioneers who challenge norms and set new benchmarks. These leaders are shaping the business and education landscapes, and contributing to the global discourse on gender equality and empowerment. Their experiences highlight the dynamic interplay between ambition and opportunity in a region known for its bold vision and innovative spirit.

Women representing Anglo-Indians abroad embody a delicate balance of honouring their rich cultural heritage while seamlessly integrating into new cultural systems and ways of life. Through their resilience and adaptability, they serve as ambassadors of the Anglo-Indian culture, bridging the gap between their roots and the diverse communities they now call home.

With grace and determination, they preserve cherished traditions, cuisine, and customs, infusing them with a contemporary flair that resonates with their heritage and present surroundings. Their ability to navigate cultural complexities with poise and authenticity enriches their lives and fosters cross-cultural understanding and appreciation, creating vibrant tapestries of diversity wherever they go.

Our sisters representing Africa are beacons of cultural pride and heritage, weaving the rich tapestry of their traditions into every aspect of their leadership. Through their work and advocacy, they promote and preserve the diverse cultures of Africa, infusing them with modern relevance and global resonance.

From the rhythms of their languages to the vibrant hues of their attire, these women proudly showcase Africa's beauty and resilience. Their leadership is not just about achieving success, but also about honouring their roots and uplifting their communities, ensuring that the legacy of African culture continues to thrive on a global stage for generations to come.

The significance of women coming together in one voice cannot be overstated. When female leaders unite, they bring unique empathy, collaboration, and holistic thinking to the table, fostering environments where everyone can thrive.

This collective feminine energy is vital in narrowing the gender gap and creating a more balanced world. These women amplify their impact and pave the way for future generations by sharing their stories and supporting each other. Their united front is a powerful force for change, shaping a world where equality is not just an aspiration but a reality.

Each chapter of this anthology offers a unique perspective, yet together, they form a cohesive mosaic of leadership, resilience, and empowerment. These stories are more than personal achievements; they are beacons of hope and inspiration for future generations of female leaders worldwide.

As you delve into their experiences, will you be inspired to pursue your path with passion, purpose, and unwavering resolve?

Welcome to a celebration of leadership, a testament to the power of women's voices, and a glimpse into the future shaped by these remarkable leaders.

Voices of Women stands not just as a collection of stories, but as the founding cornerstone of a global movement. We extend an open invitation to all women from every corner of the globe to join us on this transformative journey.

Together, we ignite a beacon of hope and empowerment, inspiring the rise of women's voices to shape a world that embraces equality, diversity, and unity.

As founding members, we recognise the power within each of us to catalyse change and drive progress. Through solidarity and shared vision, we sow the seeds of a future where every woman's voice is heard, valued, and celebrated.

Join us in this noble endeavour as we pave the way towards an improved world where the collective strength of women propels us all to greater heights.

Brenda Dempsey

Bailey Merlin embodies the spirit of a dynamic, multifaceted leader deeply committed to personal development, ensuring she continually evolves into the best version of herself. When Bailey approached Book Brilliance Publishing with her dream of becoming a published author, she was pursuing a master's degree at Harvard University. Alongside her rigorous studies, she was simultaneously working in medicine and media.

As an author, educator and bi+ advocate, she understands the profound power of community and the pervasive issue of loneliness. Recognising this, she takes the initiative to create communities where none exist. Her book, *A Lot of People Live in This House*, reflects this commitment, exploring themes of community, especially during the isolating times of a pandemic.

Bailey's life experiences have taught her that authentic leadership involves delegation and trust. She believes in empowering others to excel, often referring to herself as a 'delegation machine.' This self-awareness and willingness to share responsibility are hallmarks of strong leadership.

Entering her thirties, Bailey embraces her role as a mentor and beacon for others in the bi+ community. Her journey is a testament to standing up, showing up, and shining brightly.

As you delve into the work of this articulate and inspiring author, you will see how effectively she uses storytelling to convey her points and keep readers engaged. Bailey Merlin's brilliance and leadership serve as a guiding light for many.

Brenda

Bailey Merlin

"*I believe that female leadership is not only essential, but transformative.*
My experiences as a writer, bi+ activist, and member of an intentional community have taught me the importance of inclusivity and collaboration in leadership. Women bring unique perspectives, empathy, and resilience to the table, qualities that are invaluable in addressing complex societal issues, and fostering healthier, more equitable communities."

Bailey Merlin

Building Community When You Cannot Find It

When I graduated with my master's degree from Harvard Medical School in 2023, I was at the lowest point in my life. On paper, it didn't make sense. In the span of nine months, I had gotten married, discovered a new direction for my career, written a thesis, and published a book. Which of those peaks were valleys? Yet, even as I cracked open the sparkling wine and received gorgeous bouquets, parts of me were so burnt out that I wasn't sure I'd ever feel alive again; I wasn't sure I even wanted to. But, as most people who have spent their lives caring for others know, giving up isn't an option. And what I learnt at Harvard was that people needed me. Specifically, bisexuals needed me, and they didn't even know it.

Now, of course, I'm being hyperbolic. Bisexuals don't need anything other than not having their identity invalidated or being shamed. The one thing I'd learnt in graduate school was that bisexuals, the focus of my thesis, were sick and lonely but that there wasn't a proven reason as to why. The lack of data is a result of "bisexual erasure," which is when bisexuals are not allowed to exist in either straight or queer spaces because they aren't "enough" of one or the other.

My initial thought for my thesis was to examine the loneliness epidemic in folks ages 18 to 29. When I conducted my initial literature review, I saw that LGBTQ+ populations were more likely to suffer from loneliness than heterosexuals, and that bisexuals were far and away the largest part of that population.

But how could that be? As a bisexual, I'd only ever met four or five people who told me they were bi (which doesn't mean I hadn't met more). Yet, here was a data set claiming that bisexuals made up the vast majority of the queer folks that this research team surveyed.

"Well," I said, "maybe they just found a particularly bisexual part of the country."

Allow me to pause to let you know that I'm using the term "bisexual" here for brevity's sake, but must clarify that "bi+" is the more inclusive term used in the community because it encompasses a range of plurisexuality (i.e. pansexual, polysexual, omnisexual, etc.).

I soon realised that the research team hadn't found a particularly bisexual town, but that the United States themselves are very bisexual. While only 7.2% of the American population openly identifies as LGBT+, over half of that number identifies as bisexual. That's nearly 14 million American adults. To put that into perspective, that's more people than the fourth-largest state in the union. If we gathered up all the bisexuals for an election, we'd be (unironically) a swing state.

So, where were all the bisexuals, and why were we so lonely? For my project, I determined to meet as many bisexuals as I could and talk to them about their experiences in and out of healthcare. I talked to 40 bisexuals in three weeks, and I kept hearing the same thing:

"I'm bi+, and I don't feel like I have a community designed for me. I wish I did, but oh well…"

This refrain stuck with me. How could it not? A large part of my burnout was due to my own lack of community. In May 2023, a time when I should have been celebrating graduation and the publication of my first book, I looked to my left and found no writing community, then looked to my right and found no bisexual community. How had that happened? Were there any other bisexuals who felt like me?

A glass of liquid courage and a TikTok rant later, I found my answer: bisexual authors wanted a community made just for them. So, the Bi+ Book Gang was born. The group was started as a place where bisexual writers (published and unpublished) could join together and support each other as artists. What started as a Discord channel has bloomed into a group that meets three times a week to work on projects, gets together for social events, reviews each other's work, and has recently expanded to host graduate-level writing workshops. There are members from around the world, some of whom have just started writing, and others who are bestselling authors. The best part? Members have told me that this group makes them feel like the most authentic versions of themselves.

I aim to have a flourishing community of a thousand bisexuals connected by their love of writing. In six months, we're already a tenth of the way there. Building a community should be done steadily to ensure that each new person who joins is welcomed, celebrated, and shown the ropes. I'm in no hurry.

Despite the sheer amount of organising and planning I do for this group, I don't see myself as a leader, but as more of a facilitator. Or rather, I did. Now, I realise that they are one and the same. Now, I recognise that by starting this writing group and getting more involved in bisexual advocacy, I am, in fact, a leader.

There is a difference between good leaders and poor leaders, a topic much discussed by business influencers. I'm sure you've seen the graphics in your LinkedIn feed. Poor leadership is a pyramid where power flows up to the top. Good leadership inverts the pyramid, with the leader at the bottom as the base for everyone else's success.

You see this kind of leadership most apparently in two places: the military and the food service industry. Having only served in the latter, I can say that a restaurant's success depends entirely on its leadership. Places run with a top-down approach, leaving their workers scrambling to meet the needs of a dinner rush while managers hide in offices worrying over receipts. Blessed is a kitchen with a chef who sees themselves as a shift's bedrock. They are calm under pressure, tag out teammates who need two minutes to scream in the walk-in cooler, celebrate wins, and take responsibility for failures. With a leader that gets on the line with you or handles unruly dinner guests, though, failures are fewer and farther between, and their staff are far more willing to go the extra mile.

Why? Because when leaders demonstrate with actions that the team is "in it together," it's much easier to want to support the leader's goals. At the end of the day, good leadership is an act of service. It is not *my* goal to be celebrated for having started a group for bisexuals that should have already existed. Instead, my goal is to make a space for those bisexual writers who may never have had a community where they could be themselves, feel safe, be seen, and have a chance to flourish as artists.

Being a leader isn't easy. Sometimes, that means making hard choices about the direction of your group and telling people they can't join your party because your goals don't align. Mostly, it means that you have to organise. A lot. Most of my work around the Bi+ Book Gang is finding times for events, checking in with members, reading their work, writing feedback, and sharing publication opportunities.

One of the hardest things about starting and facilitating a group is that you have to work diligently to encourage people to keep coming back. So many LGBTQ+ groups are started with the best of intentions but inevitably fall apart because the founder(s) can't keep up the momentum. I think of these moments as growing pains, which happen every six months or so in the first two years. After that, if you've got a core crew of participants, the group can see it through for however long you want to run it.

Because membership can ebb and flow, there can be moments when you, as a leader, do not feel nourished by your community. This is a normal feeling, even if it's less than ideal. Who wants to manage events that no one comes to? Why bother keeping things going if you're the only one who seems to care? Managing to remain optimistic and engaged becomes so hard!

I recently ran into this stumbling block myself, though it was expected. Six months into the Bi+ Book Gang, I noticed that attendance in our weekly accountability sessions was lower than usual, and our Discord chat channels had little tumbleweeds in them. It hurt my feelings. How could it not? After all, I'd spent so much time and energy nurturing this little seed of community, and it felt like no one respected or appreciated that effort.

Instead of running away, which I wanted to do instead of being vulnerable, I looked the problem in the face, got online, and wrote:

> *Hope everyone is doing well. I was chatting recently about how the Bi+ Book Gang is officially in that moment where a group either makes or breaks. We've been around for more than 6 months! We've run writing accountability groups twice a week, hosted our first workshop critique group, and have such a rich server. We have members from around the world! I'm so hopeful about our future.*
>
> *However! A lot of groups, especially LGBTQ+ groups, fall apart because of a lack of engagement (my pet theory: a lot of us are statistically more likely to be burnt out, sick, undermedicated, working 2+ jobs, you get it). I'm happy that our accountability groups have been roughly the same size (I'd always welcome more folks, of course), which is a good sign for me.*
>
> *I started the Gang because I didn't have a writing or bi+ community. When I met all of you, you said the same thing. We've had some great times! But as we settle into this post-6-month groove, I'm thinking about longevity. If as many*

people aren't showing up for the groups as usual, I want to know why so I can address the issue. When we chatted about your work that first time, I told you that the Bi+ Book Gang wasn't homework. I meant it! We (and me specifically) are here for you in whatever way you need, but I don't know what you need unless you tell me.

So, let's check in: What do you need from this community?

And then, the best possible thing happened: the community responded. They were vulnerable with me and each other. I learnt of sickness, cataclysmic life shifts, writer's block, and everything else under the sun. They told me they wanted to participate in the events but that it was hard to attend because of the timing. They told me they wanted classes. They told me they felt like imposters.

From there, the community took care of itself. They comforted one another with all the right words and resources. And me? Well, I moved the accountability meeting because nothing in a healthy community can remain fixed. The only issue was that an early morning Saturday session was requested, and I quite enjoy lingering in bed on the weekends. So, I said that I'd be happy to make the session but that I'd appreciate it if someone else could "captain" it, which just means to be the person who calls time and celebrates the wins. It's a small job, but all jobs have an impact. And blessedly, someone took over the role. Sometimes, I go to the session to get some work done and just enjoy the simple comfort of someone else running the show. It's important to be celebrated, even if it's just a little check mark and a smile.

and let down by those around me, was doing everything myself. I never asked for help, never trusted anyone to do as good a job as me. For a long time, I was right. When I moved to Boston and into an intentional community with seven strangers – the very plot of my novel, *A Lot of People Live in This House* – I was suddenly surrounded by kind, considerate, and successful humans who wanted to make my life easier. Over time, I let them. Once learning that other people were just as competent as I was, I became a delegation machine. "Could you do this?" and "Would you take that?" became everyday phrases.

Life got easier. I realised that I had a good sense of people and could identify a trustworthy and reliable person more often than not. That's why the Bi+ Book Gang is now full of so many good people. Not everyone will be a reliable facilitator, and I know that. It's okay. All communities are diverse. There are core group members and folks who come and go depending on the season. A group needs all kinds to grow. My core group meets regularly, we know about each other's lives, and I have people I trust to run the show when I need time away. My trust in them means I don't burn out, which will help the Bi+ Book Gang go far longer than six months.

Enjoying this group now makes me a little sad for a younger version of myself who didn't have a writing community or bisexual community. It's easy to be bitter about not getting the things you needed when you were young. But a community is here now, and that's what matters. Now, I get to offer the things and be the person I needed in college to someone else. What's better than that?

There are so many things that I wish I could tell young me that would have made this journey to leadership easier (though I have to wonder if I'd be the same type of leader that I am now). So perhaps instead, I'll offer this advice to the young folks reading this so that they might have an easier time developing real leadership skills:

1. **Spend time with people.** This goes beyond professional development courses or liking social media posts about management. You have to get out into the world and meet people, particularly people who are as unlike you as possible. I probably learnt the most about being a person when I worked in a restaurant. Seriously, there are few places where an 18-year-old host on her way to college and a 54-year-old bartender going to night school, raising a child, and going through a divorce are going to be best friends. You have to meet people who bring out the best and worst in you to understand the full spectrum of life. It's scary, but that's what makes it so rich.

2. **Learn how to say no; the sooner, the better.** Women have the bad habit of not feeling like they can say no. This is a social problem more than anything. Women are socialised to be amenable from birth for the sake of keeping others comfortable. It's why we are often overworked and underappreciated. Learning how to turn down a project, offer, or person is essential to leadership. You cannot and should not

do everything. Choose what resonates with you and makes sense for your schedule. It's better to do a few things well than a bunch of things half-assedly.

3. **Be kind to yourself.** This, perhaps more than anything else you hear in a seminar or learn from a workbook, is the most important part of being a leader. Yes, as a leader, you are responsible for people, but you are also responsible for yourself. Hold yourself to a high standard because leading by example is necessary, but if you stumble, don't spend the rest of your life engaged in self-flagellation. Make a mistake? Learn from it, integrate the lesson, and move on. You're human, too.

My 31st birthday is in June. After the tumult of my twenties, the shift into a new decade of life has felt like a relief. I'm glad I'm getting older. I'm glad that my younger friends see me as a mentor. I'm glad that I finally have the time and resources to start communities for people who have been historically marginalised and forgotten. I'm glad that I get to see bisexual writers become better at their craft and write beautiful books, essays, and poems that will speak to thousands of others. I'm grateful for the road that brought me here, and I have no idea where it's taking me next. What a beautiful mystery it is!

From the outset, Layla proudly embraces her Bengali heritage and culture. This passion and belief empower her to take on the world, no matter her role. As she progresses in her leadership journey within the National Health Service (NHS) in the UK, Layla's pride in her work is evident.

Understanding the importance of role models, Layla surrounds herself with exemplary leaders and learns to embody the best leadership qualities. She demonstrates this through her sensitivity and kindness when working with others, creating an environment where people feel at ease and valued.

Like most great leaders, Layla's journey is marked by transitions, challenges, and resilience. Life presents shiny obstacles – some to be ignored, others to be seized as great opportunities. Layla's openness about her experience with a financial scam provides hope and strength to others who have faced similar trials. Her willingness to share her vulnerabilities, especially concerning money, highlights her courage and commitment to helping others learn from her experiences.

As Layla continues on her leadership path, she exemplifies the traits of a servant leader. She commands respect through her actions and uses her sensitivity, gentleness, and compassion to make a significant impact on the lives of others. Layla's story is an inspiring testament to the power of embracing one's heritage, learning from role models, and leading with heart and integrity.

Brenda

Layla Begum Ali

*"Be like a fragrance
and impactful on others."*

Layla Begum Ali

From the Bay of East Bengal Village to Leadership

The Pivotal Moment

Leadership in My Work as an NHS Business Planning Manager

I am an approachable person and am keen on self-improvement, both personally and professionally. In my current line of work, I am surrounded by experts, collaborators and mentors who inspire my leadership planning.

I am also a mindful person and use my cognitive empathy to understand others, build a meaningful presence and to speak to people in ways that they understand.

Self-awareness and working collaboratively with diverse groups, building rapport and relationships, are very important to me. I am what I do, and I do what I can to impact services and others without being overbearing (especially in NHS patient care services, to improve their well-being).

Leadership in My Community

My mindful leadership begins in my community, Tower Hamlets in East London. My purpose is to mentor youths, widows, single parents, and those who are vulnerable in my Bangladeshi community. My roots are here in Tower Hamlets – growing up in a council estate in the borough, and navigating my life to where I am now today. I have been exposed to many of the same problems and issues that these vulnerable people are dealing with, and want to show them empathy and help them to empower themselves.

Leadership in My Personal Life

Arriving in England aged eight, along with four other siblings from a village in Sylhet, North Bangladesh, I struggled with English as it was my second language. But I was the rebel middle child who vocalised my views and ambitions to my parents, to break out of the generation cycle and not be dependent on the benefit system. I passed my GCSEs and went to college and then university, setting an example for my younger siblings and relatives. At the age of 10, my father gave me the huge responsibility of translating English into Bengali for all his official correspondence and letters. I used to feel nervous but also had a sense of "Yay!" that my father put his trust in me.

I didn't get much support from my family as they were followers rather than leaders. They used to say that I was "intimidating" and as a strong woman, it would hinder my marriage potentials. They would say, "Layla, local men find you forward!"

But I knew deep down that my life wasn't simply about marriage but something else as well. I wanted to do some good in this world, so I rebelled, with my family's voice echoing in my ears! I challenged their status quo, showing them that I could lead and contribute to the world, beginning with my Bangladeshi home.

Recognition

Becoming more educated and understanding of my culture and faith, I learnt there were many misunderstandings and assumptions about me and my independent way of thinking. People in my culture called me a *fondit*, which means "educated" in Sylheti dialect, but it was used against me – almost as if I was "forgetting" my heritage and where I came from. However, what I was trying to do was do good and integrate into UK life, whilst still being proud of my heritage and my roots.

My adaptable and compassionate traits enabled me to work in charity, housing, social care and, now, the NHS.

Early Journey

My journey began working in the local community where I was a project support and youth worker for over 11 years. The project support role got me noticed by a corporate leader who gave me the opportunity to become more visible and join him as part of the corporate team at Head Office, as he believed it matched my talent.

I also mentored school pupils with challenging behaviour in Newham on a monthly basis to improve their self-esteem and promote a "positive presence" during their youth struggles.

Approach

My youth work allowed me to work closely with local youths from a Bangladeshi background who had low self-esteem and were involved in petty street crime, including drug dealing and theft, or were from broken homes. I recognised that I could help them because my language and faith was the same as theirs. I wanted to bring out their talents to be able to prosper like me, while building rapport, and designing roadmaps and strategies to empower them to break out of their negative behaviour patterns.

My empathetic strategies in youth work helped me combine my nature, purpose, and direction, eventually leading me to the NHS. My first leading role in 2012 was as Admin Team Lead, managing six staff. It gave me a chance to demonstrate that I could work well in a team, while gaining respect and recognition. I was also studying for a post-graduate diploma in Healthcare Leadership. I won the Emerging Leader 2014 award for internal staff competing with 12 other senior leaders for my Community NHS Trust which boosted my confidence and self-esteem, and "chuffed" my parents!

Needing a new challenge, I applied for a higher salary role in 2015, and ended up in the corporate team as a Business Development Co-ordinator, offering me the opportunity to work with key decision makers. This role came to me at the time I was supposed to be off on compassionate leave (see below), but I decided to take this golden opportunity as the Finance Director was mentoring me in a new role.

I put my sadness to one side, as I didn't want to miss this chance that I had waited over a year for. He commended my spirit and dedication which boosted my morale. I stayed in this role for over eight years, honing my skills and becoming aware of who the Executive Leaders were and how they made influential decisions.

By 2019, I was approached for the role of Business Planning Manager by one of the Directors who felt I was the "right fit" and the best person for the job. He had a lot of trust and belief in me. I grabbed this opportunity and things moved so fast, that I had to learn the role on the job! I was now visible to over 60 Senior Leads and learning executive decision-making standards, while adapting to new methods of communications as well.

Father's Sudden Death

My father's passing in 2015 was absolutely devastating and painful. I knew he was secretly proud of his "son" Layla, but he was now gone. I had to put my emotions on hold and use my resilience and leadership skills to arrange his Islamic burial.

I only had six hours to plan and arrange it as the cemetery closed at 5 p.m. on that cold Friday afternoon. I wanted him to be honoured correctly and not be kept in a cold freezer for the weekend and delay his resting, because I knew he hated the cold weather. I had to compose myself and truly focus on what he admired about me, as I knew my brothers were not coping well with his loss.

Relationship Challenges

At 28 years old, I began to try and find the right person to settle down with and have children. I was yearning to be a mother. But I kept experiencing disappointments, was alone and helpless, as in my community, most women marry young.

One Coin Scam

I focused my energy on my widowed mother, two brothers with additional needs, and a sister who was struggling to make ends meet. I was down, grieving and unmarried but I wanted to do something for them and their children.

In September 2016, a Bangladeshi family friend whom I had known for over 12 years approached me for a once in a lifetime business opportunity that would allow me to help them. He was in a leadership role in the community, and came from the same culture and faith as me. He influenced me to invest in a new digital currency, called One Coin. He said that I had to invest within the month, or I would miss out.

He convinced me to invest £55,000, my life savings of over 20 years… Two months later, I recognised it was a Ponzi pyramid scheme, and I had been conned, misled, and used as a "targeted recruit" for my networks and to lure others from my community. I was devastated by my choice because I was trusting and believed others from my community were trustworthy. I observed how other Bangladeshi leaders in these scams were misinforming locals using Islamic words such as "Insha-Allah" which translates as "If God wills" in order to gain trust.

Though I was in pain, I didn't want others to be misled and fall into the same trap, so I steeled myself and began to raise awareness about these scams. I was the first Bangladeshi to speak out publicly about them. I shared my scam experiences online, and got noticed by the BBC who asked me to feature in their investigative documentary series, *Panorama*. I was nervous and knew I would face criticism from other smart investors and from my community who called me "greedy" because I invested too much without knowing the risks and was trying to get rich overnight. However, they didn't understand that I didn't do it for myself, but hoped my returns would help my entire family. I had to take their criticism and not let it disempower me to share my story and help others using my experience.

Initial Reaction

I come from an uneducated, traditional family, with no leadership role model for me to look up to. I was nervous to stand out with my courage. However, working in the NHS encouraged me to develop my self-belief and challenge my own assumptions.

A colleague once said to me, "Layla, you need to become visible, so people notice your talent and come to you with opportunities."

Another friend told me, "Layla, you must write your story."

Calling Style

In 2021, I optimistically applied for a competitive program aimed at the British Bangladeshi Diaspora Leaders. I got selected for the program and proved my bravado. "Alhamdulillah!" I said (*Praise be to God*).

I was introduced to other leaders in my evolving journey, and gained diverse skill sets while helping young leaders back in Bangladesh. I was giving back to my country of origin, making an impact in both the UK and Bangladesh.

This leadership opened doors for me, and I was invited to Bangladesh in December 2022 on an all-expenses paid trip to meet the young leaders I was coaching.

Headhunting

I started to take the personal burden of my responsibilities and wrote about them. A Dubai-based coaching firm headhunted me to join their paid platform and coach others on my experience using my expertise.

Finding Courage and Changing Mindset Fears

I feared that as an unmarried woman of Bangladeshi origin, I would be rejected by my community and relatives as I only had the power to "influence" my own family. I assumed you had to be educated, wealthy, and born into a leadership family to stand out. I feared my directions would lead me to neglect my spirituality and work/family life balance.

Doubts

I found that my spirituality supported this gap. I was a Muslim first, and learnt about the Leader, Prophet Muhammad (peace and blessings be upon him), and women leaders from Islamic history. I began to learn about the Prophetic Leadership model in 2017 and travelled to Palestine which awakened my spirituality.

Overcoming Through Resistance

My spirituality helped me overcome my doubts and I pushed myself and set boundaries to grow. I realised my journey was mine alone and I had to take ownership of the necessary steps to achieve my potential.

Embracing Self-compassion

I owe it to my Islamic spirituality to be hard on my personal mistakes and challenges, but soft with people. That meant being kind to myself first. I had to be honest with myself and stop hoping that the world owed me something. I found that I had self-compassion for all the naive mistakes I had made. I had to rise from feeling sorry for myself, and help others who misunderstood boundaries and directions. This was truly motivating for me.

Changing My Mindset

My bad choices in life made me go through a lot of self-reflection, to change and accept. The clear self-talks helped me accept that I couldn't stay angry all my life.

Growth and Learning

In 2018, I went on a spiritual journey in Saudi Arabia known as *Umrah* to empty my confusing thoughts, and to try and find peace and clarity in what my purpose was in life. I am an honest Muslim, and am accountable to my Creator, whom I worship.

Strategies Adopted

After returning from the spiritual journey, I tried to change my behaviour; I wanted to heal and not allow it to kill me inside. I was going to learn from it and get out of my comfort zone to overcome my struggles. I started to write on Twitter about my experiences and motivational tips on life coaching.

Attitude

My attitude needed altering as I was stuck on some bad experiences and needed to talk about them without sounding broken. I wanted to stand up for myself without getting emotionally worked up. The more I spoke publicly, the more I found the courage in my own healing. I had to unlearn and accept that I am imperfect, and I don't know about everything – including digital currency.

I felt humility that there were so many people in the world suffering from sickness, living in war zones, coping with natural disasters, and things out of their control. But on the other hand, I had the power to change my thoughts and attitude, to learn the positives from the bad experiences and what it taught me.

Words and Actions

I knew that deep inside, I was a good person and cared for others. I am not a victim of circumstance, but had to remind myself that my family/friends viewed me as their hero. I wanted to live by this heartwarming tribute.

My sister says that I am "half of her family" and have always taken a leadership role in her life. For instance, when I was a student at 19, I financially supported my younger sister's desire to settle down in a marriage that was arranged by my father, and I sponsored relatives in Bangladesh and paid my own student fees.

Actions Supporting Others

The more I helped the less fortunate, the more I found that I was healing. I was now impacting the lives of others, rather than focusing on my past. I had to let go and work on my self-improvement and be selfless. Every Ramadan, I give away 2.5% of my savings to help those in need, prioritising children and youths from my community.

In 2022, before the Hajj season, I started writing about practical tips on Hajj and Umrah from my point of experience. I wanted to encourage young people to connect with their spirituality and I was emotionally expressive in order to motivate my audience.

My writing helped me heal and opened doors of opportunities, securing six interviews and a chance to feature in the *Arab News* magazine! I was finally writing about my niche subject that offered others awareness and was a joy to read.

Overcoming Challenges

In 2022, I was given the chance to speak up in my NHS role on the planning process and project updates. This skill set required me to be more empathetic and accepting towards powerful people managing improvement plans. I understood that not everyone is like me, well-co-ordinated in planning, but it was important for me to be respected in my profession.

Subject Matter Expert

Growing up, I was influenced by cultural expectations, but my education, intelligence and new-found skills enabled me to share my thoughts and ideas, communicating in plain and simple language. As I grew simpler, I found gratitude in giving.

Strategies Used

My problem-solving mindset helped steer me towards self-improvement. I was more reflective and, with new positive energy, I wanted to be the best version of myself, both at work and home. I wanted to connect with people from all walks of life and communities. I learnt that there are no shortcuts to success and instead focused on what could be done better.

Criticism

My close circle of family and friends thought of me as too outspoken and intimidating, putting men off from approaching me for marriage. I faced criticism for acting as the "victim" because I was too "greedy" to get rich with One Coin.

Some said I was too much of a "masculine woman" and didn't show emotions, which deterred men from liking me. But what no one knew was that I was protective of my emotions and only opened up to people who valued me.

Resilience

I learnt to ignore people and assumptions, and prioritised my growth – I refused to be held captive by people's perceptions of me. Some thought of me as odd, because I was now challenging their status quo and living my best life.

Proactive Attitude

My spirituality helps me focus as I take time out to pray during my lunch breaks, connecting with my Creator. I try and deal with issues that are in my control without blaming others, and keep my values and morals.

I listen closely to critics to understand if they are being constructive or meaningless. If positive, I appreciate their wisdom and try to shape my vision without losing hope. When someone criticises me, I thank them for developing my thoughts; I believe my critics are a contributor to my success.

Work-Life Balance

My spirituality is the main focal point that helps me plan my work/life balance. As well as working in the NHS, I am a carer to my elderly mother who has health issues, and support my brothers who are dependent on me.

I have another "special" role as an aunty in helping my sister's children with life guidance, coaching, mentoring, and occasional babysitting.

As an unmarried woman, I feel I am closer to my family than ever before.

Plan

The opportunity to become a mother hasn't arrived yet. In the meantime, I have the time to learn about spirituality and leadership. I fill up my annual leave either attending training sessions, travelling, or helping others. I spend a lot of time with children and enjoy their playful nature and hope that I can inspire them to be kind. My plans are purposeful to serve humanity.

Healthy Strike

My balance comes from having a strong faith and outlook, and remembering that I am but a traveller in this life. I know life will always have challenges but the key is to have hope. I think proactively instead of reactively so get things done. I keep things minimal and simple, and focus on needs rather than wants.

Valuable Lessons Learnt
Discovering the Leadership Process

For over 10 years, my thinking and coping strategies have allowed me to think outside the box to discover that I am good at helping others.

My cognitive thoughts reaffirmed this; I have the hidden ingredients for emotional intelligence and spirituality, and can connect with people on a deeper level, including those with mental health issues, the elderly, the young, widows, and those less fortunate than me.

Impact of Authenticity

I realised it was important to be impactful and have a "can improve" mentality in all my dedication and hard work. The impression I want people to have of me is as a fragrance that can be inhaled and remembered.

Test of Resilience

My leap of faith came after my father's death and losing all my life savings. I had to find humility to accept my ordeal which in turn gave me wisdom and resilience to cope.

Contribution to My Growth

My sister's young children have made a huge impact on my growth. They show me innocence and motherly love. I learn so much from them and it is only fair that I am present in their childhood so they can be raised in a loving way to contribute to the world after I have gone. I am creating a small legacy of people that I can nurture emotionally and with whom I can share my kindness.

Collaboration and Empathy

In my NHS role, I learnt that collaboration and empathy to others is vital. I am learning how to stop sounding arrogant when I suggest improvements to others.

In the summer of 2022, I collaborated with a film production team by hosting them in my home and adapting my style to communicate about contracts, boundaries, and asserting my role in the collaboration. I was now hustling with a new network – the production company and agents that had demands and needs to serve the local community – offering them a service and making referrals to recruit local people to fill in gaps in unemployment.

Helpful Qualities

Asking 'good' questions, better advance planning and not to take everything personally are powerful qualities.

Three Tips for Developing Leadership Skills

Encouragement

When I was vocal 11-year-old, I received no encouragement from home so I therefore rebelled and made some poor choices. Some labelled me as a *morabbi*, meaning mature in Sylheti dialect, but it was used as a curse against me.

I had no guidance or mentoring which impacted my teenage years. I now live by the principle of encouragement when coaching young people, so they don't have the same struggle I had with the transition from young person to adulthood.

Personal Accountability

I take ownership on my personal responsibilities, filling the gaps in my skill set and by training and taking courses. I practice what I learn on my inner circle and empower them to seek wisdom from experiences, including voluntary work.

Continuous Learning

Life is an ongoing school and each milestone achieved is wisdom gained. Never stop learning, and be humble and accepting to learning unknown things.

Tips

If you are facing any blockages, remember that as every door closes, there is another door for you to enter. You must unlock with your key that is your true knowledge, and solve the issues. It is a process, not the end. Find a coach and seek directions early as possible, go to events to network and meet people.

Mentoring

In my first NHS leading role, I had five senior mentors and a leadership coach. I was hustling with time and performance which brought me satisfaction in my work and I applied this to my personal life.

People flourish with coaching. Not seeking out coaching when I was young was one of my mistakes. Therefore, my goal is to give to others while they are young, such as my younger niece and nephews, so they can be part of the future generation of leaders.

Network

Connect and follow up with leaders you meet and ask them out for a coffee. Be honest, listen actively, and build a rapport.

Value Failure

The wealth of wisdom grew from all my failures, and I learnt to accept and move forward with it. It was better than accepting defeat or living with regret so I had to break the cycle – stuff happens but you have to move on.

Spot the Opportunities

Be confident and friendly. Try and spot opportunities and ways to navigate the what-ifs and not be a slave of fear. Build a reliable character and skill set and get lucky from taking actions and meeting incredible people – in my case, becoming a location host and networking with TV production companies.

Gap Analysis

I am fully aware that there are many gaps in my leadership skills and learning to achieve my desired process, performance, and strategic benchmarks. If I told my 8-year-old self that I would be writing my first book in 2023, the response would have been *duro*, meaning "Damn!" in Sylheti!

Rosa's vibrant personality shines through in her narrative, captivating readers. Her straightforward explanation of leadership speaks volumes, offering profound insights for those who follow her.

Working in the male-dominated tech industry, Rosa harnesses the power of her female leadership skills to unlock limitless potential. However, her mission extends far beyond personal success. Rosa is dedicated to changing the lives of people struck by poverty by empowering them with opportunities and life-changing skills.

Like all great leaders, Rosa possesses tremendous self-awareness. Through introspection, she has discovered that courage and continuous learning are the cornerstones of her life. In her chapter, she delves into the lessons that have significantly impacted her journey. Rosa inspires readers to take actionable steps in their lives by sharing her insights, fostering personal and societal change.

Rosa has never adhered to the usual stereotypes of a Hispanic woman in a predominantly male field. Instead, she forges her path, taking the road less travelled. Her deepened spirituality has fortified her, making her an indomitable female leader. Rosa rises and roars, unafraid to share her voice and brilliance with the world.

Her story is a testament to the power of self-awareness, continuous learning, and the courage to defy conventional expectations. Rosa's journey inspires us to embrace our unique paths and lead with passion, compassion, and unwavering resolve.

Brenda

Rosa Lopez Antonini

*"Let the world doubt you,
let them bet against you –
but in the end, it is your
strength and determination
that defines your success.
Rise above the noise."*

Rosa Lopez Antonini

From Bytes to Breakthroughs
A Leadership Journey Through Technology and Beliefs

To begin, I want to recap my understanding of what constitutes a true leader from my perspective. A leader embodies authenticity and leads by example. They are open-minded and continuous learners. They may possess a deep knowledge of marketing, persuasion, and business, yet they conscientiously choose not to exploit these strategies for personal gain. Instead, a leader focuses on uplifting others, helping them recognise their own worth and potential. This process involves fostering individuals' best qualities, irrespective of whether the outcomes directly benefit the leader personally.

Reflecting on my journey to leadership within my field, I realise that there wasn't a single dramatic turning point, but rather a gradual transformation shaped by a series of defining experiences.

One of my earliest and most formative memories involves a profound sense of helplessness and the inability to alter a distressing situation. I was perhaps four or five years old when my mother fell very ill. Lacking access to adequate medical care, I could only listen as adults around me discussed the grim reality dictated by our financial constraints. This experience was my first real encounter with the stark limitations imposed by poverty.

Despite the humble and materially deficient circumstances of my early life, it was not until that moment that I truly understood the impact of financial hardship on a person's existence. It was then, in the shadow of my mother's illness, that a vision for a more prosperous, unencumbered life began to take shape in my mind. This early brush with vulnerability and the spectre of loss instilled in me a profound appreciation for my family and forged a determination to relieve the hardships they faced.

I committed myself wholeheartedly to excelling in all my classes, channelling my mother's resilience and persistence, traits I identified as vital for success in any field. Throughout my journey, I have learnt that the principles of success and happiness transcend time and culture. They include setting clear goals, making the best use of available resources, persisting through challenges, working diligently, learning from failures, and maintaining relentless perseverance. Indeed, there are no shortcuts to true achievement.

I trace the pivotal moment when I recognised the need to step into a leadership role within my field back to those early years. The stark realisation that I did not want to feel defenceless, that I wanted to feel the power to change outcomes from my decisions and actions. My drive was clear: I resolved not only to change my family's circumstances, but also to extend that opportunity to others trapped in that cycle. This early resolution set the course for my leadership path.

As the years progressed, my studies and consistent engagement with books greatly shaped my life. In my professional career, the same motivation persists. I view challenges and frustrations as normal parts of life, just like moments of joy and achievement. I believe that societal norms that categorise us as being at the top or the bottom are misleading; in reality, there is never a point where personal growth ceases – there is no ultimate top. Similarly, there is always the potential to decline if we neglect our responsibilities – true bottoms do not exist, only deeper falls. Maintaining perspective on these dynamics is crucial to ensure our egos do not lead us astray.

In many situations, having numerous options can make decision-making more challenging, as the abundance of choices often leads to indecision. However, when options are limited, it can simplify the path forward. Paradoxically, constraints can catalyse decisiveness and innovation, guiding us to find clarity and courage when choices are few. Believe it or not, having limited options often paves the best path forward. When you're not overwhelmed by pursuing a grand objective, you can focus on achieving more minor, manageable goals. This approach teaches you the power of incremental progress; taking one step at a time can propel you much further than you might imagine. Breaking down a large goal into smaller, achievable steps becomes a natural strategy when your starting point is significantly disadvantaged.

Looking back, it's easier to see why each setback and misstep was necessary. It's common to judge our past selves from the perspective of our more knowledgeable and experienced current selves. Still, it's through this reflection that we build a constructive mindset, one of the most powerful tools we can foster in ourselves and pass on to our children.

Growing up, my deep dive into the study of metaphysics provided a strong foundation for developing a resilient mindset. Engaging with these profound philosophical concepts early on helped me to understand the interconnectivity of life and the transformative power of our thoughts.

The cornerstone of my courage has always been continuous learning and a willingness to experiment without fear of failure. I firmly believe that while anyone can lose material possessions in an instant, knowledge and insights gained from personal development are enduring. Cultivating a curious mind is essential for me – I view life as too short to learn all that is available. Embracing learning as a vital habit that should be nurtured throughout life not only increases awareness and open-mindedness but also equips us to capitalise on opportunities as they arise. This commitment to lifelong learning has been crucial in my ability to adapt and evolve.

I am deeply aware of how our actions affect our future and those of others, and I emphasise the importance of combining actions to improve future generations. This perspective shapes my thoughts, emotions, and responses to innovative ideas and the behaviours of others, highlighting the significance of being mindful of our interconnected well-being. Recognising that the welfare of others enriches our own lives, I strive to live in a way that considers my impact on the world around me.

My journey through life has been marked by several profound transitions, each one moulding me into who I am today. It began in a deeply religious household, where attending church and adhering to religious traditions were integral to daily life. As a child, I found myself contending with questions about the divine – specifically, the existence of suffering in a world governed by a supposedly benevolent deity. These questions stirred deep emotions within me, leading to a period where I reluctantly embraced these beliefs, adopting a passive outlook that everything happened according to divine will.

In retrospect, this phase of passivity was the most challenging period of my life. I lacked leadership in my own life's direction, resigning myself to a belief that all was predetermined, which unfortunately led to enabling negative outcomes. However, this mindset could not sustain me, and I soon found myself seeking more control over my life. This quest led me to explore metaphysics and the concept of energies, igniting a transformative shift in how I approached life. I began to take initiative, liberating myself from the guilt of financial success – a stark contrast to the religious doctrine that had once made me feel that poverty was somehow more virtuous.

As I forged this new path, I focused on pragmatic goals rather than perfection. I became less concerned with pleasing others and more willing to experiment, even if it meant facing failure. This evolution was crucial, as it taught me the importance of balance and the power of saying no without guilt – a lesson that took years to embrace fully.

Professionally, my journey was equally unconventional. In the Dominican Republic, I pursued a degree in Pharmacy – not out of passion, but as a strategic move to escape poverty and assist my family and others in doing the same. When I moved to the United States, the challenge of transferring my credentials led me to take a job at a check-cashing store, earning minimum wage. This job, while humble, was a stepping stone. It was there that a chance encounter with a customer who worked in technology steered me toward the tech field. Curious, I sought his advice on how to enter the industry, which eventually led me to a career in STEM.

Working with data proved to be a natural fit for my curious, logical, and creative mindset. I felt fortunate to have found a field that aligned perfectly with my skills and interests, though, like any path worth pursuing, it had its challenging moments. I learnt that sometimes it takes time to be in the right environment to grow and freely express creativity.

Despite my gratitude and satisfaction with my career in the technical field, I felt a persistent sense of unfulfillment – particularly, a desire to help others on a larger scale. This urge led me through a period of introspection, especially after two unsuccessful attempts to establish a non-profit aimed at helping those in the Dominican Republic. Frustrated, I found myself questioning why I couldn't simply let go of this desire if I was unable to fulfil it.

During this reflective phase, I pondered what makes people successful and why success seems elusive for some. It was then that the concept for my book, *The Zero-Sum Game of You*, crystallised as a response to these musings. Trusting my instincts, I began to write, despite my self-professed limitations with the English language – I was skilled at writing computer code but not prose, particularly at that time. Completing the manuscript took nearly a year. On the morning I was to send it to my publisher, an idea struck me:

"I will donate 60% of any profits to help young adults with their education so they can secure better jobs."

To this day, I have donated 100% of the profits, realising that this venture was the answer to my long-standing quest to help others. It became clear that assistance needed to be both financial and developmental, helping to build strong mindsets.

This experience reaffirmed my belief in taking one step at a time and following your instincts. Sometimes we need to journey through life's challenges to see how all the pieces connect, leading us to our ultimate destination. Each transition in my life, whether personal or professional, has been less about a sudden change and more about a gradual evolution towards self-actualisation.

Challenges are inherent in every journey, coming and going as they shape our paths. I have faced numerous challenges and learnt to navigate through them, and I am ready to tackle whatever may come next. Interestingly, I have yet to encounter overwhelming obstacles in my professional career. I've found that most career-related challenges can be overcome through continuous learning, effective communication, and changing environments when necessary.

On the personal side, becoming a mother marked a significant turning point in my life, prompting a shift in priorities. While my career remained important, balancing my professional responsibilities and family life became paramount.

This shift influenced my career choices significantly – I sought specific job incentives and roles that would not compromise the time I wished to spend with my children and family. Over the years, I've observed that regrets often stem from unclear priorities. Our society moves at lightning speed, and it's easy to get swept up in daily responsibilities, sometimes at the expense of neglecting our top priorities.

Being a Hispanic woman in a male-dominated field might seem to present numerous challenges to some. However, I have never allowed myself to be daunted by potential disadvantages. My career in technology has been immensely fulfilling, fuelled by hard work and a profound passion for my field.

While being a minority may have introduced certain challenges, they have not impeded my progress. This may be because competition within my technical specialties is less intense, or perhaps because I have always chosen roles that align perfectly with my expertise. Even in leadership positions, I have concentrated on innovating, designing, and developing solutions that drive business and technical growth.

I acknowledge the existence of disparities, but by focusing on my work and goals rather than the obstacles, I've achieved every position I've aspired to. This method has allowed me to navigate my career effectively, proving that with determination and dedication, barriers can often be transcended or made less relevant. This approach not only highlights the potential for overcoming hurdles, but also underscores the importance of creativity and innovation in adding value to any endeavour.

I realise that facing these challenges has been a transformative journey, revealing layers of resilience and determination within myself that I hadn't previously recognised. Each difficulty has provided invaluable lessons, shaping my character and refining my approach to both my personal and professional life. This continuous learning and adaptation process leads me to reflect deeply on my experiences. What valuable lessons have I learnt about myself through these challenges? Here are the insights that stand out.

1. **Belonging and Authenticity.** I've learnt that I have just as much right as anyone else to be here, to belong, to pursue my dreams, and to be proud of my roots. Embracing my heritage has been fundamental to my identity and the person I have become.

2. **Defining What Matters.** It's essential to clearly define what matters most to you at each stage of life. Having this clarity has led my decisions and helped me prioritise my actions and goals, effectively preventing any big regrets. For me, family is central. Therefore, I consistently try to express my love and appreciation for them as much as possible, ensuring that my actions align with my deepest values.

3. **The Importance of Continuous Learning.** Continuous learning is essential. Knowledge does

more than enhance one's ability to communicate; it opens up new opportunities and broadens one's perspective, fostering understanding and reducing judgement of others. Fostering a curious mind to research as much as I can and to read and learn from others' mistakes and successes, has saved me tremendous time and enabled me to take on higher risks.

4. **Learning from Everyone.** Everyone has something to teach us, regardless of background or financial status. Observing how individuals treat others provides a true reflection of their character. I am committed to treating everyone equally and kindly, regardless of their title or social standing. This approach fosters a positive environment and reinforces that dignity depends not on one's external achievements, but on their inherent human value.

5. **Aligning Goals with Priorities.** Our goals must synchronise with our top priorities to avoid painful regrets. Living consciously and understanding the sacrifices we make for our choices, combined with setting goals that do not compromise our main priorities, paves the way to true fulfilment.

6. **Breaking Down Goals.** Large goals can be daunting. It's essential to break them down into manageable steps. While having a final target is good, attempting to plan every detail is impractical. Life is unpredictable, and adaptability is critical. If you know your "what" and "why", the "how" can evolve as needed.

7. **Caring for Body and Mind.** Treat your body and mind with care and compassion. We only get one body and it's our responsibility to maintain its well-being. Similarly, the health of our mind is just as crucial; the thoughts we nurture and the mental nourishment we choose profoundly impacts our future.

Reflecting on the past through the lens of today, I view each up and down with new-found understanding. If given the chance to send a message back in time, I would impart these three essential tips to my younger self. Each one serves as a guidepost for navigating the challenges ahead.

1. **Master Communication Skills.** Effective communication is foundational for leadership. The ability to articulate your vision, negotiate conflicts, and inspire others is critical. While you can achieve your goals without strong communication skills, mastering them will expedite your journey and enhance your impact. Investing time in refining your ability to convey ideas clearly and persuasively will pay dividends in all areas of your professional life.

2. **Learn to Say No.** It's vital to establish boundaries and learn the power of saying no. This skill helps you balance your generosity with your resources. Particularly in financial matters, overextending yourself before achieving stability can lead to bankruptcy and eliminate future opportunities. Understand that saying no is not just a way to protect your resources, but also a strategy to focus on your most important goals and responsibilities.

3. **Understand the Costs Upfront and Consistently Add Value.** Effective leadership requires making decisions that often have complex and extensive implications. It is crucial to thoroughly assess your decisions' potential costs and implications before committing. Such foresight can avert unexpected setbacks and better equip you to handle possible challenges. Understanding the "cost" of each decision enables you to balance benefits against risks more precisely, enhancing your effectiveness and strategic insight as a leader. Always aim to add value in your role, ensuring that each decision serves immediate needs and contributes positively to your organisation's long-term goals.

Shifting from a hands-on approach to leadership towards a more profound, philosophical understanding, I often reflect on a favourite quote of mine that encapsulates this broader vision. As a recurring sign-off in my book signings, I use:

"Gratitude is our pathway to Oneness."

This phrase reveals my core belief in the interconnectedness of our actions and their significant impact on our collective well-being. In a similar vein, I frequently post a message on my social media to encourage both myself and my followers, emphasising the power of personal resilience:

*"Let the world doubt you, let them bet against you –
but in the end, it is your strength and determination
that defines your success. Rise above the noise."*

Judith Ratcliffe stands out as a formidable and likeable female leader, known for her professionalism and trustworthiness. Deeply immersed in the world of privacy professionals, Judith commands respect and admiration.

From the outset of her chapter, Judith captivates readers with a paradoxical statement on leadership. This intriguing opening fosters curiosity, compelling you to read further to uncover the deeper meaning behind her words. This characteristic of curiosity is quintessential, prompting you to ponder the significance of language in both written and spoken forms.

Judith masterfully employs storytelling techniques and metaphors, allowing readers to envision her character vividly. Her writing captures your attention, much like her spoken words, showcasing her exceptional leadership qualities. When you read her words, you can almost hear her voice, a testament to her powerful communication skills.

On a mission to dismantle stereotypical images of women in the boardroom, Judith speaks with authority and conviction. Her words, grounded in evidence and a deep understanding, resonate with the belief that women possess extraordinary abilities to effect positive change. When Judith speaks, people listen.

Judith's narrative is a call to action, inspiring others to consider the power of language and the impact of authentic leadership. She leads by example, demonstrating that women have the power to reshape the world in the most positive ways. Judith, lead on…

Brenda

Judith Ratcliffe

*"Dance like everyone's
watching you –
and invite them to join in!"*

Judith Ratcliffe

Manifestly Making It, in Public

The Paradoxical Story of a Privacy Professional, Hospital Radio Presenter and Author...

[Caveat: Nothing I say or write for
Voices of Women is legal advice.]

Describe the pivotal moment you realised it was time to step into being a leader in your field of expertise.

There has always been a Sheriff of Nottingham and there will always be a Robin Hood.

Fighting injustice has always been important to me.

While writing a dissertation on unreliable evidence, I learnt of one-such apparent injustice. Scrutinising the pitfalls of being unduly influenced by science and relying too heavily on DNA evidence to decide innocence or guilt, I discovered S & Marper v United Kingdom[1], about the unlawful retention of DNA and fingerprints by the police, of those entitled to the presumption of innocence (which includes 'the acquitted').

---

[1] S & Marper v United Kingdom, European Court of Human Rights, Applications nos. 30562/04 and 30566/04 Judgement, 4th December 2008 https://rm.coe.int/168067d216

A short while later, I wrote my first privacy-related article, about that case, for the *Expert Witness Institute* newsletter.

Short of 'defamation' and a little about the J.K. Rowling case[2], where photographers took pictures of her 19-month-old son while he was out in public in Edinburgh, privacy law appeared to be absent from law school curricula and seldom reported on by the press.

Even now, other than personal data breaches, which are more regularly news, and major invasions of privacy, very little is reported and people don't know their privacy rights (although some are starting to recognise bits of Data Protection). Even some legal professionals don't seem to understand privacy – the right to respect for your private life, family life, home and correspondence, which includes things like personal autonomy, physical and mental integrity and protection of your reputation, to name but a few of its parts – properly.

Still fewer seem to understand the inextricable link between violating a person's privacy rights and the breaking of Consumer Protection Law, and unjust trial decisions, patient safety failures and a denial of patient dignity.

They also often seem not to understand the inextricable link between violating a person's privacy and exposing customers and employees to high risks of having their voices, faces and data stolen and used to commit fraud, or other crimes, and exposing countries to national security risks.

---

[2] Murray v Big Pictures (UK) Ltd [2008] EWCA Civ 446, 7th May 2008, www.bailii.org/ew/cases/EWCA/Civ/2008/446.html

This lack of understanding is arguably one key reason why numerous arguably wrongful and harmful decisions get made daily, which undermine people's rights and cause direct and indirect harms.

I decided: *enough was enough…* and so I drew my 'sword'…

How did you find the courage to change your mindset, words and actions to strengthen and support your journey through your transition?

My family motto is *Virtus Propter Se – Courage For Its Own Sake*, or *Courage Is Its Own Reward*. I could say I've inherited some courage from my family line, which may include Marian Fitzwalter[3], who may or may not have married Robin Hood, but who if she is who I believe, was a formidable woman in her own right, having apparently even fought Robin Hood himself and equalled him during that fight in both courage and skill, if I read the tale correctly[4], as well as beating the allegedly villainous Prince John in hand-to-hand combat[5].

---

[3] Alias Matilda.

[4] *Robin Hood and Other Outlaw Tales* by Stephen Knight (Editor) and Thomas H. Ohlgren (Editor), Medieval Institute Publications, Michigan, 1997, lines 34-49

> *With quiver and bow, sword, buckler, and all,*
> *Thus armed was Marian most bold…*
> *…Whose vallour bold Robin admir'd.*
> *They drew out their swords, and to cutting they went…*
> *O hold thy hand…" said Robin Hood…*

[5] *The Graphic and Historical Illustrator* by Edward Brayley, J. Chidley (1834), pg 8.
> *"… a … fray ensued, during which it is said that John and the lady … met and fought…so stoutly did she repulse him, that he was constrained to withdraw …"*

My family tree may also include Sir Richard Ratcliffe, who fought beside Richard III on Bosworth Battlefield and is sometimes said to have been one of his chief advisors, and, I believe (since he too shares our bend-engrailed sable – my family crest), one Radulphus Ratcliffe, whose shield is in the dining hall at my Inn of Court – The Honourable Society of the Inner Temple. He was called to the bar there in 1574, was elected a Bencher in 1589[6], and became Treasurer in 1601[7]. I was unaware of his existence when I made my application to join the Inn! (A spooky coincidence, perhaps?)

I developed a 'can-do' and 'always be prepared' **mindset** through activities with the Girl Guide Association of England and Wales, which included being a Rainbow Guide Young Leader and then Leader for eight years.

I chose to ignore the usual 'this is woman' and 'this is youth' stereotypes.

I chose to be a trailblazer and lead the way – no one else seemed to be doing what I was doing or tackling it in the same way.

Words are to play with and adapt, depending on your audience and setting: formal versus informal, members of the public versus colleagues, radio listeners or committee members. Sometimes brevity is key, at other times more detail is needed.

---

[6] With thanks to Celia Pilkington, Archivist of The Inner Temple for providing the information and kindly permitting me to include it.

[7] Ibid

Shakespeare never spoke truer than when he made Hamlet say: "the play's the thing, wherein I'll catch the conscience of the King"[8]. Words can seem meaningless without context, but in a 'play', words in storytelling form are powerful enough to move people to laugh, cry, and even take action. As we know, storytelling can often bring hidden truths into the light.

My aim is to **catch the consciences** of today's 'people in power' – the politicians, the business leaders and influencers, and, of course, those with arguably the most power, if only they knew how to effectively wield it – members of the general public – the so-called 'ordinary' citizens, who are more often than not far more extra-ordinary (in terms of having outstanding skills and talents, creativity, kindness, generosity and courage) than they are given credit for being.

Actions

- I looked to my heroes, to their stories and their music.

- I found courage in the fan mail I received whilst I was a hospital radio presenter – living up to being the 'hero' I was becoming for others.

- I listened to what complainants told me, to what their problems and concerns were.

---

[8] Act II Scene II, last two lines, *The Tragicall Historie of Hamlet, Prince of Denmarke,* by William Shakespeare, Printer I. R, London, 1605.

These things helped me to retain the courage to go out and speak to people, to share knowledge through seminars and panel discussions. It became second nature to speak my truth to large audiences, as well as one to one.

[Taking something memorable with me to engage audiences before discussions begin helps break the ice and makes networking much more fun (as well as effective): **To unleash my magic, I often wear my Silver Shoes – ever a talking point!!**]

Then I took things a step further and started inviting people to join me in making a difference, by signing my petitions, reading my articles and books, and spreading the word about challenges and solutions.

What challenges did you face along the way and how did you overcome them?

Organisations lacking budget. This meant gaining qualifications more slowly, because I had to earn enough money to pay for them myself. And then there's 'paying for the privilege' of keeping them 'in date'[9], which seems somewhat daft. University and school qualifications are everlasting, and arguably professional qualifications should follow suit.

I overcame this challenge with patience and using part of my wages to pay for qualifications.

---

[9] Certification Maintenance Fee https://iapp.org/certify/cpe/

Problematic course content and poor coursebook material. These ignited the desire to improve on resources for privacy and data protection professionals, by providing practical pocket guides that share my knowledge and experience. So I started my series, *Privacy and Data Protection in Your Pocket*.

'Swords' of those in power versus my pen. A number of arguably bad laws, which appear to undermine your rights and put up barriers to getting them actioned and upheld, are currently 'in play' and are also going through Parliament as 'bills'.

Ombudsmen and regulators, who are meant to be impartial, appear to fail to stand up for individuals and appear to uphold law-breaking by government departments and other organisations. They also appear to uphold bad policies and processes (that have been arguably proven to break the law), which compounds matters, as do government committees who appear not to understand or appreciate the consequences of failing to properly protect and uphold privacy rights.

There are aspects of the above that I cannot overcome alone. However, I can help to increase the knowledge and awareness of individuals. I am currently writing my second Privacy book about rights and how to exercise them, current barriers and how those might be overcome.

The process for *even*-ing the score and putting wrongs right is a long journey, but things are, I feel, moving in the desired direction.

I used to have to ask to speak at events; people now come to me and ask me to speak.

When I have the courage to speak, I encourage others, who may feel the same way, to speak out too. It only takes one person to lead for others to join them.

My messages are picked up by others within the communities I've joined and are shared across communities. The more my messages get shared and gather momentum, the more I write and post and speak and record and share, the wider the knowledge and message goes. And it goes all over the world.

Together, we can make a difference. While we can't put genies back into bottles, we can at least undo some of the harm and halt currently harmful bills, Acts of Parliament and actions. We can bring safeguards, good laws and policies back.

By writing and supporting petitions and submitting evidence to Parliament, including to its Scrutiny Committees; by speaking at conferences and events, and writing articles and news reports, I am helping to write (or, perhaps I should say rewrite) the book, so to speak, on 'best practice'.

Slowly, I am breaking through the walls of silence.

What good can 'one' person do?

"You'll never be a barrister," I was told.

Such off-putting words by a much-respected lecturer were deeply disillusioning and upsetting at the time (particularly given all the hard work I was putting into it).

However, I chose to ignore these words, persevered, and have now been told, while at work, that I am as good as a Junior Barrister and although I am *not* **yet** a Barrister (and this cannot be denied), I was good enough to be called to the bar.

I also often advise and guide on compliance and on many different aspects of the law, without giving legal advice – I write articles and books on aspects of the law, I submit evidence to Parliamentary Scrutiny Committees and have even shown senior solicitors and barristers what was missing from their cases, such as people who arguably should be added as respondents, because 'on the facts', it appeared that they must have turned a blind eye to the alleged wrongdoing, or else, were directly complicit in it.

"You're a much more experienced Data Protection Officer than we thought..." I was told.

The rough translation of that comment is: *"We were hoping to employ someone who was naive and/or inexperienced, who wouldn't look too closely, who wouldn't challenge and/or stand up to us, when we asked them to do things that are unlawful and who would just roll over for us and do whatever we wanted, when we wanted, because we asked, or told them to."*

I have a sneaking suspicion that had I been a man and/or older, that this type of comment wouldn't have been made.

Nowadays, I like to use this as classic example of what 'not' to say to your Data Protection Officer (or any member of your privacy or data protection team) and lead into a discussion on 'why your Data Protection Officer (and their team) must remain independent' (it's a legal requirement, for starters![10]).

I have also used it as a way to flag, in blogs and elsewhere, how badly treated some Data Protection Officers (and/or members of their team) are, and how poor attitudes and behaviours towards Data Protection Officers and their teams need to change, because if you don't 'protect' us and stand up for us and stand with us, even when we tell you things you may not want to hear, how can we protect you/ the organisation and the individuals (colleagues, employees, customers, patients and more) who we serve?

"When I was your age, I was having children..." I was informed, in front of several other members of my team.

I will leave you to draw your own conclusions as to what may have been implied by that statement, but I will comment on how inappropriate it is to say that to a colleague:

- It is nobody's business whether or not a woman chooses to have children (or, if she does, 'when' she chooses to do so) and

- to comment upon it, particularly in an open area, where you know you can be heard by a number of other people, may be interpreted as a desire or intention (whether so-held or not by the speaker) to embarrass or humiliate the person, about whom you are speaking, for the life choices they have made (and/or a recklessness as to the consequences of

[10] Article 38 (3) The General Data Protection Regulation: The controller and processor shall ensure that the data protection officer does not receive any instructions... https://gdpr-info.eu/art-38-gdpr/

making such comments, where you know that others can hear you).

(This is always assuming, of course, that it was a life choice, and that there is not some other, more traumatic or upsetting reason why they have not yet had one or more children. If such a traumatic or upsetting reason is present, the consequences of highlighting the lack of children, while never to be known by the speaker, may cause further harm to the person spoken about.)

Had I been a man, would this type of comment have been made?

Women in legal arenas and indeed, within the privacy and data protection space are not always treated as well as, perhaps, they should be. There are many stereotypes that women still have to face and break down, including being expected either to 'do as they are told' or to act, dress or speak in a particular way, to get colleagues to listen to them.

Assertiveness in women isn't always welcomed, even though it would be, were we men.

Although men aren't the only ones who do this, there are many instances of bullying where some men quite literally shout women down, because they dislike being challenged, and it happens, no matter how diplomatically, politely or 'quietly' a woman may speak.

How have I overcome this?

I choose to speak at normal volumes and assertively, as often as I can, to help break down the 'quiet little woman' stereotype and wherever I witness bullying, I challenge it (at the time or afterwards).

I ask questions that make people think and when I make assertions, I back up my assertions with evidence and I would encourage all women to do the same, wherever they can. I tell stories because they engage, entertain and break barriers.

Bringing evidence to the table strengthens arguments and can help you win, even when some of the people in the room are shouting you down, in every sense of the word.

What valuable lessons have you learnt about yourself?

1. I have learnt about the high value I place on personal integrity and that trusting my gut is usually the right thing to do. I was told to dismiss a number of very old cases (over seven years old) without looking into the full facts or looking at the evidence. This didn't sit well with me. I requested all of the evidence so that I could review the case properly and then make a decision. I found the evidence that proved the complainant correct.

2. I also learnt that I'm *as good as a Junior Barrister* even though I'm not one officially – I was told this by a Legal Director, whom I assisted in a number of matters.

3. Finally, I learnt that my storytelling is powerful and compelling and helps change hearts and minds[11]. **Leadership is sometimes about being able to explain the bigger picture to others and help them understand the impacts, both positive and negative, of their proposals and/or actions.**

So, making a point of getting to understand the impact on other rights, as well as on public safety, national security and wider issues, when an individual's privacy is broken or violated, and being able to explain those through stories and storytelling activities makes me a far more effective privacy professional and/or Data Protection Officer. In addition, it makes me a better and more effective case, complaints and rights requests resolver, as well as helping me to lead changes and improvements more effectively within organisations.

Share three tips you would give to your younger self to develop your leadership skills for today's world.

1. **Treat everyone as your equal...** You will always have the confidence to speak the truth to those in positions of power. You will find that doors open and you will be able to listen better and collaborate with amazing people from all walks of life.

[11] *"[Judith Ratcliffe] uses stories to powerfully illustrate why data protection is everyone's concern..."* The Office of The Data Protection Authority of Guernsey/ Project Bijou: Theme 2: Why better engagement is needed. *VIDEO: The power of words. Using stories to dismantle legalese and communicate clearly:* https://www.odpa.gg/project-bijou/theme-2-why-better-engagement-is-needed/judith-ratcliffe/

2. As a wise person once kindly shared with me, **get into the habit of asking 'when' things will happen.** It is far more effective than asking 'why' something hasn't happened, or asking 'if' something is going to happen...

3. **Be the person in the room who unashamedly asks the awkward questions.** Others are usually thinking along the same lines, but may not be brave enough to speak. **Also, be the person in the room who sits back and lets others speak first** (while making notes about what they say, so that you can reflect on what they have said in your own response) – this can give you a greater persuasive influence.

Christi embodies the spirit of eternal optimism. With a commitment to transforming dreams into reality, her creative vision and expertise shapes the future she passionately pursues.

Life's journey is rarely linear, and Christi invites you to embrace this truth as you delve into her captivating story. One pivotal day, an Awakening occurs, altering her life forever – an experience that leaves an indelible mark on her soul.

As you immerse yourself in Christi's narrative, you will feel a profound connection, embarking on an enchanting journey. Her exquisite storytelling, while magical, is firmly rooted in the attainable. It beckons you to open your mind to the limitless possibilities that life offers.

Christi's tale is one of exploration and discovery, encouraging us all to embrace life's exciting potential. She reminds us that by opening our eyes and hearts, we can unlock a world of extraordinary experiences.

As a leader, Christi understands the strength found in vulnerability. She teaches us the importance of engaging with our emotions through her reflections, nostalgia, and lessons. Her gentle nature, combined with her resolute character and leadership, shines brightly, illuminating our world and inspiring others to follow.

Open your heart to Christi's beautiful journey and discover a reality transformed by hope, courage, and the belief in what is possible.

Brenda

Dr Christi A Campbell (PhD, FNP)

*"Stand strong in
the gentleness of it."*

Dr Christi A Campbell

Edge of Forever

The mysterious story of memories and miracles ...
their impact on life ... creation ... intention ...
and manifesting dreams into reality ...

L ife is a journey ... neither linear nor circular, but rather a beautiful ever-reaching spiral achieving new heights with each discovery, lesson and joy that is found along the way. Yes, it is indeed a journey, but I didn't have an understanding or realisation of what that meant for the first 40-some years of my existence.

There I was, living my life, moving along on the acceptable trajectory of education, family, career ... eating, sleeping, working. Just 'living' – being 'in the moment' of earthly tasks, oblivious to the fact that there might be a plan for me – a purpose for my existence – that perhaps I was already on a journey of which I was totally unaware.

We each have our own journey and to find our way and make meaning of our experiences, we make choices at each turn. Others cannot do it for us – some may help us achieve, while others may even impede our progress.

This is my story – at least a snapshot of it. Perhaps it will be of benefit, to help shed light on your journey, and illuminate your path to discovery. Be open, flow with the story, and allow yourself to tap into your inner knowing, to be activated to a greater and richer level.

What is Your Story? Do You Know?

What I have come to realise is that every moment puts us
on the edge of forever ... a beautiful place of creation ...
for exploration ... to continue to weave the intricate
and unique threads of our tapestries ...

Let's explore, so be peaceful, sit in the quiet stillness, and look inward. Explore your heart and sink into the far corners of your mind. Let go ... and soar to magical sights of discovery.

When I allow my mind to wander back through time, to float along peering at memories that expose themselves to this type of intrusion, I see pivotal times that are not always glorious. Actually, there are not many that I yearn to go back to relive. When all is said and done, I have no desire to relive anything – for that journey of heartache, mistake, growth, and glorious discovery are all moments that brought me to now. What I do moving forward is see those sparkling jewels of knowledge lining the path ahead and holding the space for discovery ... so I follow them with joy, and an open heart, knowing all is as it should be.

To get from there to now, and help bring understanding to the tapestry of discovery, I must go back and bring some of those vignettes to life. I can only speak to memories that I have – not necessarily how someone else may recall and perceive them, but I must be honest and truthful, knowing that is the only way to hold clarity and shine light on the journey ahead.

I sit with that for a moment, and the first memory that comes is a very small child sitting in a pretty dress on what I perceive to be a pew, waiting for the judge. It was the day my mother married for the second time and the day that my birth name was changed as I was adopted into this new family structure. There is a back story to this new dynamic – how my mother came to this place – but that is not mine to tell ... so onward.

When I look back on my childhood, memories that immediately pop to the forefront are not those of carefree happy times. I realise, of course, that there were times of both good and bad. But why is it that the ones experienced as "bad" are the most prevalent?? Could it be that those are the times where lessons were learnt, etched upon our psyche, where the experience was powerful enough to inform our emotional and spiritual growth? Perhaps ones that when uncovered later will have been moulded into diamonds from the pressure and fire of the experience – ready for discovery as the much-needed resource later on? I like that – truth rings from that insight.

After a sweet walk on a brisk clear day, I find myself writing with abandon because the words began pouring out as I walked – I had to come right in and begin! It is time; all is aligned and the flow is strong enough now that it cannot be denied! I have to smile because the interesting thing is that I have known for years that I needed to write – in fact, I have had at least four book titles at the ready for quite some time...

So, the vignettes ... I wonder if I need to pour out all those experiences on paper or just own that there were both good and bad as I mentioned. But conversely, it may be cathartic to put it all down, so here goes...

> I remember sitting on the back porch steps in the warm summer sun with Spike, our dog; I recall going to look for pop bottles to sell to make enough money so we could go swimming that afternoon; I remember sticky candy necklaces at the pool, a wasp sting on my head in the open showers, and the feeling of being unseen; I recall splitting one order of French fries amongst us on an evening out to Frosty Queen; I remember going in and out of hotels in Colorado looking for the best rate for a family of six to rest for the night; I remember how excited I was to get Barbie and Ken dolls from my grandma, but that memory fades into fear because those dolls weren't allowed at my house for being too lifelike; I recall the soft coolness of the grass as I rested on the way walking home from school because of a splitting headache; and the day I sat under the tall corn on the soft earth recovering as I worked an excruciatingly hot and humid summer job in Nebraska; I recall the fun of drive-in movies with the big grocery bag full of popcorn to share; the memory of walking to school with splints on my legs due to knee pain from a condition that most often affected boys; the memory of

Mom sunbathing in the backyard and giving me a pamphlet about the coming change I would experience; I remember a hairbrush being broken over my head because I didn't hold still enough; I recall sliding in big piles of pine needles in the fall ... ah, that wonderful earthly smell ; I remember my brother's pigeons; the fun of cranking homemade ice cream on a hot summer day; shopping to get two new outfits for high school; rolling up the skirts in order to fit in; singing in the choir and playing the piano; being so excited getting the lead in the junior class play and having a marvellous time performing ... just to have it all broken to pieces by a belt-whipping later that night, simply because in the melodrama, I had to hold a cigarette pretending to smoke; I remember the strictness of my parents being overwhelming and family life was volatile; my brother rebelled; moving from my hometown and my world as my little sister needed to start kindergarten in a Christian school so I would have to do my senior year in that same environment away from childhood friends ...

Wow – that all tumbled out! There is so much more, but we all have journeys, stories, and memories. We need to learn to embrace that journey, gathering the beautiful experiences to hold in our hearts and carrying with us the warmth of knowledge for the path ahead while casting aside the rest. This allows us to move forward with ease, dignity, and acceptance.

All of those childhood memories that bubbled up unexpectedly paved the path to adulthood where I continued, still not aware that I had a reason for being, but that was soon to change. Looking back to explore how all of this that is my life came to be, I can pinpoint what I recognise as the beginning of awakening ... a pivotal realisation.

In 1996, I connected with a gregarious and open-hearted welcoming spirit, a true enigma. It is easy now to recognise our paths were meant to cross at that precise moment. I was at a place of readiness. I was welcomed into that unique group of souls who expressed their wisdom through art and it was there I learnt of synchronicity. This was the beginning of awareness; the shell was cracked open and light began to illuminate untapped wisdom of my own glowing deep within, that unbeknownst to me, had been holding in readiness for just that moment in time...

We collaborated on commissioned art that referenced my Native American heritage. What started as that simple connection at an art festival that I could have surely walked past without attention, grew into the development of deep connections, lasting friendships, and special collaborations, especially with one of those amazing artists whose incredible art is a true reflection of the soul navigating its earthly journey. Those connections continue with me to this day, informing my experience of growth, development, and enlightenment.

As with every life path, not all was rosy. There were the marriages – two, in fact. With the dewy eyes of young love, I believed it would last forever but disillusionment followed. However, 15 years later, love struck for the second time. Again, I pictured being the elderly couple strolling hand in hand along the garden pathway of life, but while that didn't happen, I was able to see with clarity the purpose of both. One brought my beautiful child into the world, and one was the container from which I grew up and out into the beautiful world of expansion. I moved forward, fully embraced the power of "ME" and legally reclaimed my birth name. The strength of that was palpable; the energy around that change was euphoric.

Another pivotal touchpoint was completing my PhD studies. It would take a chapter, if not a book, to delineate all that took place during that immersive period. Suffice it to say that as one of the most transcendent of life experiences, I delved deep inside to understand who I was, what I believed, and what I was put on this earth to do. There are many stories – each with its own perfect thread – that contribute to the weaving of a wonderfully unique tapestry of experience that continues to develop and transform as life unfolds.

One of the outcomes was the opening of my integrative healing centre in 2006. It focused on holistic healing through the understanding of self, providing a healing practice that truly embodied the concept of mind, body and spirit.

Acknowledging the spiritual nature of humanity, the vision combined the traditional Western medicine approach with the wisdom of Eastern philosophy to provide complementary approaches to healing in one space. The healing centre functioned successfully for 13 years before closing its doors in late 2019, as I was feeling compelled to create space in my life for new, even greater expansion.

With meditative, prayerful guidance, I opened my heart and mind to the wisdom of the ancients. As ideas began to fully crystalise, it was time to embrace the whole of me, to step fully and unabashedly into the role for which I was born. It was time to claim and to share the gifts entrusted to me, to contribute to this world much-needed one-to-one and one-to-all truly impactful healing.

The vision of having a sacred healing sanctuary was originally delivered in a dream, formalised in my consciousness in 2005, and was realised partially by setting up the healing centre. However, it languished in the background for 18 years (maturing and growing up, I say!) roaring back into my consciousness with heightened awareness in 2023. I now hold complete certainty that it is in place and will become apparent in the near future. It is simply a matter of alignment with divine timing. I do not know the when, the where, or the how, but I do know it is so.

I have worked closely with my soul guide – a name I chose to describe the collaboration, but one that is not expansive enough to truly distinguish what our work entails – for over five years. During that time, I have come to recognise my true Beingness: I have joyfully dwelled in the presence of Sacred Wisdom; I have received messages and focused direction for my Divine purpose: I have been able to embrace that assignment from my life book, and grow beyond any self-doubt that what I am privileged to be the conduit for, is of significant healing consequence to humanity.

I used to question how the message – the healing work – would get out into the world, beyond the confines of my home, my city, my state, and even my country, because I understood the need for this to be global. I confidently held the space for miracles to happen, to somehow be thrust out onto the world stage and make connections globally – and I am almost giddy with excitement to be present in the midst of this miraculous unfolding. Within the last two years, I have made fabulous connections with beautiful souls around the world whose time it was to join this path with me. Ask and it shall be given, hold fast to your dreams, and manifest them into reality. Listen to the whispers of your Soul and follow the magical path of your destiny.

The thing is … life is fluid and as such, learning, understanding, accepting, and embracing are ever-changing, shifting emotions of knowingness. Softly but with focus, the threads of experience and change find their way into the tapestry of our lives.

One fabulous attribute of our life tapestry is that it has a beautiful resilient strength. Pulling gently on one thread of memory does not unravel the art of your existence, but rather strengthens its rightful place of entanglement within this exhibit – **YOU**, this manifest of life.

I invite you to sink into the depth of your memories and let them at first wash over you with abandon. Explore with curiosity and await with patience, for those that will move to the forefront with clarity are the ones that, as forged in the fire or gently moulded with potter's hands, contribute to the uniqueness of your journey. Reflect with gentleness upon those pivotal moments, embrace them without judgement, and allow the powerful light of understanding to heal them, whilst recognising the pure light of wisdom shining with clarity to light your path forward.

See yourself without judgement, watch how you navigated those experiences, and look for the magic in those transformational moments. Really, really look ... see, embrace, respect, honour, and love the essence of YOU.

Embrace your own unique, beautiful, sometimes messy journey because it's yours and yours alone. It has made you into the unique human you are today – it is resilient, ever-changing, a script always in production, a tapestry on the loom being created in all its splendour by your path and experiences.

Thus far, my journey towards completeness has been a path of exhilarating experience, exceptional challenge, joyful excitement, deep hurt, healing clarity, strength of being, divine wisdom, spiritual guidance, and above all – tenacity.

Change is the essence of life and knowledge is the life force of growth. Within that growth is the ability to experience expansion, all of which holds space for enlightenment. None of this works in isolation or a vacuum. There is always the ebb and flow, the give and take, with each experience propelling us along the path of our life journey. Awareness is crucial for understanding and growth.

What are we then but the stories we leave in our wake as we walk this planet? In addition, it is those whose lives entwine with ours and those that we touch along the way, often in capacities we do not know. That, then, should inform the integrity of the journey.

Writing my story has brought forth nostalgia, laughter, and, at times, tears. It has also served to further fulfil and strengthen my desire to create and maintain true healing environments for those I encounter on this life journey. Focused on honouring the Spirit in each of us, I welcome friends and guides who join me along the way as I continue to press towards full implementation of the vision given to me to fulfil. It is interesting that as I move through this process, it becomes ever clearer that I am simply the willing conduit for this work. Life is about movement, growth, expansion of heart, transcendence of spirit, and attending to tasks relevant to our unique journeys.

One of the greatest gifts on this earthly journey is understanding our purpose. Perhaps this moment in time spent with me will heighten your awareness, encourage exploration, and celebrate discovery while acknowledging your place of universal importance and embracing ownership of the purpose you are placed on this planet to fulfil.

See through the eyes of wisdom and be anchored to calm gentleness in the middle of chaos. Let extraneous noise fall away. Don't ignore your inner nudge but follow it with curiosity and embrace the magic.

Your existence is pivotal to the Divine plan. Love all of your 'beingness'; look beyond any fear to the knowingness of you; listen to the gentle whispers from your soul; learn from the past, engage in the present, and seek out opportunities for the future. What-ifs don't exist, so spend time fully present in the moment, open to the wisdom and flow from the Universe. As you Embrace the Journey, you will gain strength and purpose with my newest gift from the Divine:

STAND STRONG IN THE GENTLENESS OF IT

"I had no idea that being your authentic self could make me as rich as I've become. If I had, I'd have done it a lot earlier."

Oprah Winfrey

American talk show host, television producer, actress, author, and media proprietor

Leadership unleashes innovation and creativity as defining traits, and Natalie naturally integrates these elements into her work, helping others to grow and thrive.

At the core of her determination to make a difference are authenticity and vulnerability – two magnetic qualities that attract and inspire her community. Often, brilliance emerges from opportunities that involve significant transitions. Natalie explores this theme in her engaging narrative within the pages of her chapter.

Natalie comprehends the crucial role a positive mindset plays in personal development and champions leadership as a path to deeper self-understanding. Through her journey, she has realised that her purpose extends beyond geographical boundaries; her message and mission have a global reach. This light bulb moment ignited her resolve to embark on a mission greater than herself, embodying the hallmark of a servant leader who understands the power of influence and impact to create meaningful change.

As you delve into Natalie's chapter, you will discover a wise woman who places collaboration and empathy at the heart of her success. Natalie's story is a testament to the transformative power of authenticity, a positive mindset, and the courage to pursue a mission that transcends borders. Her leadership journey inspires us all to embrace innovation, creativity, and the profound impact of genuine connection.

Brenda

Natalie Heilling

"In authenticity, female leaders find their voice; in vulnerability, they find their strength. By embracing authenticity and vulnerability, leaders can inspire transformation and create a ripple effect of positive change in the world."

Natalie Heilling

The Energy Game

The Pivotal Moment

All too often, we live in a place that is not in alignment with who we really are, which causes us to feel unhappy, anxious, and unfulfilled. The key concept for me is mastering our energy. We are energy; our beliefs, thoughts, decisions, and actions all create our reality, and we have the power to change it. After my own journey of transformation, where clearing and mastering my energy was pivotal to my success, in 2023, I finally realised a dream I had been nurturing for years – The Energy Game.

My passion lies in helping people uncover their unique potential and embrace life to the fullest. I am an energy healer and life coach dedicated to guiding individuals on their journey to self-discovery and empowerment. I'm also the mastermind behind The Energy Game, where our mission is all about unlocking potential and fostering fulfilment. Alongside my role as an energy healer, I proudly serve as the co-founder of Research Partners. Together, we collaborate with global businesses and start-ups, offering executive recruitment support while advocating for diversity in hiring practices.

In The Energy Game, we focus on energy healing and life coaching, where leadership takes on a whole new meaning. It is about guiding individuals on a journey of transformation, and being a facilitator of growth and healing. I work with clients on multiple levels to help facilitate a desired transformation in their lives. This includes help with pain relief caused by physical illness, assisting with releasing limiting beliefs or negative emotions, and habit changing and goal setting. Some clients may come to me thinking they need one thing and when we dig deeper, the issue is something entirely different.

One such example was working with Nadine, who came to me when she was experiencing chronic pain from a medical condition. She wanted to reduce her pain and dependency on prescribed medication, as well as improve her overall life fulfilment. After a few sessions together, her pain did indeed reduce. It also became apparent that her stressful lifestyle and lack of self-care were a contributing factor to the flare-ups. This made sense because unmanaged and constant stress can often lead to physical illness.

During our time together, she learnt how to manage her stress and stop unhelpful looping thoughts. This was replaced with feeling more empowered and confident that she could create the life she desired. Within weeks, she quit her job and accepted a new job in another country to realise a dream that she had for many years but had previously not had the courage to pursue.

With over 20 years' experience leading internal teams, I've honed many qualities essential for this style of leadership. That's why transitioning into healing and coaching felt like a natural step for me. In both realms, authenticity, empathy, and empowering others have been key. These are the core tenets of my style of leadership.

Recognising the role of leadership in personal and professional growth is crucial in my line of work. Effective leadership acts as a catalyst for self-discovery and improvement, providing invaluable insights and tools for navigating life's challenges with clarity and confidence. From my experience, strong leadership encourages individuals to step out of their comfort zones, confront limiting beliefs, and embrace new possibilities.

However, coaching is not only about imparting knowledge but also about sharing personal transformations. Clients don't just come to me for my expertise; they're drawn to my personal journey of growth. By embracing vulnerability in my leadership style, I show that change and growth are possible through authenticity. This shared journey forms deep connections with clients, leading to profound transformations and personal development.

Looking back on my leadership journey, I realise the foresight and vision I had are more relevant than ever today. Leading remote teams, which has become a common challenge post-Covid, has been a big part of my career for the past 20 years. On co-founding my first business, an executive talent research business, I had a vision for a global remote team. I wanted to create a company that not only delivered exceptional service to clients, but also prioritised work-life balance for our employees. That meant providing individuals with the opportunity to work remotely, offering flexibility in working hours, and ensuring a harmonious blend between professional responsibilities and personal well-being.

When hiring team members, I didn't simply focus on skills – I also considered how remote work might affect their mental health, motivation, and job performance. I realised that creating a supportive environment for remote work was about more than just productivity; it was also about taking care of our team's well-being. These early experiences taught me the importance of empathy, adaptability, and foresight in leadership – qualities that have guided me ever since.

Let me take you back to a moment that transformed everything for me. Before 2019, I silently battled C-PTSD from a challenging relationship. Life felt like it was on autopilot, where survival mode was the norm, and I hadn't realised how far I had drifted from inner peace and happiness. Despite outward appearances of success, I struggled internally.

In 2019, the cracks began to show. Overwhelmed and falling ill too often, I started doubting I could even handle a simple holiday. In fact, the anxiety became so crippling that I couldn't bring myself to board a flight. That moment served as the wake-up call – deep down, I knew life wasn't meant to be a constant struggle. So I made the decision to change.

Therapy was a start, but it wasn't enough to regain my health. That's when I delved into research, eager to explore avenues for healing from trauma and tapping into personal growth through energy practices. This curiosity led me to incredible insights and practices that not only transformed my life, but also empowered me to guide others on their own journeys.

It was at this point that I realised I wanted to expand my leadership impact globally. This shift led me to embrace vulnerability in leadership, being open about my own journey to guide and inspire others. Suddenly, leadership became more than just leading a business; it became a way to profoundly impact people's lives, guiding them towards healing, growth, and transformation.

Shifting from a corporate leadership role, where I had spent my entire career, into a different industry, was a journey filled with inner conflict. I found myself wrestling with my ego, battling self-doubt, and facing limiting beliefs.

Ironically, one of my biggest challenges was dealing with the fear of judgement, something I often coached others about, yet struggled with myself. In fact, the fear of judgement loomed so large that I had systematically built a whole new persona, that promoted my energy offerings on a totally different social media platform (Instagram) outside of LinkedIn which is where 'corporate Natalie' lived. I justified this to myself with the belief that while the corporate world is slowly recognising the importance of energy and its influence on our lives, I worried about facing scepticism from those who saw my shift as unconventional or questionable. But in reality, most of this scepticism was coming from within me.

Finding Courage and Changing Mindset

Facing fear and resistance through the lens of an identity shift was a truly transformative journey for me. Initially, I found myself wrestling with fears and doubts that arose from the stark misalignment between who I was and the kind of leader I needed to be – one who was comfortable showing vulnerability, being more visible, and engaging in public speaking. My previous persona was very introverted and shy, so public speaking was not an option!

Recognising this misalignment was a pivotal moment, prompting me to embark on a deliberate transition from one version of myself to another. This journey involved delving deep into my beliefs, values, and behaviours, all while being open to challenging and evolving them. Stepping out of my comfort zone was daunting, but necessary. By consciously embodying the qualities and characteristics of the leader I aspired to become, I bridged the gap between my current and desired identities. Through self-awareness, changing habits, and taking action, I unlocked my fullest potential and embraced a new persona.

Transitioning into a new venture required a fundamental shift in my approach to growth and learning. As a leader who values understanding a business from the ground up, I recognised the importance of immersing myself in diverse learning experiences.

In my existing recruiting business, having already navigated the journey of building it from scratch, and achieving a level of competence and stability, my learning and growth had plateaued. However, venturing into new territory demanded a fresh perspective. I embraced the opportunity to delve into unfamiliar domains, eagerly soaking up knowledge through ongoing study, practical experiences, feedback sessions, and certifications.

As well as learning the modalities, exploring areas which had always intrigued me, such as online business and social media platforms, allowed me to broaden my horizons. Rather than viewing this as a daunting challenge, I approached it with the curiosity of a child in a sweet shop, eagerly sampling the vast array of possibilities before me.

Diving into this diverse learning journey, I naturally embraced a growth-oriented mindset. Each new insight sparked my love for learning and lit up my excitement for what lay ahead. This mindset shift not only broadened my skills, but also brought a new-found sense of fulfilment and purpose to my leadership journey.

As a leader, transparency and integrity have been my top priority. I've seen first-hand how crucial they are for effective leadership. By consistently walking the talk, I've set a standard of authenticity and accountability for my team. My goal is to inspire them to embody these values in their own actions and interactions.

Transitioning into energy healing and coaching reinforced the importance of living what I preach. At first, I was hesitant to share my diverse background, fearing judgement or confusion. But embracing transparency and authenticity actually boosted my career, aligning my professional path with my true self.

As I've mastered my energy, I've realised the immense power of our words. The words we speak are infused with energy and directly influence our thoughts, beliefs, and actions.

By aligning our words with our intentions and taking inspired action, we can manifest our desired reality and create positive change in our lives and the lives of others.

Overcoming Challenges

Transitioning into a leadership role in a new industry is not without its hurdles. I grappled with limited industry knowledge, fearing it might undermine my credibility. To combat this, I immersed myself in industry-specific resources, sought mentorship, and enrolled in relevant courses.

However, the true breakthrough was that embodied my teachings and became my own success story. I utilised the tools I teach to overcome burnout and C-PTSD, change mindset, make positive change (relocating to another country), and completely revamp my life to align with my life vision. This experience enabled me to craft a narrative of genuine transformation, rooted in authenticity and personal growth.

Building a network from scratch posed another challenge. Attending industry events, networking with peers, and engaging in online communities helped bridge this gap. Leveraging my corporate career's credibility also proved invaluable in establishing trust in the new space. I also learnt how to build and leverage my personal brand.

But the biggest challenge of all was internal, combining the two identities that I had managed to create for myself to the outside world on Instagram and LinkedIn. This was creating internal conflict and was the key to my transformation. My spiritual and corporate persona needed to merge and, in doing so, I surrendered to the fact that whoever needs to hear my message will hear it, and if it doesn't resonate, that is okay.

As the saying goes, "The expert in anything was once a beginner." Success isn't about where you start, but the determination you bring to the journey.

Transitioning to a new career path, often perceived as unconventional, inevitably brought concerns about criticism and scepticism. Some questioned the viability of my new direction, expressing worries about its impact on my professional reputation and existing business. Despite these doubts, I stayed true to my intuition.

However, in facing these challenges, I also came to realise that I can be my own worst critic. Surprisingly, the impact of criticism wasn't as severe as I had feared. In fact, many people showed genuine interest in my new endeavours. As soon as I started to broaden my audience, I was featured in the media and invited to be an executive contributor to an online publication serving leadership, mindset, and lifestyle topics. This served as a reminder not to overthink things and to trust in my abilities. It also became apparent that, rather than conflicting, my new venture seamlessly complemented my existing recruitment business, exceeding my wildest expectations.

Ultimately, I didn't let doubt and criticism hold me back. If it weren't for my own internal dialogue, I might have launched The Energy Game sooner. It's a lesson in taking risks, staying true to your passions, and embracing the unknown, all of which ultimately led to unexpected growth and fulfilment.

Navigating the balance between my professional and personal life has been a journey filled with struggles and triumphs. As a working mother and business leader, I prioritised creating a flexible work-life culture for my team, but I faced significant hurdles when my health began to suffer due to C-PTSD. I found myself neglecting my own well-being in favour of maintaining appearances at work. Hitting rock bottom made me realise the critical importance of prioritising self-care and finding a healthy equilibrium between my personal and professional life.

This realisation sparked a transformative shift in my approach to work-life balance which is also integral to my coaching programs today. True fulfilment and success stem from a holistic alignment across various facets of life – emotions, personal growth, relationships, parenting, health, and so on. Once I embraced this insight, I began to master the art of living in alignment with my values and priorities.

To restore balance, I integrated self-care practices, such as meditation and energy healing, into my daily routine. Mindfulness and reflection became essential tools for managing stress and clarifying my priorities. Additionally, I made a commitment to continuous learning and sought support from loved ones and networks, recognising that I couldn't do it all alone.

Valuable Lessons Learnt

Being authentic means being true to yourself, no matter what. This is how I am, not just in my personal life, but also as a leader. Finding my authentic leadership style was a journey, rooted in my values of honesty, integrity, and transparency.

Authenticity isn't just a buzzword for me, it's a game-changer in leadership. Sticking to my values builds trust among my team, making collaboration and engagement soar. Plus, being authentic helps me rely on my intuition, which enables me to have more confidence and clarity on which decisions to make. It's what drives me to inspire and motivate my team genuinely, boosting productivity and success.

Stepping into a new industry wasn't easy. I had to face my fears and doubts, embracing vulnerability as a leader, but soon realised the power of sharing my own struggles and victories to inspire others. Being vulnerable means opening up about my experiences, both the highs and the lows, to make a real impact and help others grow.

In authenticity, female leaders find their voice; in vulnerability, they discover their strength. By embracing authenticity and vulnerability, leaders can inspire transformation, empower others, and create a ripple effect of positive change in the world.

I've faced numerous tough situations that truly challenged my resilience, especially when those situations clashed with what I believe in and who I am. It wasn't easy; I often felt uncomfortable and had to really dig deep to push through.

One such instance is that I had become deeply attached to my identity of being a co-founder of another business. This was ingrained into my persona. It is who 'Natalie' was and what she was known for. It was how I introduced myself when people asked what I did for my career. I somehow initially felt a sense of loss and failure that this would change. I felt vulnerable talking about my new business venture. However, this new path is what I truly believe in. My persona was changing and it was uncomfortable as I ventured into this new territory, but it was essential in order to follow my passion.

Moving towards a career that can be seen as unconventional brought many doubts and uncertainties. But I had to stay true to my intuition and be resilient to keep moving forward. During this time, loneliness and isolation emerged unexpectedly. The weight of decision-making often overwhelmed me as I navigated new responsibilities. Change and uncertainty are inherent in leadership. Leading through recessions, I faced tough decisions like downsizing, while maintaining team morale.

Resilience has been my secret weapon in both my careers. It's what's helped me bounce back from setbacks, adapt to changes, and keep pushing forward . And every time I leaned on my resilience, it pushed me a little further, helping me reach new milestones.

Resilience isn't just about being tough; it's about having optimism, problem-solving skills, and support from others. It's what helps us handle life's curveballs, overcome obstacles, and come out stronger on the other side.

My leadership style highly values teamwork and understanding. Collaboration is all about bringing everyone's ideas together, which often leads to new solutions and shared victories. And empathy is about really understanding where my team members are coming from, what makes them tick, and what challenges they're facing.

These two things have been lifesavers in tough situations. When working on big projects, having everyone's input helps us make smarter decisions and come up with creative fixes. And when things get challenging, showing empathy makes our team feel supported and ready to give their all.

By making collaboration and empathy a priority, I've built a workplace where everyone feels respected and valued. And that's what keeps us moving forward and feeling like we're all in it together.

Three Tips for Developing Leadership Skills

Tip 1: Focus on Continuous Learning

The need for growth is something we all feel deep down; it's what keeps us feeling alive and fulfilled. It's not just about getting older; it's about growing personally, intellectually, emotionally, and spiritually. Without growth, we can feel like we're just going through the motions, not really living our best lives.

That's why I'd tell my younger self to keep learning and growing. Staying curious and open-minded opens up so many opportunities.

Ultimately, growth is about becoming the best version of ourselves, which is why it is so important in leadership. Not only does it help us find our passions, discover our purpose, and make the most of our lives, but it enhances self-awareness, fosters better emotional intelligence, and creates a more positive work environment.

So, embrace growth – it's what makes life exciting and meaningful.

I recommend various strategies to help:

1. Books and online courses: Explore your passions and interests by reading books and taking online courses aligned with your values. This is a great way to learn and grow, especially if your current career isn't your passion.

2. Networking: Attend networking events, industry conferences, and professional organisations to connect with peers, exchange ideas, and gain insights from experienced leaders.

3. Feedback and reflection: Encourage the habit of seeking feedback from colleagues, supervisors, and mentors regularly. Encourage self-reflection to identify strengths, areas for improvement, and opportunities for growth.

Tip 2: Seek Mentorship and Guidance

Seeking guidance from mentors is crucial for personal and professional growth. Mentors provide valuable insights and support to help navigate the challenges of leadership and life.

Looking back, one of my biggest mistakes was not investing in a coach sooner. I used to struggle to achieve certain goals on my own because I did not want to invest in a coach. What I failed to realise is that it took me longer to get where I needed to be and in some instances, I may not have reached the desired point at all. I missed out on valuable opportunities for growth, especially early in my career.

As leaders, we should always be open to learning and seeking growth opportunities. Working with coaches and mentors has been transformative for me, opening up new possibilities and propelling me forward. Thanks to mentorship and coaching, I've made new connections, found exciting opportunities, and learnt more about myself.

In short, mentorship is a secret weapon for success. By seeking guidance from mentors, we can learn faster, tackle challenges, and reach our goals with confidence.

Tip 3: Embrace Failure and Learn From It

As a society, we often confine ourselves to narrow definitions of success and failure. One of the most profound insights I've gained is the importance of redefining these concepts for ourselves. For some, success is about achieving career status or financial wealth. Others find fulfilment in making a positive impact on their communities.

For me, redefining success meant letting go of others' expectations and embracing my own definition. This shift in perspective made failure less daunting, as it no longer held power over my sense of worth. Instead, failure became an opportunity for growth and learning.

Failure doesn't have to be a roadblock. Embracing failure as a chance to pivot, adapt, and evolve is key to resilience. Each setback offers valuable insights that shape our journey forward. So, let's shift our perspective on success and failure because that is when we truly get to live.

Lyndsay is a seasoned leader who champions others by sharing their stories and interviewing them on her podcast. She knows the value of spotlighting talent and believes in creating win-win opportunities.

Leaders understand the importance of role models, and Lyndsay embodies this with her belief that "you cannot be what you cannot see." Her dedication to showcasing representation as a core element of nurturing future leaders shines through in her storytelling.

Lyndsay's chapter reveals her as a woman of substance who has internalised the wisdom of those who came before her. She leads by example, eschewing micromanagement in favour of empowering others. Heeding the advice of a former boss, she understands that by letting others take the reins, they soon discover their ability to soar.

As a powerful advocate for women, Lyndsay is thrilled to see more women pulling up chairs at the boardroom table. She deeply values the power of sisterhood, knowing that being part of a supportive sorority means having each other's backs. Through her storytelling, she illuminates the journeys of women who face and conquer adversity, bravely venturing the road less travelled to reach their goals.

Turn the page to delve into Lyndsay's world, where every story is a beacon, every interview a revelation, and every shared experience a step towards a more inclusive and empowered future.

Brenda

Lyndsay Dowd

"POWER SKILLS (we don't call them soft skills around here) are modern leadership tenets. Leaders who embrace their POWER SKILLS go from good to great."

Lyndsay Dowd

You Can't Be What You Can't See

Let me share a story that might resonate with you. Imagine spending 25 years in corporate America, with 23 of those years at IBM. During that time, I managed large sales teams and carried on a family legacy – my father, father-in-law, husband, and mother-in-law collectively put in 105 years of service at IBM. It was a legacy I was proud of, but after 23 years, I felt it was time for a change.

Has there ever been a moment in your life when a new opportunity knocked on your door? For me, that moment came when another company approached me to run one of their sales teams. I took everything I knew, along with my Big Blue legacy, and jumped on board, fully aware it would be challenging.

And challenging it was. Six months later, I was fired. If you've ever been in a similar situation, you know how devastating that can be. It wasn't part of my plan, and it hit me hard. I felt alone, embarrassed, and lost. It was as if I had a scarlet letter on my chest, making me wonder who would ever want to work with me again.

After a month of reflecting and licking my wounds, I asked myself three crucial questions:

- What am I good at?

- What do I love to do?

- How can I help people the most?

If you're at a crossroads, these questions might help guide you too. What I realised is that I excel at building modern leaders and creating an irresistible culture that drives results. This realisation led me to start my own company, Heartbeat for Hire, LLC. I also wrote a book, *Top Down Culture: Revolutionizing Leadership to Drive Results*, and started the Heartbeat for Hire podcast, which has since ranked in the top 5% globally.

You might have seen my work featured in prestigious publications like *Fortune Magazine*, HR.Com, *Authority Magazine*, Business Management Daily, and Valiant CEO, or heard me on one of the 60+ podcasts I've been featured on.

Today, I coach C-suites on long-term engagements, speak to companies about modern leadership and the importance of a healthy culture, and teach LinkedIn workshops.

Whether you're looking to enhance your leadership skills or build a thriving company culture, there's a path forward. Sometimes, the setbacks we face open doors to new opportunities we never imagined. How might you turn a challenging situation into a stepping stone for future success?

Evolving Leadership

Think about how much the world has changed in the last 25 years, and the business landscape is no exception. Naturally, leadership had to evolve as well. Consider the history of business: it began with manufacturing, a transactional environment where people punched cards, completed their shifts, and went home. This task-oriented, patriarchal approach seeped into the modern business era, influencing the white-collar world too. The mantra was clear – don't ask questions, just do your job.

As time went on, albeit slowly, the business landscape started to change. More women emerged in leadership roles, and people began craving a different style of leadership. Team-building and camaraderie became important, leadership development gained traction, and HR finally got a seat at the table.

One of the most significant shifts in the US business landscape was The Great Resignation during the pandemic. Do you remember that period when many left their jobs in droves, demanding better treatment and conditions? This movement swung the pendulum in favour of employees, forcing companies to acknowledge they needed to do better. Long days and poor treatment were no longer acceptable.

During this time, almost everyone worked from home, and for the first time, we got a glimpse into each other's personal lives – kids, pets, and home offices. This insight sparked a desire for vulnerability in our leaders, urging them to show up as their whole selves, not just as professionals.

The changing business landscape and the increasing role of women in leadership presented new opportunities. Women have learnt to navigate this patriarchal world adeptly. I often joke that women speak two languages: 'male' and 'female.' We know how to be true to ourselves, build community, and meet people where they are, a style of leadership that tends to bring out the best in teams.

Curiosity is a hallmark of the best leaders. I coach my clients to ask, "How can I be the best leader for you?" It's a humbling question, but modern leaders aren't afraid to be vulnerable. They embrace failure and hone their power skills – traits, habits, and differentiators that define good leadership. We don't call them soft skills because they are anything but soft.

Throughout my career in tech, I was often the only woman on many teams. When you're the only one, you end up modelling the behaviour you see, which can be cut-throat, mean, and unsupportive. Here's a hot tip: no one has ever been inspired by micromanagement!

Occasionally, you come across a truly great leader, and those experiences can be profound. Have you ever had a manager ask you to tell them your story? I did, and it left me speechless. I nervously repeated, "What's my story? How much time do you have?"

Are you, like me, not sure? Do you know your story and have awareness about your gifts and talents? Do you know what drives you?

At that moment, I realised I didn't have an answer. I hadn't curated my story or condensed it into a soundbite. Instead of a confident response, I gave her a shorter version of my life story. But she wanted to know more – she wanted to understand my motivation, what makes me 'tick,' and why I do what I do. The details I shared helped her understand how to support me. From that moment forward, I used this tactic with my teams.

Equally important is the question, "How can I be the best leader for you?" When you ask this, you're admitting you don't know everything. And let's be honest: nobody does, no matter how qualified they are. If you do know everything, then you're probably overqualified for the job. Asking this question helps lower people's guards. It's a trust-building moment, and trust is your currency.

You'll get wildly different answers from each person because everyone has different desires, depending on their age, tenure, goals, and experience. When you understand what they want, you're better positioned to provide what they need and advocate on their behalf. Leading this way creates psychological safety. And once you have that, your team members will step out of their comfort zones and try things they haven't tried before.

In my experience, teams thrive in creative, vibrant, and fun environments. But don't be fooled – it's not all roses and sunshine. You create a vibrant environment because, as a leader, you also have to deliver tough messages, sometimes in the form of a lay-off or a performance plan. Most leaders dread these moments, and those who care deeply find them incredibly stressful. However, when you're consistent and lead with heart, it makes those moments a bit easier.

Have you ever been in a position that you dislike? What's the worst thing you've had to tell to others?

I've had to lay people off, and I swore I'd never get good at it – and I never did. I hated it. But because I was consistent in my approach and advocacy for my team members, those tough moments were often met with the most remarkable responses. Employees would say, "I'm so sorry you have to do this."

Hearing that always stunned me because I was affecting their lives in the worst way. Have you ever faced a similar situation? How did you navigate it?

As a leader, letting people go is part of the job. But when you lead with heart, even the most difficult situations can turn into opportunities to maintain rapport. I've been able to keep connections with those I had to let go, and these relationships continue even today.

This is the essence of being a modern leader. Those who struggle the most are often the ones clinging to outdated concepts they've used for decades. Have you ever heard someone ask, "Why do I need to change?"

The answer is simple: the world around us has changed dramatically – technology, ChatGPT, remote work, diversity practices, business resource groups, and more. So, why wouldn't leadership styles need to change too?

Changing Narrative and Storytelling

Let me share an example from my time as a client executive at IBM, a coveted and challenging role. I had a $150 million quota for one account and led a team of 55 people. Our relationship with this particular client was complex – we were partners, clients, and competitors all at once. Every action was scrutinised, and visibility was high.

When I presented my business plan to my new boss, Sherry, detailing how I wanted to approach the client, she stopped me about two-thirds of the way through and said, "Girl, I've got your back. Now fly!" Her words took my breath away and still gives me goose bumps today. What happened next was incredible.

Sherry's confidence booster made me realise that I didn't have to fear failure. We could try things we had never tried before and connect with parts of the business we had never spoken to. I took Sherry's message and shared it with my extended team. We dug deep, communicated, connected, and supported each other. We embraced new relationships and new conversations, collaborating in a much stronger partnership.

As a result, we closed the most significant deal our two companies had seen to date – over $23 million. We crushed our numbers and created a paradigm shift, changing our relationship with the client on every level. This all stemmed from Sherry's simple yet powerful remark: "I've got your back. Now fly!"

Failure is part of growth and success. How you, as a leader, embrace, celebrate, and learn from failure is vitally important. Have you experienced a moment where a leader's confidence in you made all the difference? How did it change your approach?

Leading With Heart

The most significant message I share with leaders is to give your team the space to do the jobs they were hired for. Let me share a story that illustrates this perfectly.

I had a wonderful boss, Adriana. She was fantastic and promoted me twice. The first time she promoted me, she asked, "How do you want to run the business?"

I looked at her curiously and said, "You want to know how I want to run the business? You mean you are not going to tell me what to do?"

Her response was a game-changer: "Yes, you know more about this space than I do. You've been in it longer. How do you want to handle it?" I was delighted by her insightful leadership style.

Inspired by her approach, I turned around and asked my team the same question: "What haven't we tried and how can we do this differently?"

I branded my team 'Mavericks and Hustlers,' and they proudly wore that badge. Adriana created an environment of trust and autonomy for her leadership team, and as a result, her managers were incredibly loyal to her. To this day, Adriana and I are still very dear friends. She instilled trust and faith in me, which I, in turn, instilled in my team. This created an exciting environment of fun, grit, and high performance. The impact she had on me was profound.

Now, let's look at an example of what not to do. The woman who fired me had zero power skills. After a particular call, she bluntly stated, "I don't like how you represented yourself on that call. I don't like how you represented the company, and you didn't do a good job. Fix it for next time."

How do you think I did the next time? I was so worried about the words coming out of my mouth that I couldn't rely on my instincts, my sense of humour, or my superpower of reading people.

This role became terribly unhealthy for me. I was always anxious and not sleeping, waking up at two in the morning to check if I had sent that email.

When a leader instils doubt in their employees, they will never get good performance. Moreover, the way they treat people permeates throughout the organisation. My team saw how she was treating me and didn't like it. They became protective of me and always stepped up when I asked for help. They wanted her off my back so I could get off theirs.

This woman wanted a true micromanager, something I refused to be. It was a tragic example of poor leadership – one I have derived countless stories from to teach leaders a better way.

Have you ever experienced a leader like Adriana who empowered you or someone who undermined your confidence? How did it affect your performance and approach to leadership?

Bad Luck Creates Destiny

Sometimes, bad luck sets you on the path to your true purpose. When I was fired, or as I like to say, "shoved out of the nest," it led me to start my company, Heartbeat for Hire. This was the moment my true purpose in life became clear – to modernise leadership and help leaders build healthy, high-performing cultures that drive results.

Through my book, speaking engagements, podcast, LinkedIn, press, and all my social platforms, I aim to cast a wide net. You can't know what good leadership is if you've never had a good leader. When you think about it, how many times have you raised your hand when asked if you've had a bad leader? Probably 100% of the time, right? But how often have you experienced a great leader? If you're like most people, barely half raise their hands.

This is why sharing stories of positive leadership is so important. Some people are naturally great leaders, but leadership is also a learned experience. POWER SKILLS are the tenets that make modern leaders, and we all need more of those.

Time for Voices of Women

Women have waited long enough for seats at the table. Now, it's thrilling to see women pulling up chairs and sitting down! There is important work ahead. Surrounding yourself with incredible women who inspire, challenge, and cheer you on is crucial. Community is vital when you're trying to do something difficult.

Have you ever noticed how much easier it is to pick up a pay cheque than to build something yourself? But every time I waver, the women in my community remind me that I'm exactly where I'm supposed to be. That support system has been monumental in my success.

When you think of women's voices, remember that everyone has incredible stories – some have been told, and many are still waiting for their moment in the spotlight. I'm a natural storyteller, and that's how I start each episode on my show. I ask my guest to share their story, focusing on the vulnerable situations or circumstances they had to overcome to get where they are today.

A Little Advice

If you're looking for advice, the first thing every woman needs to do, regardless of age, is leverage recognition. This POWER SKILL lifts others up. You don't have to be a people leader to do it. A candle doesn't lose its light by lighting another candle. The best leaders are generous. Have you ever shared someone's excellent work with others? Whether it's sending a note to their manager, writing a recommendation, or recognising them publicly, we all have the ability to do this. Great performance should be recognised, and by shining a light on others, it doesn't take it away from you. In fact, it reflects well on you as a generous person, employee, or leader.

Next, dive deep into LinkedIn. I have been on LinkedIn since 2006, and initially, I only visited it when I got an award, a promotion, or was passed over for one. I undervalued the importance of building my personal brand.

You are never too young or too old to build your brand. In today's world, projecting who you are beyond your job title is essential. What do you want people to know about you? Remember, when someone Googles you, your LinkedIn page is often the first thing they see. Make it speak for you.

Another recommendation is to pay it forward. Have you ever had someone say, "Can I call you sometime and ask for feedback?" Always say, "Absolutely!" because others did this for you. Women are amazing at passing the torch – it's how we learn, grow, and challenge ourselves. As you age and mature; remember that you are modelling behaviour. If you are genuine and lift others up, they will follow your example and do the same.

One exercise I encourage everyone to do is to build their 'brag book.' Every time you receive recognition or a promotion, add it to your brag book. I kept a folder in my email called "Pats on the Back," where I would save accolades, kudos, or notes of encouragement from colleagues. If somebody sent my boss an email praising my work, it went straight into the folder. It's impossible to remember all the nice things people have said about you off the top of your head, so the brag book serves as a wonderful reminder of your accomplishments. This living document travels with you from job to job, and when you're interviewing for your next position, you'll have all your achievements at your fingertips.

Remember, these are your accomplishments. These are facts, not feelings. Don't confuse the two. Some women feel that talking about them sounds boastful. However, you need to get comfortable discussing your achievements with confidence and pride.

Leading With Heart

My vision for the world is to see far more people leading with heart. Be kind to each other, lift each other up, and be the change you want to see; don't wait for someone else to do it for you.

Let me leave you with this: when you lead with heart, despite difficult situations, you can maintain rapport and even strengthen relationships with those you have to let go.

Have you ever noticed that the leaders who struggle the most are often the ones clinging to outdated concepts? They might ask, "Why do I need to change?" The simple answer is that the whole world around us has changed dramatically – technology, remote work, diversity practices, and more. Why wouldn't leadership styles need to change too?

When you embrace modern leadership, you inspire others to do the same. Imagine asking your team, "How do you want to run the business?" How empowering is that? It builds trust and fosters innovation.

On the flip side, think about a time when a leader instilled doubt in you. How did it affect your performance and morale?

Leadership isn't just about the successes; it's also about handling the tough moments with grace and empathy. Whether it's delivering difficult news or navigating complex relationships, leading with heart makes all the difference.

So, how will you lead? Will you be the kind of leader who lifts others up, embraces change, and creates a culture of trust and innovation? The choice is yours, and the impact can be profound.

Tiba's story begins with a powerful revelation: courage is the first step in any transformative journey. As a leader, she understands that initiating change in one's life requires immense bravery. In the face of challenging situations, Tiba finds that profound lessons emerge, helping to make sense of the pitfalls and obstacles that impede happiness and progress.

An effective leader rises to challenges, even if it necessitates a change in direction. Tiba knows that transformation is not a solitary endeavour; it thrives on collaboration and the guidance of mentors who offer solutions and drive growth. Embracing this realisation, Tiba committed to a new direction, embarking on a purpose-driven mission to help others realise their potential.

With her Iraqi heritage, Tiba weaves a rich tapestry of values into her leadership. Her cultural roots infuse her work with a depth of empathy and understanding that transcends boundaries. As she continues her leadership journey, Tiba creates ripples of brilliance, illuminating a path for others to follow.

What sets Tiba apart is her dedication to capturing and sharing inspiring stories that have the power to change lives. Her narrative is a testament to the impact of courage, empathy, and purposeful action. Now, it's time to delve into her story and discover the essence of this captivating female leader.

Brenda

Tiba Al-Khalidy

"The journey of leadership begins with a single step of courage, guided by purpose and fuelled by resilience."

Tiba Al-Khalidy

Embracing Leadership
A Journey of Courage and Purpose

In the vast expanse of our lives, we often encounter pivotal moments that stir within us the call to lead – be it in our careers, relationships, or personal growth. For me, the realisation occurred during adversity, igniting a transformational journey into the realm of coaching and leadership.

The Awakening: A Call to Purpose

I vividly recall my time as the head of the accounts department in a law firm – a role that should have felt fulfilling, but instead was impacted by bullying and a toxic work environment.

The experience of workplace bullying left a profound impact on me, shaping my decision to embrace change and pursue a path of coaching. Bullying can be devastating, eroding self-esteem and diminishing self-belief. It creates a toxic environment that stifles growth and undermines one's sense of worth.

The relentless experience of workplace bullying began to take a toll on my mental health and well-being. I reached a breaking point where I no longer recognised myself and found it increasingly difficult to enjoy life. The toxicity of the environment forced me to suppress my true self, leading me to shrink into a diminished version of who I truly was, stifling my voice and passions.

It became clear that I craved a life aligned with my values, one where every moment was lived authentically and joyfully. In my quest for a new direction, I discovered coaching – a transformative journey that began with seeking solutions for my own healing and growth. Engaging multiple coaches allowed me to gain clarity and perspective until I found the right guide who helped me heal and rediscover my purpose.

It was during this transformative process that I realised my calling: to become a coach myself and empower others on their own journeys of healing, growth, and personal and business development.

Drawing from my background in accountancy and business, I envisioned a path where I could leverage my expertise to support others in realising their full potential and living authentically aligned lives. This awakening ignited a profound desire to contribute positively to the lives of others through coaching and mentorship.

In the face of this adversity, I made a conscious choice not to let the negativity define me. Instead, I channelled that experience into transformation. Coaching played a pivotal role in this journey, empowering me to reclaim my confidence, and recognise my value and my strengths.

Through coaching, I discovered the power of self-awareness and resilience, enabling me to rise above the impact of bullying and begin to make a new path aligned with my true purpose. Coaching not only provided me with practical tools and strategies, but also instilled a deep sense of empowerment and belief in my ability to effect positive change.

The weight of these challenges led me to a profound realisation: I was already a leader in many aspects of my life, navigating work, family, and personal growth.

This awareness was not new to me; from a young age, I discovered the joy of empowering others. I vividly recall being seven years old, sitting in our garden, helping my friends with their daily homework. In Iraq, our homes were built with large front gardens enclosed by high fences, providing complete privacy. I would set up a makeshift classroom with a blackboard and eagerly explain lessons to my friends.

This act of empowerment not only brought me joy but also served as a coping mechanism after my father's passing. Helping others and witnessing their growth became a source of solace and strength during challenging times, laying the foundation for my innate ability to guide and coach others towards their potential. It brings a smile to my face now, as I reflect on how I'm continuing this journey over 40 years later, operating from my own garden once again, but this time in the UK.

During this realisation, I made a bold decision – to transition into the coaching world. I converted a space in my garden into an office, a sanctuary dedicated to empowering others. Fuelled by purpose, I immersed myself in learning, undertaking every coaching course available to equip myself with the tools to facilitate growth and transformation.

My journey into coaching was not just about pursuing a new career path; it was a profound shift in mindset and purpose. The decision to step into coaching was rooted in a deep desire to make a positive impact and help individuals navigate challenges with resilience and clarity. This transition marked a pivotal moment – an awakening to my true calling as a leader.

Embracing Change: A Mindset Shift

Throughout my life, I have faced immense adversities that have tested my resilience and shaped my journey. Losing my parents at a young age and enduring the hardships of war in Iraq and displacement were profound challenges that left lasting scars. At one point, I found myself on the brink of despair, grappling with the aftermath of a suicide attempt that left me in a coma for three days.

Emerging from these dark moments, I gained a profound perspective on the value of life and the strength of the human spirit. These experiences, though incredibly difficult, have fuelled my unwavering belief that no matter how tough life may seem, there is **always** hope and the possibility of creating a life filled with purpose and joy.

I share my story not to dwell on the past, but to inspire others to persevere in the face of adversity and to embrace life's challenges as opportunities for growth and transformation. You can overcome any obstacle and emerge stronger on the other side, ready to embrace a life filled with resilience, courage, and profound fulfilment.

Even through the challenges I encountered in life, each adversity served as a powerful teacher, imparting invaluable lessons that transformed my mindset.

Firstly, these challenges taught me the importance of kindness, both towards myself and others. Embracing kindness brought infinite inner peace and fostered a sense of empathy and compassion that guided my interactions and decisions.

Secondly, adversity taught me the art of restarting, to persevere and rise again after setbacks, cultivating resilience and determination.

Finally, facing limitations spurred creativity, finding innovative solutions despite constraints, unlocking a world of possibilities even with limited resources.

These profound lessons became pillars of strength, shaping my approach to life and leadership, and ultimately contributing to my growth and evolution as a coach and mentor.

As I ventured into the coaching landscape, I encountered numerous challenges. One of them was navigating an industry flooded with unregulated practitioners and inflated promises.

My response was simple yet resolute: integrity and authenticity. I remained strong in my values, choosing authenticity, and ensuring that my coaching practice upheld the highest standards of service and ethics.

The logistical challenge of balancing work and family life was another hurdle. However, the physical separation of my coaching space – a sanctuary in my garden – provided a dedicated environment for focus and productivity. This space not only facilitated professional growth, but also enabled me to maintain a healthy work-life balance, allowing me to be present for my family while pursuing my passion.

Lessons Learnt: Courage and Resilience

Reflecting on my journey, I learnt invaluable lessons about myself and leadership. True leadership is not merely about skill; it's a demonstration of courage and resilience. It's about embracing change, confronting adversity head-on, and taking responsibility.

Through a lifetime of transitions, I learnt the importance of self-compassion, a trait essential for any leader. Leadership isn't simply about guiding others; it's about nurturing oneself with kindness and understanding.

My experiences taught me that leadership is not a destination, but a continuous journey of growth and self-discovery. It requires a willingness to adapt, learn, and evolve – a commitment to personal development and a deep belief in one's ability to effect positive change.

When seeking a coach to guide you on your journey of personal and professional growth, it's crucial to take your time and conduct thorough research. The coaching landscape is vast, and while many coaches have good intentions, not all will be the right fit for you. It's essential to align with a coach whose values resonate with yours and who possesses the qualifications and expertise to address your specific needs.

A mismatch with the wrong coach can potentially exacerbate your situation rather than facilitate positive change. If you don't immediately connect with your first coach, don't be discouraged – finding the right coach is a process that requires patience and persistence.

Invest the time to explore different coaching styles and approaches until you find the perfect fit, one that empowers you to thrive and achieve your goals effectively.

Tips for Aspiring Leaders

Nurturing Growth and Purpose

To my younger self – and to anyone embarking on a leadership journey – I impart guiding principles to cultivate growth, purpose, and resilience.

Firstly, follow your passion with unwavering dedication. Explore diverse paths and align your career with your deepest passions. True leadership flourishes when rooted in genuine enthusiasm and commitment to what you love. By pursuing your passions, you not only excel in your chosen field, but also inspire others through your authentic enthusiasm and dedication.

Secondly, cultivate self-compassion as you navigate challenges and responsibilities. Leadership requires empathy, starting with kindness towards yourself. Embracing self-compassion fuels the empathy needed to lead effectively, fostering a nurturing and supportive environment for yourself and those you lead. Remember, leadership begins with self-understanding and compassion.

Thirdly, embrace purpose as a guiding light. Define and refine your purpose, allowing it to evolve with you throughout life's journey. Your purpose infuses every endeavour with courage and determination, guiding you through challenges and inspiring others towards meaningful goals. Let purpose be the compass that aligns your actions with your values, igniting passion and resilience in your leadership journey.

Next, and most importantly, believing in yourself is key in leadership. Banish self-doubt and cultivate confidence in your abilities. Believe that you are capable of achieving great things and making a positive impact. Confidence empowers you to take decisive action, inspire others, and navigate challenges with grace and resilience.

After believing in yourself, never give up, despite facing obstacles. View challenges as temporary waves – some propel us forward in our journey, while others seem to push us back.

Approach setbacks as opportunities for growth and learning, leveraging each experience to strengthen your resolve and determination. Perseverance in the face of adversity is a hallmark of effective leadership.

Taking full responsibility of your life goes **beyond** managing your business, career, or finances – it encompasses your mental and physical health as well. It's not solely the doctor's responsibility; you must take charge of your well-being both now and in the future.

Furthermore, do not let the past dictate your present or shape your future. Part of effective leadership is the ability to respond appropriately to situations, whether they are small or monumental, demonstrating readiness and accountability in all aspects of life.

Lastly, incorporate mindfulness into your leadership toolkit. Learn and adapt mindfulness practices to enhance decision-making and promote well-being. Mindfulness fosters clarity of thought, enabling you to approach situations with calmness and insight. By integrating mindfulness into your leadership approach, you cultivate a more grounded and intentional leadership style.

In summary, these guiding principles provide a roadmap for aspiring leaders seeking growth and purpose. By following your passions, cultivating self-compassion, and embracing purpose, you lay a strong foundation for authentic and impactful leadership. Belief in yourself and perseverance through challenges further fortify your leadership journey, empowering you to overcome obstacles and inspire others. Additionally, incorporating mindfulness practices enhances decision-making and fosters a more grounded leadership approach.

Embrace these principles with intention and commitment, and watch as they transform your leadership style and impact.

Cultural Influences and Leadership
A Tapestry of Heritage

Growing up in Iraq amidst rich cultural traditions and close-knit family dynamics, I was immersed in a tapestry of values that shaped my approach to leadership. The importance of community, resilience in the face of adversity, and unwavering perseverance were ingrained in me from a young age. As the youngest of eight siblings, I learnt the art of responsibility and empathy, supporting my family through challenging times. These early experiences instilled in me a deep sense of duty and compassion – a foundation upon which my leadership journey would later unfold.

My heritage played a pivotal role in shaping my leadership philosophy. In Iraqi culture, there is a profound emphasis on hospitality and generosity, traits that I carry forward into my coaching practice. I believe in creating a welcoming and inclusive environment where individuals feel valued and supported, a reflection of the warmth and hospitality I experienced growing up. This cultural heritage infuses my coaching sessions with empathy and understanding, fostering genuine connections that empower individuals to unlock their full potential.

Navigating Transformation
From Adversity to Empowerment

Reflecting on pivotal moments in my journey, I recall facing immense adversity that tested my resilience and determination. As mentioned, the trauma of losing my parents as a child and living through a war left permanent scars on my spirit.

These experiences taught me invaluable lessons about resilience and courage. Each challenge became an opportunity for growth and transformation, fuelling my unwavering belief that no obstacle is insurmountable. Through sheer determination and the support of loved ones, I emerged stronger and more determined than ever to embrace life with purpose and conviction.

Empowering Others
The Ripple Effect of Leadership

One of the most rewarding aspects of my coaching journey has been witnessing the transformative impact of empowerment on others. As a coach, I have had the privilege of guiding individuals through their own journeys of self-discovery and growth.

One particular client stands out – a young entrepreneur who was grappling with self-doubt and uncertainty. Through personalised coaching sessions, I helped her uncover her strengths, clarify her goals, and develop a roadmap for success. Witnessing her transformation from self-doubt to self-assuredness was incredibly fulfilling and underscored the profound impact of coaching in fostering personal and professional growth.

I believe in the ripple effect of empowerment – that by empowering one individual, we have the potential to inspire countless others. As I continue to refine my coaching practice and expand my reach, I am committed to uplifting individuals and communities, fostering a culture of resilience, courage, and purpose. Each success story fuels my passion for coaching and reinforces my belief in the transformative power of leadership. In essence, leadership is made up from courage, purpose, and resilience. It is about embracing change, nurturing growth, and inspiring others to realise their full potential. As I continue on my journey as a coach and leader, I remain committed to these principles, knowing that each step forward brings me closer to empowering others and living a life of profound purpose.

If you're reading this now and find yourself thinking about your own purpose, wondering what path to pursue, or how to make a meaningful impact, consider reaching out to a coach. Coaching offers a valuable opportunity to explore your aspirations, clarify your values, and uncover your unique purpose in life. A skilled coach can guide you through a journey of self-discovery, providing personalised support and tools to help you navigate challenges, define your goals, and align your actions with your true calling. Investing in coaching can be a transformative step towards realising your full potential and living a life that resonates deeply with your passions and values. Take the first step today! Book a session with a coach and embark on a journey of purposeful growth and fulfilment.

Eve embodies the essence of the Voices of Women movement. She believes that the power of our voices lies not just in being heard, but in being understood. This understanding fuels our strength and confidence to speak out.

In her narrative, Eve takes readers back to her childhood, unearthing hidden traumas and encouraging us to embrace our younger selves to heal. By doing so, we uncover our true nature, laying the foundation to rebuild our lives with authenticity and resilience.

Leadership often emerges in the most unexpected moments, like a phoenix rising from the ashes. Eve is one such leader, embracing her role with the regal grace of a queen. Her journey highlights the consciousness of leadership that strikes at unlikely times, but is undeniably transformative.

Determined and hard-working, Eve is a woman on a mission to help others communicate effectively in difficult circumstances, empowering them to create better lives. Her conviction is rooted in the importance of being understood, especially during challenging conversations.

Through her story, Eve inspires us to find our voices, embrace our past, and lead with compassion and strength. Her journey is a testament to the power of understanding and the impact it can have on our lives and the lives of those around us.

Brenda

Eve Stanway

"How you live you life depends on the story you tell yourself."

Eve Stanway

The Road to Leadership Is Paved With Learning

I believe that for us to know that our lives truly matter, our voices must not only be heard, but deeply considered and understood. Our voices cannot simply be background noise, but must resonate in a way that inspires reflection and sparks action. As a leader in the field of talking therapy, I see my role as pivotal in rousing and motivating individuals to break their silence to share their words, feelings, and perspectives with others. There are many theories about why talking therapies are effective, but I am convinced that their power lies in the transformational act of articulation – whether through speaking or writing. As we express ourselves, our words transition from mere thoughts to something tangible, capable of being shared and understood by others.

It has taken a lifetime to reach this conclusion, and my journey began in my troubled childhood.

An Unusual Childhood

A great leader inspires confidence and moves other people into action. As a child of divorced parents, my father relied upon me to take care of myself and my brother. From a very young age, I understood that my actions mattered and that it was my duty to look after my family. Even though I was still a child, I gave up the notion that I should be looked after. It became my responsibility to ensure that my brother, my parents, and I were safe and taken care of.

When my mother left us when I was only seven years old, the burden of responsibility became even heavier on my young shoulders. The flip side of being given many inappropriate and unreasonable duties for one so young was that I was also empowered from a young age to believe that my thoughts and opinions mattered. Children made to grow up too young often become extremely competent, if damaged adults.

My father suffered from episodes of mania and depression. During his manic times, he was charming, persuasive, and charismatic, able to convince me and others that anything was possible if we followed his instructions to the letter. During his subsequent months of depression, in the face of his increasingly bizarre demands and vitriolic temper, I was left to pick up the pieces, required to take charge and motivate him and my brother to do the necessary things to keep the family fed, housed, and safe. It was a huge responsibility.

When I was 11 years old, we found ourselves stranded in the West Indies. My father had constructed a 70-foot catamaran originally intended to compete in the Round the World Yacht Race. His big dreams were exciting; however, my father was as reckless with money as he was with people's feelings. He would spend his money and sometimes that of others around him. Due to his mismanagement, the boat became wrecked and unseaworthy, and our financial sponsor lost hope of it ever sailing in the race. We were abandoned and as a result, my brother, my father and I lived aboard the vessel, stranded on the side of the lagoon in Sint Maarten, Netherlands Antilles.

We had no money other than the 25 cents needed to fill our 25-litre water can with free water.]To eat, I had to go fishing using a multi-hook line and bait borrowed from local fishermen. We also had some food stocked on our boat, which was over a year old. One night, I prepared the usual soaked beans, barley, and rice in a pressure cooker. I carefully wrapped the fish in grasses and placed it by the fire to heat the pressure cooker under the boat. It took 30 minutes to cook the beans and pulses, and after cooling it in the lagoon's salt water, we opened it to eat. To our horror, we found some unexpected stowaways in the pot....

Weevils! Weevils in all the rice and beans, which meant that we had no food left to eat. Although technically, we could have eaten the weevils, my brother and I couldn't bring ourselves to do it. Dad came home late that night, so I planned to talk to him in the morning. I wanted to tell him that we had to be deported back to the United Kingdom because we had no food and no way of getting it. Even at a young age, I believed that in the UK, people couldn't starve because there was a benefit system, the NHS, and help for people in need. In the West Indies, we were under the American system with no social security.

I remember putting everything I had into that conversation because I knew I had to convince Dad that we needed to return immediately. I needed to inspire my dad's confidence to believe in himself and take action to take me and my brother to a safe place. At the time, I didn't realise that I was a leader from that point, though my apprenticeship had started much earlier. Looking back, this was the moment when I first discovered leadership. Leadership isn't necessarily about doing something yourself, but it's about motivating another person to do what needs to be done. Leadership involves inspiring yourself and others to a common purpose, a common goal.

Growing up without my mother, I now know that I would have benefited from a strong female leader to show me what I was capable of. For me, this is the biggest lesson; both men and women need women who are able to lead and can demonstrate leadership. Much of my work is centred around the importance of supporting fathers and mothers to be the inspirational, calm leaders with boundaries their children need, which, of course, I never had. During the teenage years, this leadership morphs into coaching which helps to launch a healthy new adult to swim on the vast pond of life.

Life Lessons as a Teenager

Someone wise once said, "Resilience is the art of learning how to put up with shit!" Sadly, this is what so many people are taught. Put up with mistreatment and unfair behaviour, stop complaining, and work harder – well done, you are being resilient!

Of course, this is complete nonsense!

I have always loved horses. At the age of 19, I worked as a groom in Newmarket caring for three horses from 6.30 a.m. to 9.30 a.m. each day. One day I was riding one of my horses, Great Gusto, at a fairly slow pace and one of the cheek pieces of his bridle snapped. Imagine a large, oat-fuelled racehorse and absolutely no directional control as the bit slid out of his mouth and the rest of the bridle slipped from his head! The lesson learnt was that leather tack needs to be cleaned and oiled regularly, or it becomes brittle and liable to break. Leather can retain its resilience and strength only by being kept pliable and soft.

Resilience is not about denial, or being hard and unyielding. It is about being flexible, able to bend and come back into shape. Resilience, like leather bridles, needs daily care and attention, otherwise a person may snap at a critical moment. That is when not only themselves but everyone else involved can become endangered. Just like that moment on the gallops in Newmarket, when my horse and myself plus other people and their horses out that day were all endangered by my out-of-control horse. All for the time and care to pay attention to a small but essential piece of equipment.

Our bodies and minds, our relationships, and our actions need to be soft, subtle, and strong so that we are less likely to snap and cause danger to ourselves and others. Resilience is not putting up with things until we break. It is taking care of ourselves and watching out for what we and others are going through to ensure that no one gets broken.

As a leader, I have learnt that maintaining myself and my well-being is the best way of keeping those I lead safe. In turn, attention to my resilience models that it is okay for others to give themselves the care to be strong and resilient themselves. Bend and bounce back, rather than crack and fall.

Lifelong Learning

I think the way we see the world is shaped by the stories we tell ourselves about our past. For me, feeling uneducated pushed me to learn more. I was educationally neglected; it could almost be called abuse. My mum didn't go to school much, but both my dad's parents went to university. My dad attended a grammar school, and his dad was the headteacher at Halifax Grammar School. I still don't understand why he didn't send us to school!

Despite this, I developed a love for learning. I taught myself up to my O levels by going to the library in Penrith every day. I managed to sit my O levels by writing to schools and ended up camping near a school to do them, wearing second-hand clothes and standing alone among the other students. I passed six, simply on my memory and determination.

Looking back, I see my story is like many others who fight for their education, knowing it is the key to freedom and choices. Since finishing school, I've never stopped learning, earning two degrees, a master's, and many other qualifications. I'm always reading something new, and even though I say each course will be my last, I dream of studying art at university.

I spent time attempting to justify what I knew by gaining more and more qualifications as an adult, to prove I knew what I had not learnt while growing up. Learning has been my path to freedom; however, understanding my role in leadership has been the route to authentic living. At last, I understand I'm not so different from others, and sharing my knowledge is a way to lead. When we find our way out of difficult situations, it's important to help others do the same.

Crunch Time

Discovering that I could be my own leader came in a moment of transformation that was truly mundane. It was early on a Thursday – I noted it in my diary. I had dropped my son at school, and I was rushing to get my daughter to her school before 8.35 a.m., the usual hectic school run with not enough time. I had so much to do and could feel the pressure on my shoulders and chest. My skin was fizzing with urgency driving for the Formula 1 Mum's driving team – we have all been there!

I felt pure rage that I was being forced to do everything, that throughout my marriage, I had to drive, cook, parent, earn, and work and yet, it was never enough. Every day I woke up tired and pushed myself relentlessly.

That day, as I drove up our driveway, my foot slipped causing my car to lurch suddenly forwards. I slammed the brakes on – when I say I was a cat's whisker from driving into the wall of our front room, it was.

I burst out crying and shouted, "Why is life so hard? Why will no one show me how to do this?!"

My neighbour looked around, startled. She had heard my pain and anguish.

"Are you okay?"

At that, I simply collapsed. I felt about as low as I could imagine. I was meant to hide my pain and carry on. Now I had failed even at that. In that moment, I saw that I spent so much of my life strategising in the tiniest detail how to fit in the needs of others, that I was no longer leading my own life.

I was used to talking to others about what was happening in their lives, finding out where the problems were and helping them make a plan, inspiring them to move forward. I simply had not ever thought I might be able to do this for myself.

At this time in my professional life, I kept being promoted and encouraged to leadership positions. I could not see in myself what others were seeing. I felt bad for being grateful to be noticed and felt that I did not deserve the recognition.

Being a leader, inspiring others to lead, means stepping through your own humility to be what others need. Even stepping into leading myself, meant answering my own call for change. I needed to lead the changes in my own life.

Self-Doubt

One of my main concerns about becoming a leader was feeling out of place. My background seemed so different from everyone else's, that I doubted my abilities. Most of what I learnt came from figuring things out on my own. My education involved reading enough to pass exams and then finding the necessary knowledge to get by. When you're taught something, you know how to do it, but when you figure it out yourself, you're left wondering if you did it right. Feeling like an outsider and doubting my knowledge made me view myself very differently from how others saw me – capable, adaptable, and creative.

The first time I was asked to lead, I was surprised. I even looked around to see if they were talking to someone else. Surely, they didn't mean me!

I was the personal assistant to the head of the corporate banking law department at a top law firm in London. My boss, Michael, was a calm, wise man who wasn't bothered by the fast pace and pressure of billing clients every six minutes, which is common in city law firms. One day, HR asked me if I wanted to manage the whole team of 40 secretaries. They thought I was the perfect person for this. I usually said no to such requests, but this time, Michael asked me why I thought I was different from what HR saw in me.

I was good at my job, knew the procedures well, and got along well with people. He suggested I should trust HR's view and see what happens. This seemed like a big risk to me. However, he told me it was their risk, not mine; they decided to offer me the role. I could decide whether or not to accept it, but they saw something in me that they needed.

The discussion with Michael truly made me think and I often reflect on it. Great leaders aren't usually the ones who want to lead; they are the ones who are chosen to lead. It's important to take time to help a new leader see the value in being chosen and understand that being no longer needed by those who chose you is a sign of success.

The toughest challenge for me was to accept that my knowledge was valuable. My learning style, which emphasises observation, quick adaptation, and creative problem-solving, has shaped me into a leader capable of tackling challenges from multiple angles, but I had to overcome my self-doubt to embrace these qualities. Ultimately, leadership requires confronting and managing self-doubt to take accountability for failures while giving credit to the team for successes.

Discovering My True Voice

Each and every one of us needs our voice to be heard. It is our sacred duty to be curious in our listening and seek to understand the minds of those in our world, to nurture the voices of men and women that we come in contact with so that they can be free and know that they are welcome in our hearts.

When another person makes the time to truly listen to or read our words, they imbue them with meaning, allowing for a shared understanding of our individual experiences of the world. To me, this is the essence of leadership in my field: to inspire, guide, and support men, women, and children in feeling safe enough to express themselves, and to encourage everyone to listen genuinely and empathetically to others.

In my practice, especially when dealing with the complexities of divorce, break-up, and emotional overwhelm, I want to offer strategies for navigating these challenges and empower individuals to articulate their deepest thoughts and feelings. This process facilitates healing and promotes profound personal insights and growth, helping them move beyond their current pain and discover a renewed sense of self.

I believe that leadership in talking therapy is about more than guiding; it's about instilling the confidence to share their innermost selves and ensuring they are heard with empathy and respect. Often this involves sharing specific techniques for clearing the path of blocked communication between individuals and coaching them to have the confidence to express themselves in a new way.

By championing open and judgement-free communication, I aim to help people navigate their emotional landscapes, transforming their experiences of adversity into opportunities for understanding and development.

My commitment to this approach is not just about aiding in individual healing, but also about contributing to a culture that values empathy, understanding, and respect for the diverse narratives that define the human experience.

A true leader rarely seeks the role. This means that many lead without realising. The view we have of a leader is someone with the spotlight following their every move. Many true leaders remain in the background of these starlets, not realising that they possess true leadership's defining qualities. It took the breakdown of my marriage for me to understand that I am a leader. I could no longer whisper directions, inspire, and motivate from behind the curtain so as not to upset the leading man! I was forced to 'lead' my own life.

As I discovered my own voice, my confidence in my ability to lead grew. Now I know what I stand for: free will, choice, understanding, and a curiosity to learn. People often talk about being authentic and honest, but those can feel like big steps if you don't know who you are. Yet, I've learnt that honesty and authenticity are crucial. Being open about my doubts, fears, and worries makes it clear to those I lead that their perspectives and choices matter as much as or more than my own.

Initially prevented from speaking for fear of punishment or that no one would care, my journey to understanding myself and my story stalled until I learnt the importance of writing it down. A series of key figures in my life had sought to impose a certain world-view on me, using criticism of my handwriting, grammar, and spelling to silence me – to keep me from fully knowing myself and preventing me from gaining the understanding which would be the key to my freedom. Aimed at silencing me, they inadvertently highlighted the power of voice and the importance of breaking through barriers to self-expression.

Even during those tough times, I found myself in leadership roles. I was chosen as Chair of Governors at my children's school and put forward for many other leadership roles. The difference was that now I knew that others saw something in me, even when I doubted myself. Criticised for taking on roles that took me away from my duties at home, I discovered that leadership through control does not inspire you once you know the meaning and value of your own thoughts.

Journaling and self-discovery have been transformative. Writing down my thoughts and feelings taught me to listen to myself in a way I never thought possible. This process has not only helped me to understand my mind, but also to appreciate the power of my voice. It's as if writing has given me the keys to unlock parts of myself that I didn't even know were hidden.

Through this exploration, I've realised the importance of vulnerability in leadership. Sharing my struggles and uncertainties openly has paved the way for more genuine connections with those I lead. It shows them that it's okay to be imperfect, that it's okay to have fears and to face challenges. This openness can create a culture of trust and mutual respect where everyone feels valued and heard.

In embracing my own story and sharing it with courage, I've learnt that leadership is not about directing others, but about guiding them through shared experiences. It's about creating an environment where everyone can learn from each other, grow together, and support one another in pursuing common goals. My journey from doubt to confidence has shown me that true leadership is rooted in authenticity, compassion, and the willingness to be seen, warts and all. The act of sharing our truths and inviting others to do the same, fostering a culture of openness, learning, and mutual respect. This, I believe, is the essence of true leadership.

As someone who leads women, it's important to teach them that hard work isn't the only way to add value. Women do put effort into what's important to them and their loved ones; however, it's also important to look at and encourage all the different things that make us valuable and complete as individuals. Women are inherently valued for what they give to others, often told that looking after themselves is selfish or time better spent helping another person.

Society's misdirected over-emphasis on giving and being selfless causes many women to lead unbalanced, stressful lives. By aligning with their true values, a woman can balance giving to others with caring for herself. She can see that by looking after herself, she can offer better quality care and support to others for a longer time without depleting her health or creative enjoyment of life.

Leading others means doing the right thing and offering a positive example to those around us. Deciding to act in accordance with your values will show others that this is the best way to offer value to the universe and live a life of abundance and gratitude. Compassion, understanding, and love are at the foundation of leading women and men to step into their own power.

Leadership is the ultimate act of collaboration and cooperation. A leader is nothing special within a team; they simply hold the role of leader. In many teams, this role can move as one or another person within a team takes charge of their area of genius or expertise. A good leader finds consensus because they care about doing so. I have often seen women marginalised by men who were not motivated to take everyone with them in decisions. Often, the key thing that gets in the way of collaboration and empathy from a leader is shame. The shame of making a wrong decision, of being shown up. So the question is – should a leader be able to get it wrong?

Yes! Being wrong is integral to the process of success! The ability to show compassion and empathy for the mistakes of yourself and others is the building block of successful leadership. A leader is not a leader without a team; progress is impossible without mistakes. Transformation takes place when mistakes are acknowledged and discussed without fear, shame, or blame.

If I could return to my earlier self, I would encourage myself to start writing and journaling sooner. I would write for myself, as without true caretakers to show me how to learn, writing may have been a good substitute.

I encourage the people I mentor to invest in their passions and be sure to take the time to learn the lessons that come beyond the books, lectures, exams, and shiny certificates. Many years ago, I paid for a beginner's French course. I studied for six months and by the end, I knew enough French to understand the quotes in the book I was reading. I cannot remember much French now. But that course, and the money and time spent, was not a waste as I learnt what I needed to enjoy that book.

Investing in that experience, I used time and money to pursue my simple goal. My intention was to understand what I was reading and so I turned my attention to achieve this, i.e. to learn basic French. I encourage everyone to learn for whatever reason as long as they are learning for themselves, not simply someone else.

Mentoring and compassionate leadership provide a view from which you can calibrate and check your own experience. I would say that becoming a caring mentor and leader is a path to our higher purpose for all of us. Using what we have learnt to help grow and nurture others to be leaders and mentors is a responsibility we all share. I believe that we all have a part to play in growing and supporting individuals, children, and groups to learn to challenge criticism, inequality, and repression. We are all responsible for ourselves and ensuring that as we rise, we raise those around us, creating true transformation through leadership and heart-led encouragement of others to be leaders in their turn.

"You are never too old to set a new goal or dream a new dream."

C. S. Lewis
Author of *The Chronicles of Narnia*

"The mind, once stretched by a new idea, never returns to its original dimensions."

Ralph Waldo Emerson
American essayist, lecturer, philosopher, abolitionist, and poet

Mimi's radiant soul illuminates her path as a spiritual female leader embarking on her most profound journey yet: the inner journey. This courageous decision to delve into the depths of self-awareness fuels her mission to guide others along their spiritual paths, demonstrating how introspection sparks growth and transformation.

Like all great leaders, Mimi has confronted adversity, battled inner demons, and overcome challenges to transcend conventional belief systems. She openly shares her journey with unwavering courage, revealing a resilience that knows no bounds. Her ability to bounce back from setbacks is a testament to her indomitable spirit.

Beyond personal success, Mimi redefines leadership, embracing its spiritual dimensions of love and peace. She selflessly dedicates herself to catalysing change in humanity, igniting a powerful drive that propels her forward, gathers momentum, and inspires followers to join her cause.

In her quest to address the world's challenges, Mimi harnesses innovation and creativity within the workplace, grounding her vision of 'Thinking on Purpose' in practical action. Discover more about this remarkable woman's story of courage, transformation, and resilience as she navigates the path of servant leadership with unwavering dedication.

Brenda

Mimi Bland

"Never doubt your power and ability to greatly impact humanity."

Mimi Bland

Gifts and Spirit of Leadership

Childhood Foundations

From my earliest memories, at around four years old, I realised I was here for a particular reason and have always felt different from others. The dreams and visions that came to me at night led me to this belief. At first, I never knew what these visions of religious and historical martyrs meant. One particular character held a plaque with my name in his hands, on which was written 'The Chosen One' in bold capital letters.

I was curious and excited at the same time and couldn't wait to tell my parents. However, their response was not what I expected. In fact, they told me never to speak to anyone about it and that I should keep quiet. As the obedient daughter, I never talked about it again for fear of being accused of lying and being punished. As a child, I had no voice.

It's never surprising when you reflect on your childhood that you find the spark that lights up your adult life. Of course, your learning and experiences create the pressure required to generate that brilliance within.

Realisation of Purpose

I have an absolute drive to help others, being non-judgemental and showing love and compassion. I managed to keep going even in my darkest moments as an adult. At one point, I was locked in the cupboard under the stairs with nothing more than a potty! My crime was that the person I loved thought me too disgusting to be seen and heard. I genuinely believe that all the pain and suffering endured in my life was a lesson for me to learn self-love. I can now share my knowledge and experiences to help heal pain and suffering, by Leading, Inspiring, Motivating and Empowering others through my LIME Effect Model.

Attaining a better life through the spirit of love, compassion, harmony, sharing knowledge, and universal life principles will inspire alignment and change in humanity. In his teachings and philosophy, Dr Joe Dispenza instils the belief that we can change our brain and reality by changing our thoughts. When you adopt this belief, you will shift your mindset and raise your vibrational frequency, enabling you to create and choose the life that you want to live.

My mission is to impact humanity and raise our planet's consciousness. I do this through my company, New Life Academy Ltd., leading as a spiritual mindset mentor and teaching the power of self-mastery. My company gives me a forum and platform to offer humanity a service to enable everyone to master their mind and emotions. I teach breath work, allowing you to stay present and become self-aware of your mind, body, and spirit.

In addition, it allows me to lead, inspire, motivate, and empower others to reach ultimate happiness and live a fulfilled life of love, worth, joy, and purpose through the LIME Effect.

My Why

Like all great businesses, I have a vision. I want to live in a world where the pain and suffering of humanity can heal through the power that lies within ourselves. I have discovered that our thoughts also relate to our experiences. In essence, my experiences have shown me that the world is perfect. However, we and our perceptions influence our feelings and emotions, and sometimes, they do not serve us as the best version of ourselves.

Over time, we have become lost in greed, jealousy, envy, and possession addiction, and the impact of these negative feelings is lessening our happiness and causing our pain. Working with my clients reveals the human conditioning of living in fear and survival; with this mindset, they become workaholics. One of my clients was obsessed with being the best in his field and lost his work-life balance. Consequently, his marriage broke down, his children refused to speak to him, and he started drinking. His lowest point came when he experienced thoughts of suicide.

He came to me on a recommendation and we worked on discovering the root cause of his feeling of unworthiness. Unsurprisingly, the root cause took him back to his childhood experiences of feeling inadequate in his parents' eyes.

Fuelled by my vision of a better world, I aim to inspire and engage with world leaders to show how a different mindset, with new perceptions, will change how we live our lives. When you encounter an obscured perception, it hides what you see instead of revealing what is in front of your eyes.

Shaping Beliefs

In reality, I believe we are spiritual beings who have a human experience. What led me to this belief stems from my background and upbringing, where I felt overwhelmed by mental, physical, and emotional abuse by others.

One day, after my morning meditation, I realised that perception and learning from our surroundings create our existence. Other people, such as teachers and parents, knew no better. They were living in the existence of habitual, repetitive actions that were misaligned and blocked from true human potential.

Over the last 40 years, along with my life lessons and experiences, I have researched and learnt from many masters in the spiritual psychology field. I have developed a method and a way of being through my alignment, which aligns more with my real reason for being here. My aim is to spread this knowledge as quickly and widely as possible.

A Pivotal Moment

Having suffered bulimia for 10 years, inspired by *Mirror Work* from Louise Hay, as well as my deep Christian and spiritual beliefs, I learnt to use my words to command the results I wanted in my body. Within two days, bulimia left my body.

Recognising that my gifts and knowledge could help and assist others when they were at the very lowest in their lives – threatening suicide and unable to see a way forward – fuelled me to step up as a leader in my field of expertise.

It was my time to use my gift of seeing the good in people, communicating with them in their time of need, and offering them the resolution and self-belief they could be and do anything they desired.

The revelation of my gifts of divine listening, understanding, and compassion led me to understand immediately how other people's current despair is usually linked to turbulent times in their past. Being stuck in these repeated patterns caused distress. There is a huge gap in the knowledge and understanding of our spiritual essence. Our spiritual being cannot accept going unnoticed, so I jumped at every opportunity to make a meaningful contribution.

This drive wasn't simply about personal ambition or recognition; it was a realisation that I had accumulated enough experience, insights, learning, divine knowledge, and belief to guide others to find their belief system and drive positive change within them.

This awareness accompanied a sense of responsibility and a desire to share my gift and knowledge with others and lead, inspire, motivate, and empower them to excel in their endeavours.

Leadership

Leadership isn't simply about achieving personal success, but also about fostering peace, harmony, love, growth, and development in others, ultimately creating a chain reaction that impacts humanity.

Moreover, I noticed a lack of strong spiritual leadership and direction in addressing feelings, challenges, and opportunities within us. Seeing this void compelled me to find various ways to share my message and experience, facilitating my adoption of a leadership role. The intention was to help steer the course and inspire others to pursue ultimate happiness and true life success.

This drive propelled me to take proactive steps towards leadership in business, such as seeking opportunities to mentor other leaders, business owners and influential people, initiating collaborative projects, and actively contributing to advancing spiritual mindset knowledge and process. It was a moment of self-realisation of my gift, talent, and determination to leverage my expertise for the greater good, and it marked the beginning of my journey as a leader in my field.

I moved into the business industry to meet and inspire leaders of corporations. By working with leaders with many employees, we can spread the message more effectively and empower people with a positive mindset aided by a clear, balanced understanding of life's purpose. When more and more people adopt this way of being, we will start to see the change required in humanity. In the business and industry sectors, I receive many requests from business owners and senior executives to offer a structured plan to help them become better, more informed, and balanced leaders who value and share the new knowledge and new behaviours with their employees, friends, and families.

The biggest challenge on this path is to have total conviction of my beliefs and core values. I had to find the courage to be different, accept discomfort when stepping outside my comfort zone, and realise that change can sometimes be uncomfortable and daunting. American activist Rosa Parks is an example of a woman of courage and leadership. She invigorated the struggle for racial equality, becoming the 'first lady' of civil rights in 1955 after refusing to give up her seat for a white person.

Embracing this discomfort as a necessary part of my personal growth, I set clear intentions for my objectives, to offer a new way of thinking and personal realisation that could be called strange, odd, or even freaky! I was an outcast from the generally received way of thinking, sometimes even accepting ridicule from close family members. Seeking support, guidance, and feedback from mentors and peers in this field who had experience in leadership was invaluable in helping me navigate the challenges of transition. I learnt to ask for guidance without feelings of weakness and soon realised that asking for support is a strength of character which creates growth.

Embracing a Growth Mindset

Another vital aspect to consider is adopting a growth mindset, as put forward by Carol Dweck in her groundbreaking *Mindset* book in 2006. A growth mindset is described as "motivation theory". Dweck says, "The hallmark of successful people is that they are always stretching themselves to learn new things." By ensuring that you adopt this positive mindset, you will soon discover its benefits, such as embracing challenges, self-empowerment, and focusing on the process and not the result.

Having adopted a growth mindset and committing myself to continuous learning and development, I constantly seek opportunities to expand my knowledge and skills through formal education, workshops, seminars, or self-directed study. It is up to you to find how you learn and then take action to create a better you.

Knowing that setbacks and obstacles are a natural part of any transition and growth process, I practised resilience by learning from failures, staying adaptable, and maintaining a positive outlook rather than being derailed and demotivated. Three traits are common to leaders with remarkable resilience: determination, focus and discipline, enveloped by a crystal-clear vision.

Finally, I took consistent and deliberate action towards my purpose and desires. I built momentum that involved changing my mindset, words and actions, actively implementing new behaviours and habits aligned with my aspirations to heal all pain and suffering.

By embracing these steps and committing myself to personal and professional growth, I found the courage to strengthen and support my continuous journey. It is of utmost importance that I follow my truth. Pausing to reflect on my core beliefs and taking time out of my life to pursue a total understanding of my gift, I have worked tirelessly to find a way to share this knowledge with as many as possible.

Facing Challenges Head-On

Do not be fooled; we are all faced with challenges. One of the most significant challenges in my life was self-doubt and struggling with pre-programming from others in my youth and past relationships. The consequence of this programming bred a feeling of low self-worth.

Stepping into unfamiliar territory, I often questioned my abilities and whether I was truly worthy of success and betterment. Was I good enough? Did I deserve success?

Having always been told I was useless and would not achieve anything, I focused on building self-confidence through positive self-talk, affirmations, and celebrating small victories at every turn. Even now, every new venture is a great opportunity to learn and grow. I am truly grateful for all opportunities that come my way and thrive upon times and experiences that feel uncomfortable and cause nervousness.

Steps To Maintain Motivation

To stay motivated, I focused on the bigger picture and the positive impact of my spiritual role. I celebrated milestones and achievements along the way, seeking inspiration from successful leaders in my field and surrounding myself with only positivity and inspirational people and ventures.

Through this process of life transition, I have learnt several valuable lessons about myself.

Resilience: I discovered a more bottomless reservoir of resilience within myself than I previously realised. Setbacks and challenges are inevitable, but how we respond to them ultimately determines our success. By embracing resilience, I was able to bounce back from adversity more assertive and more determined than before.

Adaptability: Transitioning into a spiritual leadership role often requires adapting to new situations, responsibilities, and expectations. I learnt to be flexible and open-minded, willing to adjust my approach based on changing circumstances and feedback from others. This adaptability enabled me to navigate unfamiliar territory with confidence and agility.

Self-Awareness: Engaging in self-reflection helped me develop a more profound self-awareness. Learning to recognise my strengths and weaknesses more clearly allowed me to play to my strengths while proactively addressing areas for improvement. This self-awareness also enabled me to understand better how my actions and decisions impact those around me effectively.

Empathy: I have an in-built gift of empathy. Empathy is vital in building strong relationships and fostering a positive environment, as it is essential to client trust and understanding. I utilise my spiritual gift of reflection, listening and seeking to understand their perspectives, concerns, and motivations. Cultivating empathy, connecting with my clients on a deeper level and inspiring greater collaboration, fostered trust and delivered positive results.

Courage: Transitioning required courage to step outside my comfort zone, take risks, and confront difficult situations. True courage isn't the absence of fear but the willingness to act despite it. By embracing courage, I could tackle challenges head-on and lead, inspire, motivate, and empower with confidence and conviction.

Creating a Platform

My New Life Academy shows people how to reset their minds and thought patterns so they begin to understand their emotions without reacting negatively, as this does not bode well for a happy life.

We are constantly and negatively imprinted by the media, news and the general life control methods we are expected to live by. My purpose is to teach people the art of self-mastery, to be able to stop reacting to external conditions and instead start creating the life condition they wish to manifest and experience.

Thinking on Purpose

Mental well-being at work is crucial, so my methods of 'Thinking on Purpose' are well-received and implemented to help with this new stimulating way of learning and working. I am seeing many changes for the better. It is refreshing that many business leaders value 'Thinking on Purpose' rather than reacting to emotional stress from external pressures. It allows them to be more proactive and concise with desired outcomes, but in a more caring and compassionate way to heal humanity from its poor state of mind, which causes stress, pain, and suffering.

As an empowered and influential business owner, my advice is straightforward. If you are an inspired individual with creative aspirations, I would stress that you follow your true calling. Do what you feel you want to do. When something doesn't feel right, listen to your body's messaging system and decide to change when you are not as happy as you could be. Follow your inspiration and keep working on your internal mindset and emotions to maintain alignment with your desired outcome. Always think about your purpose, and that action will always guarantee success.

Be authentic in your offering, honest, caring, open to change, open to messages that come to you, and open to taking a chance. Your mindset will work for or against you, depending on how you allow it to act for you. It requires focus and constant repetitive messaging to remain on track. We get distracted easily; work challenges, families, and leisure are all distractions, and you must learn to segment and prioritise them.

Be wise with your time, work smart, and be realistic with your plans, but do not be limited in your passion and dreams. Realise that everything is possible. We are a very creative and inspirational species; our limitations are often created in our minds or by our friends' or family's negativity, supported and aided by society's negativity, our country's political agendas, and the media.

If you want to succeed in life, following your mindset plan is essential. Do not be distracted by the variances that constantly appear in your path. Use my 'Thinking on Purpose' method, act with intent for betterment and sound, and always follow your gut instinct!

It's imperative to have a work ethic of immense focus. Work every day of the week on your plan, refreshing it constantly, always researching and learning. My life's mission is to help humanity, and my work ethic fuels my drive to achieve that. Due to patriarchal repression, women are, unfortunately, many years behind men. These historical restrictions are still happening in many countries worldwide. In recent years, the erosion of some of our freedoms has impeded our progress.

Female Mission

Women must strive to be the very best they can be. We are fantastic multitaskers; it's our nature to handle many of life's requirements simultaneously. In business, this is a tremendous natural gift. Our minds work differently from men, so we must acknowledge and enhance this asset. We remain competitive, calm, collaborative, and driven by different goals and purposes, which translates into a more balanced and compassionate workplace.

We value things that men do not; we are less ego-driven and more community-driven. Women in business should be proud to be women and not try to emulate men in their actions and decision-making processes. Companies need to be more open to this compassion and collaboration. Less ego, jealousy and competitiveness will make for a much more equal community where wealth and success will be shared more amongst us in the future.

Many businesses need compassion and a more sharing approach. Collaboration and teamwork are essential in business today. Women have an in-built instinct in this arena, which can only benefit them in the business role. We must value this and enhance our surroundings by sharing our talent with everyone in the most empowering way possible.

I feel empowered due to the self-gratification that I am, at last, thinking and acting in a way that is my true calling. My human existence is now in line with my core.

I am following the path that makes me happy. I am not pretending to be someone else, but being genuine and authentic, telling my truth. No matter what reactions I receive, I stay faithful to my heart's calling. My thinking is purposeful, and I follow an implemented plan with daily inspirational habitual traits.

My thoughts are pure, and my goal is honest and open. I am truly following the calling from an inner and external force, and am thrilled and grateful to do so.

My Message

My message of inspiration to the business world is to be honest and in line with your true calling. Follow your passion!

Your mind and body know what it is here to do. Life throws many curveballs at us daily, but we are more than equipped to handle them. If you are clear in mind and body, your soul is content that you are being genuine and honest with yourself to be who you want to be. Clarity of mind will lead you to live the life you desire. With this approach and integrity, the business world will be better by natural progression.

Words of Wisdom for Young Leaders

What three key messages would I teach young leaders?

1. **Have self-belief.** Know that you are different and embrace it. Do not fear being different and gifted. Believe in your truth and thrive on the challenges of showing others your viewpoint.

2. **Never let others tell you what you can and cannot be, do, or have.** Listen to their viewpoints respectfully, but dare to stand alone and stand up for your true inner beliefs and core values. Listen to your inner compass that guides you. Your gut instinct is never wrong. We all have an innate ability to pick the right path for our time. Follow it!

3. **Have faith and trust in the process of life.** Believe that you can manifest your desires; anything you desire in life can and will come to you if you follow your true path. Do not be afraid to follow your heart's desires – when you do, you will succeed.

I have become an empowered woman in business with opportunities and new inspirational platforms to share this skill and knowledge in as many formats as possible.

Final thought: as a female leader, I believe that 'Thinking on Purpose' enables you to step out fearlessly and boldly speak your truth to empower those who see the light and are looking to live life on their terms with love and happiness.

Andrea is a woman driven by a profound mission to transform lives. Relentless in her pursuit, she continually seeks new ways to make a meaningful impact on those around her.

By sharing her story, Andrea unveils the lessons that have shaped her journey, embodying the essence of a true leader. She imparts these invaluable insights with the grace and integrity that defines her character. Andrea's unwavering belief in the potential of others not only uplifts those she encounters, but also mirrors the brilliance within herself.

Central to Andrea's philosophy is the practice of introspection – a strategy she uses to navigate life's decisions with clarity and vision. She eloquently discusses the power of self-awareness, inviting readers to embark on a journey of self-discovery. Her narrative, though simple, carries a profound resonance that captivates and inspires.

Compassion and leadership weave into the very fabric of Andrea's being. This unassuming yet formidable woman earned a prestigious Queens' New Years Honours 2022 for Diversity and Inclusion and outstanding voluntary work. This honour stand as a testament to her unwavering dedication and impactful service.

Andrea is a beacon of brilliance, a guiding light for women everywhere. Through her purposeful living and humble example, she leads the way, illuminating the path for others to follow.

Brenda

Andrea Malam BEM

"Be the person that builds the
bridge through diversity
by believing in yourself
and following your dreams."

Andrea Malam BEM

Emotions, Empathy and Community Leadership

Each one of us has a story to share. Some have more than one. But do you want to simply be a story, or do you want to inspire and encourage others through your story?

Traditionally, as women, we are expected to keep a lid on our feelings, even though this might not be a fully realistic expectation. Life throws various challenges our way, but we must remember that our inner strength will help us decide and choose the way we respond. We all have choices. But do we always make the right one?

The biggest challenge is getting ourselves heard. Getting the message across, using our voice, and owning our story.

However, I took a step further into my power by starting to share my experiences with the community in which I work and live.

My need to be myself turned into my passion and that is what led me to my purpose. I wanted my story to be the reason someone else feels they can have a dream, build on it, and see it come true.

My need to set the right example for others gave my life meaning. It gave me my goal; my vision, my aim and my mission, while making a difference in the community.

My vision: To create a world where individuals are free to step into their courage and connect within, to reveal and share their compassion, strength, and wisdom for a better world.

This includes setting boundaries, raising standards, and bringing a change in their perception of aspects of inclusion, diversity and equality.

One of the noblest missions that an individual can engage themselves is in starting a charity or a non-profit account. That is exactly what I did!

I learnt to recognise and take advantage of opportunities for progression and success. Unearthing my purpose and giving direction to my actions helped me define my unique value.

My aim: To serve humanity and inspire others to live the life I live. But what does that mean? Does it mean I am creating and building dreams with certainty?

For me, serving humanity meant I was serving the needy, the vulnerable, and the underprivileged. That was a challenge. But who doesn't like a challenge?! I know that in a way it was ambitious, but I desperately wanted to contribute to the world by making a small mark.

Saving Dreams: My Mission

No matter how big or small your dreams may seem, there is no better time than the present to reach for them. Everything I aim to do has been purposeful, be it in my career, home life, profession, or passion. One small step can make a big difference. I am determined to make a difference in the world.

My charity Saving Dreams supports communities in the United Kingdom as well as in Nepal, India and Kenya. We are so grateful to all our supporters in our mission towards trying to find the solution to poverty and suffering.

Running a charitable organisation can be a rewarding and fulfilling way to make a positive difference in society. It works towards connecting, supporting, and empowering underprivileged children and their families.

The aims of Saving Dreams are to:

1. alleviate suffering and maintain human dignity

2. enable children to escape poverty and offer opportunities to become model citizens.

But running Saving Dreams also comes with many challenges and risks to be aware of and prepared for, such as:

1. Legal and Regulatory Compliance to the governing body that regulates charities, which in the UK is the Charity Commission.

2. Long-term financial sustainability with a sound and strong strategy and management system.

3. Human Resources and organisational structure with roles and responsibilities, such as trustees, staff, and volunteers.

4. Dealing with external factors, such as government policies, donor and fundraising priorities, public opinion, natural disasters, and safeguarding.

How Did It All Start?

You are what you tell yourself you are. What you tell yourself, you will become. This will always ring a bell in my head!

I was born and lived in India until the age of 24, before moving to the United Kingdom.

India is where I received the best start to school education, while England offered wonderful opportunities for my career choices.

When I was settled in England, I thought I was happy doing all the things women do. I was married with two kids and a steady job in the Civil Service. However, my role as a woman in the family always seemed to carry many cultural and social burdens. I kept wondering who else had to fill this role in their families. Was there any support for them in the community?

I used to be a people-pleaser and learnt a hard lesson after experiencing loss and trauma. I was too close to people suffering and knowing they had not long to live.

I have helped numerous people, including family and friends, to come to terms with the unavoidable and the inevitable. This is where empathy played a big part, and I knew I could help and support others going through the same experience.

In the past, I had always suffered from self-doubt. Self-doubt kills more dreams than failure ever will. My lack of ambition did not come from just giving up. It simply was from not knowing what I could do that could be effective and delivered promptly.

I also had the fear of being judged or feeling hurt. Fear is an emotion that I got stuck in. I let go of many opportunities because of this. I began to lose who I was.

Then one day…

I closed my eyes and pretended I was in a meeting with my manager, my inner self. I imagined we were working out our differences.

This was when it occurred to me that it was time to reach out to the wider community. I started to re-engage with my inner ambitions and went after my dream life. When you let go of the need to please, you are free to be yourself.

I faced the challenges head-on, turning my mindset to new opportunities and developing new skills.

I was always called the Strong One in my family when I was a child. The biggest challenge that I had to face in my early years was having to be 'the strong one', supporting others. Looking after each other was very common. At a very young age, I faced the death of loved ones, and other traumas in the family and our circle of close friends.

We make our own choices based on how we feel and the environment around us. I had a choice to be either 'the strong one', or become a victim of circumstances.

And there was no way I was going to become a victim, because I knew I could be the strong one, and from being the strong one, I realised I could support others too. By supporting others, I was supporting my inner self.

The Art of Knowing Thyself

No one in this world can be you, better than you. No one can know you better than you know yourself. I became my own healer. Grief forced me to look deeper into myself and my life. I realised I was different from a lot of people that surrounded me. I then knew I had the right to show emotions without being ashamed.

Embracing who you are and bringing your true self by showing up is an authentic way of proving your integrity.

I taught myself to be better at empathy. It helped me relate to others on a basic human level with determination, and understanding people with different opinions and voices. The knowledge you gain from empathy can help you to use appropriate non-verbal communication.

Emotionally intelligent people know how to empathise. They understand that empathy shows emotional strength, not weakness. They learn to be supportive and empathetic, and to speak from the bottom of their heart.

Having empathy is seeking to understand before you seek to be understood. Empathy helps to relate to others on a basic human level, to focus on the other person's perspective and to be in their shoes. The more we build positive relationships and develop cooperative connections, the more enriching our lives tend to be.

This was my niche. I was an Empath. An Empathetic Leader!

Being a Leader

To be a successful leader, you need to be ready to:

- become empowered to develop skills and life experiences

- learn from your mistakes.

Mistakes cannot be buried. We all must face up to them one way or another. The biggest mistake most leaders make is to create self-doubt and stress.

Vulnerability, once considered a weakness, has become my strength. It is what makes me human.

One of my leadership roles was being a support officer against bullying and becoming a mental health first aider.

Many people noticed how my courage had started to cause role reversals.

With vulnerability comes power and courage. Sometimes the simplest of gestures can make a huge difference in someone's life. It also helped me build trust and relationships in my community, giving them confidence in my ability and credibility as a leader.

This made me a caregiver as well as an empath. A caregiver with emotions – kind, empathetic, and emotional. We all need a moment to feel our emotions. I once went on a neurolinguistics course which helped me to read another person's understanding and read their body language. It helped me support and encourage others to be themselves, showing them the possibilities are endless.

As a multi-award-winning leader and ambassador for diversity, an author, and an empathetic speaker, I have it within my power to inspire others to achieve their goals with emotional support, connection and empowerment.

What are the best qualities that must be present in a leader that inspires others? As an introverted leader and role model, I have seen many failures, flaws and issues in the system. We have a platform, but no voice. At the same time, we find ourselves in positions where we are expected to have all the answers. So, what do you do?

The key is to recognise the signs of failure and commit to making small improvements to help yourself and others.

Some of the top qualities that we as leaders should have are vision, passion, integrity, commitment, accountability, confidence, empathy and self-awareness.

Emotional Intelligence (EQ)

In addition, with so much change in the world, emotional intelligence (or EQ as it is widely known) is the go-to quality we all need. We are all human beings, and being human means being emotional. We all have an emotional layer within our bodies. We should use it with love and to try and remove all negative energy.

Emotionally intelligent people have excellent leadership skills. They have high standards for themselves and set an example for others to follow.

Emotional intelligence has always been an important workplace skill. Having this skill helps us to be constructive and navigate changes and performance. It also helps us understand our emotions and those of others. We should learn to think of our emotions as an asset.

As EQ experts, we help people perform better at work. It helped me become a better leader, mentor and coach. It supports me in helping others become better leaders; I can help identify the obstacles standing between them and their goals.

The necessary skill sets for a good EQ are divided into four domains:

1. Self-awareness: Knowing what you feel and why. Being aware of your different moods as and when you have them.

2. Self-regulation: Expressing your feelings in the right way while staying in control. This is crucial.

3. Social awareness: Having the power to communicate effectively and clearly, to build strong, authentic connections.

4. Relationship management: Seeing the issues from someone else's perspective. Building positive relationships and developing cooperative connections.

Building a strong support network around us can provide us with the emotional and mental support we need to overcome the various leadership challenges.

Emotional Burnout: Know the Symptoms

Emotional burnout is often accompanied by a range of symptoms, such as constant fatigue, irritability, apathy, and finding it hard to concentrate or remember things.

Additionally, you may feel helpless, hopeless, or trapped in your situation.

Classic signs of burnout are:

1. Self-doubt: Doubting your decisions and second-guessing your choices.

2. Low self-esteem and self-worth: Constantly questioning yourself.

3. Imposter Syndrome: Feeling that you don't deserve your success, despite your achievements.

4. Exhaustion: You find yourself trying harder and harder to prove yourself.

When you notice any of these signs or symptoms, then it is important to pause and take a breather. Your mind and body have become an overflowing stress bucket, causing many problems.

Ask yourself:

• What is important to you?

• What is it that you truly want that matters?

How Do You Identify the Sources?

It can be caused by a variety of factors, such as being overwhelmed by work, having too much responsibility with little or no support, and dealing with constant change and conflict. If your values or beliefs clash with your work or organisation, it can lead to emotional burnout as well.

You need to take action to address the sources and symptoms of your stress. If not addressed, excessive or prolonged stress can lead to physical and emotional exhaustion, fatigue, anxiety, and illness.

It is also a good practice to engage in creative activities, connecting with supportive, positive, and inspiring people who will listen and empathise with you.

One of the ways that I tackle this is by volunteering in my community and making that small difference. It takes me to another dimension. It helps me make new connections and find support at the same time.

Building resilience with positivity helps with recovering from stress, adversity, or change. If you want to build resilience, you need to cultivate a positive, optimistic mindset that focuses on solutions, and embraces change and uncertainty as learning opportunities. This new mindset will help you manage your emotions by seeking feedback and recognising your strengths and emotional skills.

The Way Forward

It is beneficial to find meaning, purpose or passion either in your working life or your personal life. Learn some new skills, take on new challenges, or explore new opportunities. We cannot change the past or present, but we can try and do our best for the future.

I became my own hero by turning the obstacles into opportunities.

Over the years, I have achieved many accolades and received many awards. These include:

- Publishing my autobiography, *Saving Dreams*, and my anthologies, *Anglo-Indians Abroad* and *Bias Breakers*. I have also featured in *The New Woman* anthology and several lifestyle magazines.

- Being commended for exemplary service and receiving an Honorary Doctor of Advanced Studies.

- Being awarded a BEM (British Empire Medal) in the Queens' New Years Honours 2022 for implementing change in diversity and inclusion across law enforcement.

- Winning various awards such as the Admired Global Indians Award, NCA Diversity Role Model Award, Women of the World Lifetime Achievement Award, and Indian Achievers Forum Award for Nation-Building.

There is no time like the present. We are all stories, diverse stories and likely to be memories too. So, make sure you cherish and treasure these moments for the future.

Four Simple Steps To Achieve Your Dreams

- Put your dream on a vision board

- Believe in yourself

- Build your own confidence

- Evaluate your dream regularly

Make your dreams a reality.

I have achieved my dream!

You can too!

Sometimes, those who doubt themselves as leaders turn out to be the exact opposite of their belief: great leaders. Often, when we travel back in time and observe childhood, we begin to make sense of behaviours, traits, and personalities. Tracy's journey into leadership is a testament to this transformation. Once her passion for leading was awakened, she discovered it was only the beginning of a much larger journey.

The road to success is neither paved with gold nor straightforward. However, a determined Tracy was keen to find her way. Influential leaders learn to recognise and harness their gifts, and Tracy did just that. She knew where her strengths were and soon focused on them, creating a new way of making a difference where she was in charge.

It is well-known that leaders transition many times throughout their careers, and Tracy is no stranger to moving from country to country. Tracy's ability to adapt and thrive in various environments has enriched her leadership style, making her a more empathetic and effective leader.

Tracy's story reminds us that true leaders often emerge from the most unlikely places, driven by a deep-seated passion and a desire to make a difference. Her journey is a powerful example of how embracing one's strengths, adapting to new environments, and maintaining a clear purpose can lead to exceptional leadership. Tracy has found her path and inspired others to recognise and unleash their potential, no matter where their journey begins.

Brenda

Tracy Ho

*"True impact knows no boundaries!
Authentic female leaders refuse to be
mere followers of trends or expectations,
but fearlessly embrace their values and
passion. They envision success not only
on a global scale, but also in the lives they
touch locally. Through their inspiring
presences, female leaders ignite the flames
of greatness in those around them."*

Tracy Ho

From Self-Doubt to Self-Mastery
My Leadership Journey

A Reluctant Leader Emerges

Leadership is an intriguing and multifaceted trait that can be both innate and learnt. I never thought – or believed – that I could become a leader. It was an unplanned path marked by personal growth, resilience, and a deep desire to serve others. Reflecting on my journey, I realise that my experiences, challenges, and triumphs have shaped me into a leader who continuously evolves while staying true to my values. This narrative is a testament to the power of perseverance and the importance of authenticity in leadership.

Early Years
The Seeds of Leadership

My journey began in school, where I was an active and outspoken student. Participating in debating at secondary school was particularly transformative, teaching me logical thinking, persuasive speaking, confidence, and leadership. These skills were further honed through extracurricular activities and community service, where I developed project management and communication abilities by working with diverse groups. Whether it was a charity drive or a school play, I found myself naturally taking on leadership roles. I learnt the importance of teamwork, the value of effective communication, and the satisfaction of seeing a project through to completion.

My mother's approach to parenting also played a crucial role. By allowing me to make my own decisions, she nurtured an outgoing, flexible, and adaptive personality. This set the stage for my professional development and my eventual realisation that bigger organisations are not always better suited for personal growth. Each of these early experiences planted the seeds of leadership within me, even though I did not fully recognise their significance at the time.

Stumbling Blocks
Confronting the Self-Saboteur

My journey was not without obstacles. My biggest adversary was being a self-saboteur – the self-doubt that led to illogical decisions and procrastination. This inner critic cost me opportunities and promotions, impacting my income and personal brand. From doing academic research, to running projects and creating content for my corporate clients, self-doubt would creep in and I would second-guess my abilities and decisions. It often led to procrastination, as I feared that my work wouldn't be good enough. These cycles of fear-induced self-sabotage were detrimental, not only to my career, but also to my self-worth and finance.

A Paradigm Shift
Redefining Success

Early in my career, societal expectations heavily influenced my decisions. I resigned from a management trainee job at a Fortune 500 company, succumbing to external pressures favouring a government role. This decision, driven by the perception others had of stability and suitability, was a significant misalignment with my passions and work preferences.

The transition to a government role was challenging. Everything from daily tasks, team culture, and work approach to the level of autonomy, was vastly different from my values. The bureaucratic environment stifled my creativity and innovation, making it difficult for me to find joy in my work. I often felt like a square peg in a round hole; I did not want to mould myself to fit it either. I truly felt that the work environment and opportunity was limiting. I was unable to fully utilise my skills and talents. Retrospectively, this period was a turning point, pushing me to re-evaluate my career choices and prioritise my happiness, purpose, and fulfilment. This experience taught me that success should not be defined by societal standards nor the expectation of others, but by personal satisfaction and alignment with one's values and passions, which are the corner stones of great leadership.

After a two-year struggle in a bureaucratic workplace, I managed to transit into a corporate communications and media relations role, where I earned much job satisfaction and career growth. I worked extra hard, hoping to learn and catch up on the time 'lost' in government.

One of my strengths was building trusting relationships with clients and the media. I felt so happy that I was able to put my strengths into good use. I was promoted several times and received colleagues' recognition. Two years later, an opportunity came internally. It matched with my career goal at that time – gaining international exposure. I moved to Singapore to lead the office, covering Southeast Asia markets, recruiting, training and managing a team, and building client and media relationships from scratch.

Working in Singapore was a profound experience. The city's fast-paced environment and multicultural workforce provided me with a broader perspective on leadership and business. However, the intensity of the work took a toll on my health, leading to severe burnout.

It was during this time that I turned to coaching, seeking guidance on how to manage my stress and refocus my career goals. Coaching became a lifeline, helping me reset my work routine, gain clarity, and develop a vision for my future. Such experience had actually open my eyes on my real strengths and passion, shifted my mindset on my career potential and what kind of leader I wanted to be.

Sailing the Boat
My Entrepreneurial Journey

Personal branding was totally an unknown concept to me in my corporate life. I would never assert myself in the workplace and although I worked around the clock, often taking on at least two people's workload every day, I never thought of telling others. Simply thinking those were my responsibilities, I would wait for my managers to appreciate my efforts, but nothing came of it.

As well as not getting the recognition and income that I deserved, I didn't receive sufficient support from the company. After being consistently underpaid and overwork, I came to a realisation that I needed a change.

Friends have always been my biggest source of support. Whenever I felt lost, some great friends would be around me giving honest feedback and genuine advice. We formed a 'circle of trust'. All executives or entrepreneurs, we met regularly to share our problems and give each other feedback and ideas.

One of my Singaporean friends confronted me. "Tracy, don't you think your loyalty is killing you?"

His statement hit me deeply and prompted me to pause and reflect. Finally, I tendered my resignation and made a decision that surprised my colleagues, my friends and family.

After being a 'victim' of poor self-positioning and self-branding, I am determined to be an advocate on personal branding, leveraging my strengths, experiences and passion to help like-minded, value-driven executives and entrepreneurs.

In January 2016, I founded Frame & Fame Personal Branding. Driven by my passion for personal brand consulting, executive coaching and communication training, this venture allowed me to gain huge satisfaction in helping others succeed by understanding their purposes, maximising their strengths, and communicating their brand narrative effectively.

Starting Frame & Fame was both exciting and daunting. I was stepping into uncharted territory, but my passion for helping others kept me motivated. I found joy in working with clients, helping them discover their strengths, and crafting their personal brands. Some clients came to me feeling stuck in their career; they were underpaid and overworked. Through coaching and consulting work, they were able to redefine their passion and purpose, and speak assertively to challenge the status quo.

Some clients were existing or want-to-be business owners. They came with a big ambition in their head, hoping to sharpen their personal and company branding, building the perception that they want to nurture trust and buy-in from ideal customers. Some senior executives faced challenges in building their voice – from narrative development to voice projection. I worked with them to build a powerful image, build a strong voice and create consistent, compelling messaging for them to be seen as a real leader in an organisation. I aspire to help my senior executive clients across cultures and nationalities to transform by elevating their executive presence in a global workplace.

I have helped hundreds of senior executives, managers and business owners to make their own transformation, rising to the next level. Each success story reaffirmed my belief in the power of personal branding and the importance of authentic communication. Building a business from the ground up required resilience and adaptability.

I began to confront and overcome my limiting beliefs. I realised the importance of addressing these internal challenges head-on. Each time I overcame a self-doubting moment, I felt a renewed sense of confidence and purpose, which propelled me forward on my journey. My unwavering belief in my vision kept me going.

Crossing Borders
A Global Perspective

In the early years, Frame & Fame focused on supporting like-minded entrepreneurs. We had a rebrand in 2019. We finished repositioning our brand narratives, redesigning our personal branding services for primarily senior executives and corporate managers, redeveloping marketing and communication materials. I felt excited and ambitious to bring the business into heights.

But then Covid hit… While keeping some online personal branding services, I took this time to strengthen my professional knowledge and hence widen our service scope.

I spotted a missing piece in the puzzle. We had strong experience and knowledge in coaching executives to navigate in Western and Asian work environments, but we were not as strong in providing counsel and communication-related advice in the Gulf region, which has a different set of culture, values, beliefs, and business approaches.

I decided to make a move to Dubai to explore the region with my own feet! My experience in Dubai from 2022 to

2023 further enriched my global perspective. Working on a project supporting the communications function for a blockchain NGO during COP28 was eye-opening. I immersed myself in Middle Eastern culture, attended events, delivered keynote speeches, and received an award for my influence in the personal branding space.

However, the year also presented significant challenges. The different ways of doing business, varying perceptions of work quality, pricing differences, and expectation settings were tough to navigate. It was one of the most challenging years in the last decade; I lost money and struggled to build relationships in a place where no one had heard of me. It was difficult to discern who was genuine and who was a scammer, leading to costly lessons. Bringing my family along added to the stress, but also turned out to be one of the most enriching experiences of our lives.

Dubai broadened my world-view and gave me greater confidence in designing and delivering international communication and business etiquette programs for clients in the UK and Hong Kong. It also made me a more resilient leader.

Perfectionism and Procrastination
The Fear Factor

During the challenging and stressful time in Dubai, I had multiple levels of self-reflection and business reviews with my coach and mentors. One of the significant discoveries I made during my self-reflection was that procrastination is rooted in fear rather than laziness. This fear-induced procrastination hindered my growth. I realised that my fear of success was a significant barrier. (Correct! Fear of success is a bigger to me than a fear of failure!) I was so afraid of making mistakes that I often delayed starting projects or completing tasks.

After finishing the project at COP28, I took a pause and started working with a coach to de-stress and freshen my mind. Coaching helped me understand that my inner fears were holding me back. I learnt to embrace imperfection, adopt a growth mindset, and implement strategies to overcome procrastination. I learnt to see mistakes as opportunities for learning and growth, rather than as reflections of my worth or abilities. This shift in perspective was liberating, allowing me to take risks and pursue my goals with greater confidence. I broke free from the grips of fear and took meaningful action towards my goals.

Seeking External Guidance

The Value of Coaching

Despite being a coach myself, I acknowledge the importance of hiring a coach. External guidance helps me reflect on blind spots and reinforces my commitment to focusing on what truly matters. This perspective empowers me to confidently say no to distractions and stay aligned with my core values.

Having a coach has been instrumental in my personal and professional growth. Coaching provides a fresh perspective and helps me see things that I might have missed. It also holds me accountable, ensuring that I stay on track with my goals and commitments. This external support has been invaluable in helping me navigate challenges and stay focused on my vision.

Getting clarity on what my values truly were, I decided to leave Dubai. I had a strong desire to rebuild the momentum for the business. In addition to Frame & Fame Personal Branding, I decided to kick off a new brand: Tracy Ho Executive Coaching.

The first thing I did was to search for like-minded people as teammates. I care about the candidates' values, passion and career objectives. I also want to make sure I created opportunities for them to shine with their strengths as I strongly believe the business success roots in the people. It is a collective effort to make things happen!

Values and Leadership Philosophy

My leadership philosophy is grounded in prioritising efforts where they yield the most significant impact. Embracing curiosity, cultivating a global mindset, and nurturing resilience are key themes in my journey. I believe in creating space for others to see things differently and challenge societal stereotypes that box individuals into limiting roles.

Practical Strategies for Balance

Balancing work and personal life has always been a challenge, but I've developed strategies to manage it effectively. By planning my schedule two weeks in advance, I ensure that I have enough time for my work, my family, and myself. Setting boundaries has been crucial in maintaining this balance. I have learnt to say no to tasks that do not align with my priorities, allowing me to focus on what truly matters. Incorporating regular self-care routines, such as exercise and meditation, has also been essential in maintaining my overall well-being.

Personal Transformation

Embracing Authenticity

One of the most transformative aspects of my journey has been the embrace of authenticity. I believe that true leadership comes from being genuine and transparent. By sharing my own struggles and vulnerabilities, I create a safe space for others to do the same. This openness fosters trust and connection, which are essential for effective teamwork and collaboration.

Embracing authenticity has been a game-changer for me. It has allowed me to lead with confidence and connect with others on a deeper level. By being true to myself, I have been able to inspire others to do the same. This authenticity has also made me more resilient, as I am no longer trying to fit into someone else's mould. Instead, I am embracing my unique strengths and using them to make a positive impact.

Empathy and Positivity
Key Leadership Traits

Another key value is empathy, which has been a cornerstone of my leadership journey. Understanding and valuing diverse perspectives has been crucial in building inclusive and innovative teams. By practicing empathy, I have fostered a culture of collaboration and mutual respect in my teams, and have navigated conflicts and found solutions that benefited everyone involved.

Positivity, another essential trait, has been instrumental in overcoming challenges and maintaining motivation. A positive outlook enables me to view setbacks as opportunities for growth and learning. It has been a source of strength during challenging times and I have been able to overcome obstacles and stay motivated. My positive outlook is contagious, inspiring my team to stay hopeful and resilient.

Leadership in Action
Navigating Challenges and Achievements

Throughout my career, I have faced numerous challenges that have tested my leadership abilities. Each experience has been a learning opportunity. One particularly challenging period was when I had to lead my team through a major organisational change. The uncertainty and resistance from team members were daunting, but by maintaining open communication and demonstrating empathy, we were able to navigate the transition successfully.

Another notable achievement was the successful launch of a website development project that had been stalled for months. By fostering collaboration and encouraging innovative thinking, we were able to overcome the obstacles and deliver the project on time.

These experiences have reinforced my belief in the power of resilience, empathy, and effective communication in leadership.

Vision, Mission, and Purpose
A New Chapter in the UK

I have now relocated to the UK to embark on a refreshed entrepreneurial journey. My vision is to help aspiring executives to be seen, heard, and be known by their audience. I aim to sharpen their leadership communication, strengthen their executive presence and influence, and help them make a bigger, positive impact on the people around them and the world we live in.

My purpose is to leverage my passion, energy, and communication strengths to help those around me gain clarity and shine with their authenticity. By integrating personal anecdotes, values, and lessons, my journey encourages aspiring leaders to trust their intuition, embrace their unique strengths, and pursue their passions with authenticity and courage.

My mission is to empower aspiring executives to succeed in a multicultural environment. I want to help them navigate the complexities of a diverse workplace, build their personal brand, and develop the skills needed to lead with confidence and authenticity.

Tips to My Younger Self

1. Trust your intuition and be true to your values and purpose. Do not be overly concerned with the opinions of others. Find your own path and embrace it wholeheartedly.

2. Develop genuine confidence by understanding your strengths and leverage them in your pursuits. Seek out platforms that align with your passions, build a strong network, and apply your strengths to make a meaningful impact. Your unique shine will inevitably emerge.

3. Assert yourself and be self-aware. Set goals, regularly reflect and review your actions and progress, and be open to feedback. Embrace challenges as opportunities for growth and continuously strive to improve yourself.

Embracing the Journey

My leadership journey has been one of continuous learning, resilience, and personal growth. From the early days of self-doubt and societal pressures, to the rewarding experiences of building a business and helping others succeed, each step has shaped me into the leader I am today. Embracing authenticity, valuing empathy, and maintaining a positive outlook have been key elements in my journey.

I am committed to helping others unlock their potential and make a positive impact. My vision, mission, and purpose guide me as I strive to create a more inclusive and authentic world. By sharing my story, I hope to inspire others to embrace their unique journey, overcome challenges with resilience, and lead with authenticity and purpose.

I am excited to collaborate with diverse individuals and organisations, learn from new experiences, and continue growing as a leader. My journey is far from over, and I look forward to the opportunities and challenges that lie ahead.

With a renewed sense of purpose and a commitment to making a difference, I am ready to embrace the future and continue my journey of self-mastery and leadership.

"It is our choices... that show what we truly are, far more than our abilities."

J.K. Rowling

Author of the much-loved *Harry Potter* novels

Affectionately known as Action Amanda, Amanda Frolich possesses an energy that electrifies any room she enters. This magnetic presence is the hallmark of a remarkable leader, driven by a vision to instigate lasting change in every endeavour she undertakes.

Amanda has been a guiding force for children for over three decades, and now she embarks on a crusade to empower female leaders to reconnect with their inner child and embark on transformative journeys. Her charismatic leadership style inspires others to embrace their playful spirit and make a profound impact on the lives they touch.

Transitioning into a new career phase, Amanda finds fulfilment in mentoring others and has established THRIVE, a community where men and women gather to foster growth and collaboration. As Amanda continues to ascend on her leadership journey, her story serves as a beacon of inspiration, urging others to view challenges as opportunities for growth and resilience.

Discover more about this extraordinary woman who encourages us to harness our inner strength and persevere in adversity. Amanda's journey is a testament to the transformative power of authenticity, passion, and unwavering dedication to making a difference.

Brenda

Amanda Frolich

"The heart of true leadership comes from learning, growing, and guiding others with the wisdom we have gained."

Amanda Frolich

From Action to Leadership

My name is Amanda Frolich and for the last three decades, I have been known as Action Amanda. If you were to ask anyone who knows me, they would tell you that I never stop moving and that I am passionate about physical activity, healthy living, and more importantly, FUN!

I am so proud to wear the badge of Children's Champion! I will always be committed to excellence when it comes to education and influencing preschool children to be healthy and active through high-energy activities and my own bespoke catalogue of songs carefully composed to be both educational and engaging. My song *The Catchy Song* knocked *Baby Shark* off the number one chart spot TWICE!

Having worked with preschoolers for around seven years, I started my business over 23 years ago, which means that I now have a total of 30+ years' experience and I can honestly say that I have enjoyed every one of those years.

The funny thing is that I didn't set out to be a leader, although I always knew my passion lay in working with preschoolers; I loved watching the children grow and develop, and I knew from day one that I had a special gift for engaging little ones.

It was a series of difficult events that would ultimately shape my future; I found inner resilience and self-awareness through these challenges to face my vulnerabilities head-on, using them to grow and thrive. It is no coincidence that my latest venture – a series of one-day events for independent businesses – has the title THRIVE!

I believe that the heart of true leadership comes from learning, growing, and guiding others with the wisdom we have gained. I am constantly changing and developing, responding to opportunities, and striving towards my goals; I absolutely love connecting with people and helping them to grow, especially my fellow female leaders in business; championing others is at my very core.

My journey has been fraught with challenges and I am not afraid to own up to my mistakes or admit that I haven't always made the right decisions; but I think my success comes from the fact that I refuse to be defined by them, or to let them hold me back – quite the reverse, in fact.

I strongly believe that within every mishap, there is a lesson to be learnt, and every mistake is an opportunity for growth; to use the knowledge you have gained to do things differently and become even better.

The Early Years

My journey began in sports, leisure, and fitness as a fitness instructor and sports coach for a company called Play Sport, providing free activities for children in the summer and organising fun events, table tennis, darts, and ball games for the over fifties in the winter. After two years, I was hungry for a new challenge.

Keen to expand my CV, I became a recreation assistant, earning qualifications in 14 different sports and becoming a certified fitness instructor and sports coach. My career took a pivotal turn in 1991 when I participated in a musical movement course. It was here that I discovered my passion for teaching preschoolers.

During the course, I met my inspiration, Jane Loukes. Watching her at the Family Fun event, I was captivated by her energy and the way she connected with the children. She was like a modern-day Pied Piper of Hamelin, with children hanging on her every move. I knew then that I wanted to be just like her, inspiring and leading children with the same enthusiasm and joy.

Inspired to take action, I set up a little class in a community centre in Acton, London. I was soon asked by one of the mums to do a session for their child's birthday party and Action Amanda, the children's entertainer, was born!

I soon realised that I could add much more pizzazz to the classes that I'd originally taught, and a trip to IKEA saw me equipped with some little bunny rabbit ears, which then grew into a whole selection of props from fireballs to pompoms, and streamers to dinosaurs. Later, I connected these props to songs and the Early Years Foundation Stage curriculum, bringing a new level of engagement to my classes. This idea worked so well that I started using a similar approach for children's parties.

There is nothing like a challenge to unleash creative thinking and a true leader will embrace innovation and, in my case, produce something better than I'd first imagined. Ultimately, it's about enjoying the ride and welcoming change and new ideas. A fixed mindset will never see you achieving your fullest potential.

The Dawning of Leadership

When I think about leadership skills, it takes me right back to my childhood. When I was about 10 or 11, I would often visit my cousins in Basingstoke. I was always the one to suggest what to do.

"Come on, guys! Let's go and play rounders or cricket!"

They never argued and always followed my lead; some might say I was bossy, but I like to think of it as having innate authority!

There's no doubt that people will trust someone with the confidence to lead and take action, and I do believe that many of us have this within us from a young age; it's just a question of tuning into this younger version of you once more.

Working in London opened many fantastic opportunities for me. I was fortunate to meet many celebrities, with my first big gig being David and Victoria Beckham's World Cup party. The most famous celebrities I've worked with to date are Brad Pitt and Angelina Jolie.

In business, it is so important to leverage all of your best experiences to grow your brand and attract more of the same calibre of clients. As a consequence of having worked with such big-name celebrities, my client list quickly grew to include music and TV stars, like Peter Jones from TV's *Dragons' Den*. But I wasn't content with just that success; I wanted to make it even bigger.

Franchising

Knowing When To Walk Away

My journey to success has been peppered with a few costly lessons in terms of time, effort, and money. Many colleagues and other business owners had been telling me that scaling my business could be done through franchising, and I was certainly keen to try.

I met a woman at a marketing networking event who told me she could help me to franchise my business. She would provide me with a new logo, website, and everything I needed. It was a hefty investment for me at that time, but I was keen to grow my business and I had never been afraid of risk... so I went for it.

After some more poor advice and significant further investment, I realised it was time to cut my losses and my dream of franchising ended. Sometimes, the bravest thing is to know when to step away.

The Dubai Story
Unfinished Business

I was offered an amazing opportunity to work in Dubai.

When entertaining at a party, a grandmother exclaimed, "Amanda, Dubai needs you! There are no entertainers like you."

This was a golden opportunity to expand my business further. I returned home from the party and announced to my husband, "Jason, we're going to Dubai!"

We arrived in Dubai and whilst Jason was sunning himself on the beach, I was running around with my briefcase, looking for some marketing and exposure.

I rocked up to the national newspaper and proclaimed, "I'm an entertainer and I want to make it in Dubai. Can you do a story about me?"

Sure enough, they did! Fortune favours the bold. As a leader, you need to take decisive action; it's the only way to get results. It is part of my DNA; when you focus on your goal, you will soon find ways to make it happen. And bold is what you need to be.

In my hotel, I had seen a copy of *Time Out, Kids Dubai*. I jumped into a cab and instructed the driver to take me to Media City.

I burst into the office asking, "Can you write a story about me? I'm going to be doing some entertainment in Dubai."

I envisioned entertaining at the Atlantis on the Palm and the Jumeirah Beach Hotel – these are high-end hotels and I wanted to make a real name for myself. All great leaders must have a vision and take the appropriate action to make it happen after all. You need clarity, confidence, and charisma. I believe that the Universe will conspire to make it your reality - the Law of Attraction works; trust me, it's not just 'woo-woo', it's real science!

It took me eight visits to create my new reality and make my dream come true. I entertained at the Atlantis on the Palm, ran a family event at the Jumeirah Beach Hotel, performed at the Dubai Marina Mall, and trained staff at several exclusive children's nurseries. I had glowing testimonials from each venue.

I reflected on my success and thought, *Do I really want a franchisee, running around Dubai, a six-hour plane ride away, that I can't control?* No was the answer. So, although I 'parked' Dubai, in the words of Arnie… *I'll be back!* I still do not know what that will look like, but it will undoubtedly be uniquely Action Amanda.

Taking on HMRC

A significant triumph of mine was taking on HMRC. I had been going through an intense VAT inspection for almost six years. I had to prove that my classes were educational rather than simply 'entertainment'.

I knew that education classes are exempt from VAT but that did not stop HMRC from pursuing me for £350,000.

They questioned the educational status of my classes despite my commitment to linking everything to the EYFS curriculum, the statutory government curriculum for early years! The VAT consultant alone was costing £400 an hour and I soon ran out of money.

Always resourceful – that's what leaders are – I found a VAT consultant on a pro bono basis who helped me, then pointed me in the direction of a litigator and a barrister who took on my case. I also enlisted the help of professional colleagues to support me and help me fight my corner. Leaders surround themselves with good people – we are definitely stronger together and I knew I couldn't do it alone!

Following two more long and complex years of fighting, we won the case – something of which I am unbelievably proud. This victory was a significant achievement for myself and the children's activity sector as a whole. We now know that education classes are exempt from VAT!

When I look at my life, it's been a roller coaster ride of events, but there are always more lessons to be learnt.

I feel lucky, but would argue it's much more than luck. I am a high achiever, but I am also persistent. I am not afraid to put myself out there, to take risks, to see and be seen. It's the best marketing system I know. The ripple effect of bringing happiness to so many people is satisfying but you have to operate with authenticity at your very core. You have to be true to yourself and your values. You must have total belief in what you do and have an unwavering desire to serve and give value; it is only when you truly serve others that you will reap the rewards tenfold.

I don't like the word 'failure' because it implies that things have gone irretrievably wrong when, in fact, some of the biggest business success stories have come from 'mistakes.'

I have never stopped moving forward with my dream, and whilst the specifics of that dream may change as I evolve, I will always want to be recognised as the primary thought leader in my industry. I have often been told that there is no one like me and that is the biggest compliment I could ever receive; I was born to stand out!

Now, with a published children's book under my belt, my dream of turning Action Amanda into a children's cartoon series is well and truly underway; I will always embrace the next new challenge.

Making a Difference

On the rare occasion that I sit still enough to ponder my success, I do wonder what has led me to this point and I think it's a combination of my grit, energy, and resilience.

I believe life is what you make it. You've got to go out, meet people, and make connections; do the networking and build genuine relationships. You have to put in the hard work and, more importantly, be OPEN to new opportunities; find your purpose, and success will naturally follow.

For me, leadership means having someone to look up to, a role model. Someone who's been there, seen it, and done it. Someone who has gone through all the trials and tribulations of business. I seek out leaders who become more like mentors, people whom I aspire to be and who I admire. I have to believe in their qualities and share their ethos.

My daughter also wants a career working with children and is now training to be a midwife. I am so proud that working with children has passed down a generation and I hope that I have been a role model to her.

Leaders can and do falter, but carry on, no matter what awaits. Surround yourself with great people; our success will be determined by the company we keep. I have no time for negativity. One of my passions is watching other people succeed; the ability to be genuinely pleased for another person's success is a real leadership quality in my view.

As a businesswoman and leader, I enjoy working with other female business owners, giving them advice and sharing my knowledge, experience, and expertise. And I think because people have seen my journey and what I've achieved, they tend to listen to me. As leaders, you must embrace your achievements. It is not about bragging, but simply stating facts to illustrate your position in the marketplace. Confidence is about knowing your worth; arrogance is thinking you are better than everybody else. I will never be afraid to learn from others – especially those I respect and admire.

My three top tips for aspiring, young women leaders are:

1. Recognise the light within you and always have hope in your heart – hope is what keeps you going in the face of adversity.

2. Find a mentor – someone who brings out the best in you and is not afraid to challenge you or keep you accountable.

3. Be the best version of you. Own your mistakes and use them to grow; sharing your stories will inspire others to find hope, take action, and achieve their dreams.

"You may encounter many defeats,
but you must not be defeated.
In fact, it may be necessary to encounter
the defeats, so you can know who you are,
what you can rise from,
how you can still come out of it."

Maya Angelou
American memoirist, poet, and civil rights activist

Dr Leslie Davis demonstrates remarkable strength by openly sharing the mistakes she made as a young woman. Her tenacity and determination to learn from these experiences are palpable as you engage with her chapter.

Great leaders are unafraid to reveal their stories of adversity. Dr Leslie understands the power of this vulnerability, as it allows others to see themselves in her – a hallmark of genuinely remarkable leadership. While many hide their painful stories in shame or fear of judgement, Dr Leslie shows that true strength is found not in what happens to us but in how we respond.

Her experiences have shaped the purpose that drives her work today. Dr Leslie is committed to helping others escape toxic relationships and find healthier paths. Her empathetic understanding empowers her to share these crucial lessons with them.

Driven to be the best version of herself, Dr Leslie has pursued a doctorate to deepen her impact, launched her podcast called *She Matters with Dr Leslie Davis*, and founded a non-profit organisation supporting Black single moms. She stands as a beacon of brilliance, embodying the formidable leadership needed in today's world.

Through her chapter, Dr Leslie invites you to witness the power of resilience and the transformative strength found in vulnerability. Her story is an inspiring testament to a determined individual's impact, encouraging us all to rise above adversity and lead with compassion and courage.

Brenda

Dr Leslie Davis

"The femininity of your voice matters, now and always."

Dr Leslie Davis

For Such a Time as This

They say opposites attract and I definitely met my toxic counterpart in the first guy I dated. The 16-year-old version of me was quiet, yet opinionated, and she was also a people-pleaser. She didn't know it, but she had clear signs of an anxious attachment style, resulting from the abandonment she experienced in her childhood. She often silenced herself to make sure she didn't say anything to ruin the chances of having a long-term relationship with her charismatic boyfriend. She always had a lingering feeling that she was in competition with the other girls at his school and church.

And one day, she found out that she was right. She devastatingly discovered that she wasn't the only romantic interest in his life. With a fire lit in her soul, she wanted to tell him how she felt, but she had yet to realise the power of her voice.

College relationships were challenging and uncomfortable. Being one of the few Black students on campus, there were few options for a dating partner, although I was open to dating a man who was from a different cultural or racial background than my own.

During my junior year, I met the man who would forever become a part of my life, as he later became the father of my child. I was overwhelmed with love for him, but this love was toxic.

The experience of heartbreak was not a rare occurrence for me as I've had a fair share of heartache since my teen years. Raised in a home with Christian values of love and honour for others, violence in relationships was foreign to me. I had never experienced violence other than seeing a random fight at school, but one day, that all changed.

At the age of 22, just a few weeks after the birth of my son, I became a survivor of intimate partner violence for the first time. As my son was in the NICU fighting for his life with a rare heart condition, I was at home fighting for my right to breathe. Strangled by my then-lover, I was in shock.

How did this happen to *me?*

Why did this happen to me?

The statistics say that most victims of domestic violence often witness this type of trauma at some point in their childhood. But this was not my story. Experiencing violence in what I thought was a loving relationship, created confusion, embarrassment, and anger.

For years I was afraid to say anything about my experience. At the time of the incident, I was scared to call the police for help because I was scared that I would be arrested if the perpetrator lied about what really happened. Even worse, I feared that the Department of Children and Family

Services (DCFS) would take my son away from me. I had heard countless stories of female victims of violence losing their children because they endured physical assault with their children present. In fact, at the time I was working as a caseworker helping some of these women regain custody of their children.

I never told my story because I was afraid that people wouldn't believe me. I was afraid that my friends would judge me. I was afraid that the people who loved me would want to hurt the man who hurt me. It was never my desire to see him suffer just because he hurt me, because I thought I loved him.

To be honest, I was afraid of losing him. Fear kept me silent and immobile in this relationship. My silence pushed me towards darkness, into a mild state of depression. But no one ever knew because I knew how to operate as a Strong Black Woman and wear a mask to show everyone that I had life figured out.

This relationship was not the only time I endured emotional and physical abuse. Unfortunately, I found my way to broken souls who wanted to break me. There was always this sense that I could help them become a better human. But the truth was, their willingness to change was never anything I could control or manipulate. It was not my responsibility to make them want to be a better person.

Every time I considered leaving a toxic relationship, I found an excuse to stay. As I later learnt about the various forms of power and control in relationships, I realised that my unwillingness to leave a toxic relationship was because

I was trapped in a cycle of abuse. Had I known that there was a cycle, I probably would have refused to take part in it, and would have ended these toxic relationships much sooner.

People know me as someone who is quiet, observant, and who speaks when words need to be said. As a young girl, raised as an only child by a single mom, I was surrounded by my friends whose families seemed quite large and loud compared to my own. Many people thought I was shy, but that was hardly the truth. I was actually quite curious and didn't feel the need to use my voice unless someone directly spoke to me. In relationships, I vocalised what I wanted and needed from my partner, but my requests were often ignored, and I was met with silence.

The calling to be the voice of single mothers who have struggled in romantic relationships became loud and clear in 2022 while being interviewed for the BRAINZ podcast on the topic of "What Does a Toxic Relationship Look Like?"

Without notification of the interview questions, I was caught off guard when the podcast host asked me about my mission to empower women around the world to break free from toxic relationships. He wondered if I had any personal experience that motivated me to become passionate about helping others in this way. At that moment, I was faced with an option to speak my truth or remain silent.

Pondering the opportunity to be vulnerable and transparent with a complete stranger, my heart and mind began to race. I was flooded with the possibilities of what could happen next if I told my story. What would my clients think of me if I told my own truth? Would my family and friends see me differently? Would they be upset with me because I robbed them of the opportunity to support me when I was in pain almost 20 years ago? Would I be judged by the listeners who learnt that I endured multiple toxic relationships as I searched for love? Would I be judged for staying as long as I did?

Was any of that important? **NO.**

As one who prides herself on never being sugar-coated, I said what needed to be said. I amplified my voice to tell my truth. My voice boldly told the story of my participation in several toxic relationships. My story includes several experiences of intimate partner violence, and this was a story I had never told. Fear of judgement kept me silent for years. Who was I to be the voice of single moms, empowering them to be in healthy relationships, when it took me 39 years to finally find my way to love?

My passion to advocate for and empower Black single moms who struggle in relationships, became more evident during my PhD journey. As I developed my dissertation, I created a podcast as a free psycho-educational resource for Black single moms who may suffer from depression and suicidal thoughts as a result of experiencing toxic relationships. I named my podcast *SHE Matters with Dr Leslie Davis*, with the mission of bringing awareness to the mental health struggles of Black single mothers in America.

SHE Matters has become more than just a podcast. In 2023, I launched my mission to empower single moms around the world. SHE, the single mom, is me, and I am SHE. With this mission, I fully accept the role of being the voice of single moms who desire healthy relationships, but fail to identify the path to love. I accept the mission of empowering these women as I combine my life experiences and professional knowledge as a licensed clinical professional counsellor and relationship coach.

Looking back at my life, I never saw myself as a leader, mostly because I was very much a loner and enjoyed observing others from a distance. I have always felt different from my peers and often struggled to truly connect with others on a personal level. I was never part of a group of friends, and all of my friendships were developed individually, with none of my friends having any connection to each other. My friends all know that I am fine being behind the scenes, although I am quite opinionated and tend to have a mouthful of suggestions on how to solve relational problems.

To think of myself as a leader in my field is uncomfortable. I struggle to identify with the word "leader", as a leader is one who commands others. Leaders can direct others without building relationships with their followers. I prefer to view myself as a mentor, one who is experienced and trusted. Mentorship requires connection and relationship. My close friends are my mentors and most of them have always challenged me to step into the light of telling my story of being a single mom.

In 2016, I started a non-profit called Hearts in Faith to create a community of support for single moms in my community. I was perfectly fine being in the background but there was one particular woman, who was also a Black single mom, who saw something great within me. I'll never forget the day we had coffee at a local café, and I shared my vision for the organisation. She spoke life into me and challenged me to reveal myself to the world. She highlighted the fact that I was the exception to what most people believe about Black single moms in America. I wasn't poor. I had a decent relationship with my son's father. I had a reputable career as a supervisor at a child welfare agency and a master's degree in professional counselling. I was on my way to becoming the first entrepreneur in my family. The statistics didn't tell my story and it was time to use my own voice to become a light to other single moms in the world.

Becoming a leader came with unexpected challenges. One may think that challenges arise from external sources, but I have found that I have been my biggest obstacle. I often get in my own way when facing opportunities for success. Right before a pivotal moment, my mind begins to wander and self-doubt creeps in. At times, I suffer from imposter syndrome. Imposter syndrome is very real, mysterious, and sometimes debilitating. I explain to my clients that imposter syndrome is simply a toxic relationship with yourself. When I finally chose to change my vision, see myself as a mentor, and change my focus on becoming a leader in my field, I opened myself to connecting to others and focused more on relationship building.

Becoming a leader in the field of mental health has taught me that the way I do what I do matters. My therapeutic style and authenticity have been appreciated by my clients and welcomed by the world. How do I know this? In 2023, I was honoured by the International Association of Top

Professionals as the Top Mental Health Counsellor of the Year. When I received this notice, I immediately thought it was a joke. Why would anyone nominate me for this prestigious award? How did the organisation even know who I was, a young Black woman from a small town in Midwest America? Again, I was used to being in the shadows, humbly healing broken hearts in my therapy office.

One of the most valuable lessons I've learnt about leadership is to trust my instincts and challenge my fears with evidence of what I know to be true. As a Black woman in a leadership role, I have been questioned by my peers and experienced microaggressions from other leaders. I've been challenged with thoughts of worthiness and my right to belong in spaces where I was invited. Yes, there were times when I felt I did not belong in professional capacities because I looked different and my background was nothing like the other leaders in the room. I was forced to use my instincts to recognise when I was being discriminated against and blocked from opportunities to climb the ladder of success in my career.

As imposter syndrome and discrimination plagued me, I challenged my insecurities with the truth. The truth was, I was always the only Black girl in my classes, the only Black cheerleader, and I had the courage to overcome racism in the small town from where I came. The truth was, I earned my master's degree while working full time in a stressful career, as a single mom to a heart warrior who endured two open heart surgeries during the time I attended school, and I completed an internship at a local domestic violence shelter. The truth was that I had the respect of leadership in my field as I was often promoted and asked to hold positions of leadership in various agencies where I worked. The truth was, I was made for this as I had always been separated for the purpose of developing the tenacity and boldness needed to be the voice of single moms around the world.

I choose to live my life with no regrets. I am a firm believer that all things happen for a reason and for my good. But if I could speak to the younger versions of myself, there are a few moments in time I would like to revisit. To the high school version of me who thought no one really liked her, I'd say, "Who you are today is who you will need to be in order to be who you will be tomorrow. Listen to her." The quiet, observant and neglected version of myself was needed in order to observe the behaviour of others and to provide a sense of safety for others to tell their own story.

To the college version of myself, who often felt misunderstood, never smart enough to engage in conversation with her peers, and just needed to find her place in this world, I'd say, "Be fearless and speak your truth, even when it's uncomfortable for others to hear it." Silence was the killer of connections. If I had spoken my truth, especially when I was uncomfortable, I could have avoided heartbreak in friendships and romantic relationships.

To the woman in my twenties, who always found herself looking for love in all the wrong places because she never thought she was good enough to experience love, I'd say, "Your pain has purpose, but you are not obligated to stay in a place of being abused and neglected in a relationship. When you speak and they refuse to listen, that doesn't always mean you need to cater to their brokenness. Love will come but you first have to love yourself." If I had loved myself first, I truly believe I would have been enlightened to my strengths and purpose much earlier in life, and I would have been more intentional about the people I allowed to enter my life.

To the woman reading this today, you were created "for such a time as this." (Esther 4:14). As the world begins to attempt to silence the voices of women, it's time for your voice to rise.

As a leader or mentor, one must be before one can do. All of your life experiences and knowledge have brought you to this moment, and there is someone who needs to hear your story to know that they too have purpose in their pain. Be mindful that your behaviour and responses to life's challenges will always speak a message to those who refuse to listen but are always watching in the shadows. I am certain there is someone who is waiting to be inspired by your words.

We often get in our own way of experiencing self-love and realising our personal goals. The piercing voice of fear often wrecks us to the point we no longer recognise our own voice. I dare you to silence the voices of fear, hatred, and any messages of intimidation that are sent to prevent you from stepping into your God-given power to change the world.

If you ever become a victim of imposter syndrome, remember this: *The femininity of your voice matters, now and always.*

In the tranquil embrace of East Lothian, amidst the quaint charm of a Scottish village, lives Laura Bosworth, a beacon of change in the world of recruitment. With a heart pulsating with determination, Laura embarked on a journey to redefine inclusivity, shattering the glass ceiling one opportunity at a time.

Laura's journey towards inclusivity isn't simply a professional crusade; it is deeply personal. A diagnosis of multiple sclerosis – a formidable adversary lurking within her own body – brought her face to face with the realities of disability. Initially hesitant to disclose her condition, she grappled with the fear of being treated differently, of being defined by her diagnosis rather than her capabilities.

As Laura navigated this tumultuous terrain, she realised the transformative power of voice – the power to amplify the voices of the marginalised, the power to challenge the status quo, the power to inspire change.

Laura's message to women resonates with the clarity of a Scottish dawn – every woman has the power to lead, to inspire, to effect change. In a world rife with challenges and uncertainties, it is honesty, integrity, and inclusivity that serve as guiding stars, illuminating the path towards a brighter tomorrow.

Brenda

Laura Bosworth

"Inclusion is the cornerstone of true leadership, where honesty paves the path and female trailblazers light the way. Embracing diversity isn't just a choice – it's the essence of progress, where every voice matters and every perspective enriches the journey."

Laura Bosworth

The Power of Voice
Leading with Inclusivity and Integrity

Living in a little village in East Lothian, Scotland, does not diminish a Braveheart from living with purpose on a mission to create change. I have a business focusing on an inclusive search for senior strategic positions within financial services, the investment sector, and a few other sectors. I'm not limiting myself these days. As a driven individual, I set up my business at the tail end of 2020. It was in lockdown and the idea had been niggling away at me for such a long time to build a business that I could be proud of and would make a positive impact in my communities.

My communities comprise people I network with, people in the sector I work in, and people who open that community up equally. The desire was to work with individuals to find their exact role, but I believe there's a precise way of doing it. Unfortunately, many businesses are not as inclusive as they think they are. Otherwise, we'd be in a very different position today.

Before working in the recruitment sector, I worked in the financial services sector. Over the last 25 years, the industry has lacked an inclusive process for attaining more senior positions in the industry. It's no shock, I guess, that most individuals working in very senior roles, such as CEOs and COOs, are white men, with a certain level of socio-economic background. This is not reflective of society.

The injustice of the hiring procedure never being a fair playing field, and the idea that it has always been an old boys' club, sparks the fire in my belly. Dead man's shoes comes up often as well. From my perspective, the initial sign that this would become my life's passion was the unfairness I sensed when taking in-depth details about job opportunities. There was an automatic assumption that a certain type of person would be favoured for the position – whether gender, education, socio-economic background, etc.

This insight spurred me to look into inclusivity, particularly on the gender side. More recently, this has now widened to encompass everything, from ethnicity or socio-economic background, gender, where someone comes from, as well as their accent. Witnessing unfairness and being party to it has made me realise I don't want to be part of the problem in the future. I want to find solutions for organisations.

I know it isn't easy. There's no blame, but there is bias, and everybody has bias. We need to understand how to check our bias at the door effectively when we're hiring and make sure that it's not driving forward our interpretation of what we're seeing in front of us.

When I was about 21, my body went through some weird experiences, including double vision and a numb right-hand side. Over the years, I went back and forth to a neurologist, then eventually, in 2018, I was diagnosed with multiple sclerosis. I am, for all intents and purposes, disabled. That is a sure-fire way to get that disabled parking Blue Badge! Initially, after being diagnosed, I didn't want to disclose this life-changing information to my employer. I was quiet, not secretive, but I wasn't necessarily shouting it from the rooftops.

My inner thoughts grappled with the idea that I didn't want people to feel sorry for me or treat me differently. I think of it now as being purely selfish; I didn't want to lose out on anything. Inclusion is very close to my heart because I understand how it feels to be on the other side. In the past, I never really thought any differently about taking forward the application of someone who was disabled, whether physically or neurodiversely. I never thought about how to advertise positions to attract this sector of society, or how we could have conversations that would ensure they had everything they needed to go forward for roles.

My own diagnosis opened up a whole different level of understanding and empathy, especially when it was not evident that they had a disability. Each individual is very aware of how it can impact their work and how they go about their daily life.

It's been a long journey in terms of my diagnosis. It's not entirely normal, but neither is it abnormal for MS to take some time to be diagnosed. When I eventually received the diagnosis, it provided an opportunity to understand what the future might hold. However, it's not written in stone because every day's a party in my brain!

It has been a challenging way to learn about disability, but at the same time, I'm not going to let that stop me from doing what I'm doing; it's probably giving me that extra firepower in terms of action.

It takes much courage to speak out and speak up about MS, yet it's another way of attracting people who otherwise might not have a voice. It's about alleviating guilt, shame, or worry that these individuals will not be included and, in turn, be marginalised even more. And that's certainly what we don't want. That's the opposite of inclusivity.

Being a Voice of Women is all about supporting others to find and use their voice; for me, it centres all around inclusivity. We must join together to share our messages.

I think it's so important to both have a voice and use your voice. I know I'm privileged because I speak to individuals in various organisations and stages of their lives. But by using my voice, particularly with my background, I have an opportunity to start levelling that playing field. I also give people advice and pearls of wisdom that I've picked up when it comes to careers and climbing, whether it be the corporate ladder or self-development.

Over the years, I've spoken with numerous people and understood their fears, what's holding them back, and what pushes them forward. I have come to an understanding of what it is to be human and to drive your career forward. Your job is not the be-all and end-all, but whether we like it or not, it's a massive part of our lives. It's how we put food on the table, a roof over our heads, and give our children the best start. Therefore, it is an essential part of your life.

However, what is unfair is that most, if not all, of the hierarchical structures in business today do not effectively mirror what society looks like today. We must undertake considerable work to change the status quo. Thankfully, we are moving forward in the right direction; it's just unfortunate it's relatively glacial! But I know I'm not alone in working towards those goals.

My goal is to utilise my voice to highlight the injustices within the recruitment process and spotlight individuals who are accelerating progress in addressing these issues; disability advocates, gender equality, and so on. This is an excellent opportunity to express the importance of ensuring that individuals can hear others' stories and understand they're not alone. We all have challenges one way or another, and many are not as impossible as we believe; with suitable role models to pave the path ahead, people can find a way to overcome their obstacles.

This brings me to the core role of *Voices of Women*, which embraces passion, purpose and leadership as a woman.

I believe leadership is about taking people on a journey with you, not necessarily telling them what to do, but helping them to find their own path, their truths, and what they want to do in the long term. This way of working also enables people to learn from their mistakes as I give extensive feedback. I am probably in the minority of recruitment consultants who spend more time with people who don't get the job than those who do. Learning from every positive or negative experience is so important.

Another aspect of leadership, especially being a woman leader, is the opportunity to use different skills and knowledge, particularly regarding gender equity. Let's be honest: I see great women who don't know the greatness in themselves. So, one of my jobs is to push people and drive them to find their passion and that extra 'something' that will make them step up to the next level effectively rather than staying in their comfort zone.

In addition, I have noticed that many women find all the reasons and excuses why they shouldn't do something, as opposed to why they should. It is an extremely prevalent belief but over the years, I have found that these limiting beliefs are entirely solvable. When there is a problem, there is always a solution. Sometimes, one simply needs to flip the lens.

I am a woman, a leader, disabled, and in a minority, so I'm ticking lots of boxes. You could say I am in a club I don't want to be in. Yet it is about turning that around and using it to my advantage. I ask myself how can I create and influence change, using use all my skills, knowledge, and expertise. When presenting candidates, usually men, I ask myself how I can influence the gatekeepers to ensure women are also in that pool.

I have a little story to share with you. A few years ago, I had to find a senior person to fill a top position in an investment company. The hiring team was adamant that only a man would be successful in the position. Unconvinced, I took up the gauntlet; I don't shy away from a challenge but also, I wanted to prove the team wrong. I made it my life's work for four weeks to find a group of women who could do this job.

It was hard work, and it wasn't just a case of going out to the market, telling women about the fantastic, shiny job and getting them to apply for it. I had to make them understand why they could do it, why they were a good fit for the job, and how securing the job would be an achievement, as well as what **they** could offer the business.

Whilst many men could do the job very well, the organisation needed to be challenged to consider a more diverse senior leadership team and it was up to me to show them that diversity didn't mean reducing their expectations. It was frustrating as I knew that many of the women would and could do the job remarkably well.

For me, this particular investment company lacked diversity in its leadership team. I felt it was the wrong commercial decision to go for someone who would be 'a good fit'. I wanted them to hire someone who would be more than this, someone who would bring something new and different to the table. The position needed to be filled by someone confident enough to deliver in the role itself, as well as to go against the grain and have enough self-belief to stand up and feel that they were the right person in the right job at the right time.

It is all about speaking to the right person at the right time if they are having a bad day at the office or thinking about a change of scene. I can't be everywhere all the time, however much I would like to! I would speak to people and tell them a story and get them hooked. I needed to find out what that hook was because everybody wakes up on a different side of the bed. Some days, you'll wake up in an excellent mood, open and receptive to conversations, and some days, the last thing you want to discuss is your career or why you'd be a good fit for a job. So, ensuring I spoke to people at the right time was probably the most important factor.

When I consider the traits that make an effective leader today, all those I have met who fall into that category have things in common.

Some of the best leaders I've ever worked with or had the opportunity to meet are those who are real, showing authenticity and make you feel they are genuine, and/or 'let you in' a little. A leader needs to be honest and show some vulnerability because otherwise, they can seem almost unreal and fake. You see many individuals leading in a way that they think a leader should lead, which is often out of date and out of touch.

Those leaders that buck these old-fashioned trends are happy to put their stamp on it and have their own natural leadership. To me, it is obvious when I speak to someone in a senior position if they're comfortable with who they are; it's really obvious if they're very uncomfortable, too. They don't put as much emphasis or weight on what they say, whereas the great leaders make you want to hang on their every word and match them by giving them the very best of you.

When presented with the opportunity to be part of *Voices of Women*, it sounded like a great project. Women's voices need to be talked about more and be at the forefront of everyone's mind. I also believe that *Voices of Women* is more than a book; it is a community of 22 women who are leaders and who want to effect change. It is the birthing of a movement, with every contributor united in having a voice and a determination to share it. By contributing and sharing stories and passion, the collective mission begins to gather speed, and the compound effect will enable it to grow. Beyond these pages will be an opportunity to meet everyone else and I can't wait till that day!

I am now turning my attention to the future. I have a daughter aged 13, and I believe it's essential that we pass on wisdom, but not in a synthetic way. My daughter is very much like me! She's very headstrong. She's pretty stubborn. She knows her mind. Even if she's wrong, she'll never admit it. But I have always asked her to be honest with herself as it is so important. As a mum, it's great if she's honest with me, but I think it's more important that she's honest with herself and how she's feeling. If you're happy in your own skin, you'll be able to lead much better.

My daughter has recently become the captain of her football team, which is fantastic; at first, she didn't think it was a big deal. But she has an important role when they play competitive football; emotions run high, and she's the one who has to ensure that the team are working together, not letting emotions get the better of them. She has to ensure everyone is organised and is kept on track; it's such a huge responsibility. In the beginning, she genuinely thought it was having to choose heads or tails at the start of the game, and that was it! But she has now realised the importance of the position. She has discovered that she has a voice and valid opinions, and that she should never allow others to not listen to her and to close her down. It is crucial that she feels respected, listened to, and comfortable enough to be herself as well.

Passing on pearls of wisdom to the younger generation is our responsibility to ensure we create a fantastic and fair world for us all. The most important thing is to be yourself and be happy in your skin. Because when you're yourself and happy in your own skin, you **shine**. And that's what we want for our children and our future leaders. Honesty and authenticity are vital. With maturity, insight and experience, you can tell when someone is spouting nonsense! So, for me, honesty is the number one trait because how can you trust someone if they can't be genuine, especially to themselves?

My one message to women around female leadership is that **everybody** has the opportunity to lead. It may not feel like you do, but regardless of who you are, somebody is watching you and you are a role model, influencing or making an impact on someone else's life. When you think about it this way, you could be the most important person in somebody's life without realising it.

Don't let the side down; lead with an honest, open, fair heart!

Having dedicated three decades to the medical field, Carolyn's leadership experience is nothing short of extensive. She champions the fresh perspectives of female leaders, whose diverse insights drive modern goals focused on gender equality.

Early in her medical career, Carolyn noticed a troubling disparity in patient care. Determined to make a difference, she became a passionate advocate, tirelessly exploring ways to elevate the standard of medical services.

Understanding the crucial role of education in professional development, Carolyn pursued further training to provide the highest level of patient support. Her intrinsic motivation and the wisdom gained over time fuel her unwavering commitment, a theme vividly reflected in her storytelling.

In Carolyn's narrative, you'll discover her many heroes, none more influential than her grandfather. His words, resonating deeply within her, propelled her forward, inspiring her to make a lasting impact on countless lives. Even today, she draws strength from his wisdom.

She steps forward daily, driven by a leadership ethos that nurtures and empowers the next generation. Her experience, lessons, and expertise are a testament to her journey and a legacy poised to leave an indelible mark on the world.

Get ready to delve into Carolyn's inspiring journey, where each story offers a glimpse into her profound impact on the medical field and beyond.

Brenda

Dr Carolyn M. Rubin

"True leadership blooms
like a steadfast flower –
not loud or demanding to be seen,
but ever-present and graceful.
It is the strength of a woman that
turns the wheels of progress
with a touch both gentle and firm."

Dr Carolyn M. Rubin

Rising Above

Women in Leadership, Challenges Faced, and Lives Embraced

Women in leadership play a vital role in various healthcare fields, breaking gender barriers and promoting diversity as CEOs, medical directors and in research. They contribute fresh perspectives, foster inclusion, and inspire future generations. Gender equality in leadership positions is a crucial goal for a more equitable society. It promotes diverse perspectives and ensures that talent and potential are recognised and utilised, regardless of gender.

Through education, experience and expertise, for the last 32 years, I have dedicated my life to healthcare as a patient advocate focused on ensuring patients have access to care. As a servant leader, my work and actions help set people up for success, providing guidance and inspiration to be their best. When you create such dramatic change in others, it is often seen as transformational leadership.

Like many of you, I take pride and enjoy inspiring and motivating others to achieve their goals and exceed their expectations. This journey has allowed me to be a compass for others, helping them navigate their challenges and watching their dreams take shape. The results I've witnessed far surpass my initial career expectations.

My journey in healthcare began as a pharmacy technician. I soon realised there was more that could be done to assist patients. Motivated to make more of an impact, I became a Certified Medical Assistant working in urgent care, pre-op, and family practice, providing patients with quality financial care. In contrast, the physicians provided quality clinical care. I understood healthcare was not simply about treating ailments, but caring for the entire person, body, and soul.

Not long into my journey, I was asked to teach at the college where I received my medical assisting degree. When you love what you do, it becomes clear you are committed to your goals and others watch that meaningful drive to make a difference. It does not go unnoticed.

As an instructor and mentor to many, I focused on setting teams up for success to meet their patients' needs from the time they made their appointments. The aim was to empower patients with knowledge, include them in changes, and work alongside them, recognising their growth and providing support. This impact extended far beyond the patients. By choosing to nurture the talents of those around me, I empowered them to become better caregivers to the patients they served.

I remember the medical assisting program I was blessed to help launch. The first class had eight women looking to start a new career. From graduating high school to making a life decision to change professions, these women now looked to me for guidance and instruction. They worked hard and they were passionate about making a difference. They graduated with top honours, received the highest scores for their internships, and passed their certification with flying colours. During graduation, they honoured me with a glass apple inscribed, "To our angel, love, the class of 1999." The evidence was in plain sight that purpose-driven work reaps greater results and the ripples go beyond your expectations.

During this insightful time when work was filling me with continued motivation, the home front took a turn for the worse. I received news that my grandpa was seriously ill. Through my conversations with him, one constant message, a common theme, kept coming up. While the care he was receiving was great, he didn't feel like they were listening to him. We have all experienced this: you walk into the office, and with heads down, someone says, "Please sign in," and without eye contact, you are handed a clipboard, asked to complete it and return it. Upon receipt, they take the clipboard or ask you to set it down and have a seat. What have they seen? What have they heard?

Experience has taught me that my legacy in healthcare was more than about touching countless lives; it was also about the culture I fostered. During a conversation with my grandpa, he said, "Promise me one thing: every day you go to work, walk through the door with the eyes of a patient; if you do that, you will always be successful."

These wise words of my grandfather became my motto from that day forward. This vital message would be shared whenever I trained, spoke at conferences, or mentored teams. We must start listening with our eyes. Through many conversations with patients and staff, I realised there was a way to create an ethos where the patients knew they were being heard.

Teamwork thrived, and a sense of purpose prevailed throughout the office where 35 people vowed to make a difference. We created a culture where patients felt good, even when they felt bad. The values of our team were evident when we created a mission and vision statement that was posted for the patients to see.

The vision statement read:

> We are creating a culture where listening with our eyes becomes an art to foster deeper connections, understanding, and empathy in every interaction.

The mission statement read:

> Our mission is to empower individuals and communities to harness the power of visual listening. To enable people to truly "see" one another. Through the art of listening with our eyes, we inspire compassion and enrich lives.

The patients were receiving quality care clinically and quality support from the team. Word travelled about the changes we were making, and I became known not only for training and mentoring programs, but also for my unwavering commitment to compassion and care.

My reputation as a servant leader grew as the years went by. The result of this dedication was my promotion to leadership positions not because I sought power, but because my colleagues recognised my ability to bring out the best in everyone. As you scale the ladder, it is prudent to lead with humility, always putting the needs of the team and patients before your own.

Few people admit to being afraid of failing, especially when they are highly trained, educated and held in a position of influence and impact as a leader. You never start out to be a leader; for me, it was always about making a difference. But as you grow, you begin to dream, and do not always believe that opportunities will present themselves for you to achieve your vision.

I now know that self-belief is crucial in achieving your goals and you must work hard on developing that belief within you. Finding myself in a position very few women had experienced, a new fear arose within me. I was afraid to let down those who entrusted me. When fear gets in the way of your purpose, finding a mentor to help you is a way of igniting motion once again. The next step was to work with a woman mentor and executive coach to ensure I was the best I could be.

When working with this coach, I realised that I controlled my own destiny. 'Ah-ha' moments like these allow you to turn your fear into a celebration. It was essential to start adding value to myself so I could continue to add value to others. Through multiple courses, I started shifting my thoughts and writing down my "Why", making a conscious decision to continue making a difference, regardless of my role. Knowing your WHY is crucial to maintaining intrinsic motivation and committing to your goals and vision.

It meant shattering glass ceilings and actively working to create pathways and opportunities for those who would come after me. My desire was to use my leadership role to inspire and empower the next generation of women to reach for their aspirations and contribute to positive change in society. My commitment to mentorship and support is critical to who I am.

Strong women in leadership don't just break barriers; they build bridges for others to cross.

It wasn't always easy, and breaking through barriers sometimes meant helping others understand servant leadership, which was natural to me. Servant leadership empowers others with the tools they need for success, a philosophy rooted in mentorship, leadership, and personal development. I embraced the challenges and realised they were opportunities to continue to learn and grow. I sought new information, skills and experiences, understood that it required effort, and recognised that setbacks and failures are a part of the learning process. Giving up was not an option and I needed to persevere through obstacles and setbacks, as they were stepping stones towards my success.

I reflected on my thoughts and beliefs and challenged myself to replace fixed mindset thinking with growth-oriented thoughts. Sharing my knowledge and enthusiasm for growth with other women allowed me to celebrate our achievements and recognise growth as a journey – small victories matter!

Maintaining a work-life balance wasn't easy. I worked in a "man's" world, where boundaries between work and personal life did not exist. I had to learn to say no and be selective with my commitments. The next change was learning to block time for myself on my calendar, delegate tasks to team members, and focus on quality over quantity. Working with mentors to learn how to unplug and disconnect, even if for a short time, became part of my journey to success. As a leader, I wanted to show that it's possible to succeed in your career while maintaining a fulfilling personal life.

Attaining the milestone of 32 years in healthcare provided the opportunity to reflect on my journey. I witnessed great advancements in medicine and technology but knew that the essence of healthcare would always be about people – being a servant leader. My heart swelled with pride, knowing I had made a difference, not just in patients' lives, but in the hearts of my mentees.

My story became a source of inspiration for many, a reminder that leadership is not about titles or authority but about service, empathy, and making the world a better place.

My impact as a servant leader extended far beyond the exceptional care I provided to patients. I was deeply committed to nurturing my colleagues' talents and potential, and became known as a trusted mentor.

Healthcare professionals sought out opportunities to work alongside me. I was always willing to share my knowledge and experience, patiently guiding them through healthcare challenges. My mentorship wasn't just about teaching clinical skills; it was about instilling the values of empathy, compassion, and dedication.

Every free moment, I would gather mentees and share stories and insights from my journey, emphasising the importance of truly understanding each patient's needs and fears. I encouraged my colleagues to listen, not just with their ears, but with their eyes and hearts.

Under my guidance, many blossomed into exceptional healthcare providers, and I always recognised their achievements, celebrating their successes with them as if they were my own. The accurate measure of leadership is the positive impact it has on the lives and careers of colleagues. I would always tell them that if someday they took my job, I knew the leader within them was shaped by the training, mentoring and experiences provided by my philosophies.

I knew that to continue to add value to others, I would need to build on my foundation. Investing in my growth and personal development is vital to be better equipped to impact the lives of those around me positively, and it was an easy yes for me when these opportunities appeared. It further created opportunities where my self-improvement journey could enrich my life and the lives of others. It wasn't about perfection; it was about becoming a source of inspiration and support, providing positive interactions and being authentic. I wanted to make a difference, not only in healthcare but in every facet of life.

Becoming a life coach seemed like the next logical step for me. It would allow me to help individuals achieve their personal and professional goals, support them to overcome challenges, and lead more fulfilling lives.

I frequently thought about my grandpa and my promise to him; he was my source of inspiration and his words were my motivation, allowing me to open more doors to impact healthcare within other countries and industries.

Getting into other industries proved more difficult than I imagined. Although my life has been centred around serving others, training and mentoring them to be the best patient advocates and leaders they could be, breaking the glass ceiling was challenging. During this time of expansion, I endured many setbacks. I had held an interim VP position for nine months. I automated processes, managed the business and expanded contracts during this time. However, I was not offered the post on a permanent basis, because I did not have a master's degree. My work, business impact and dedication during my interim period were not even taken into account.

I kept pushing forward, becoming more resilient as obstacles appeared in my way. I would turn to my mentors for advice, joining networking groups to empower change and continue my journey to learn. Engaging with networking groups provided the opportunity to communicate my aspirations and achievements to others. This powerful belief allowed me to participate in organisations whose initiatives included collaboration and support with other women, mentorship, and friendship. Currently, our support for each other grows daily as we work together to make a difference in the lives of others.

Have you heard of the Law of Attraction? As we continued to bring positive experiences to others, we saw more positive outcomes for ourselves. Our energy level was high, and our hearts were full. We were grateful for the opportunities we were receiving to go out and help others find the success we were experiencing. I found myself mentoring others in multiple industries. Leaders striving to be better, teams looking to grow, and corporations wanting to become better servant leaders. I failed forward many times but never looked back each time I got up; I kept moving forward.

My dedication to mentorship ensures that the spirit of servant leadership continues to thrive for many generations of healthcare professionals. Become a beacon of inspiration, reminding everyone that authentic leadership isn't just about serving patients; it is about serving and uplifting one another, creating a healthcare community bound together by a shared commitment to compassion and excellence. Empowering others with the tools and knowledge they need for success is a powerful way to contribute to personal and collective growth. My commitment to this principle will positively impact various aspects of healthcare, life and work.

An opportunity arose for me as a Certified Team Member of Maxwell Leadership. I was excited and blessed to join 120 coaches providing leadership transformation to more than 6,500 people over a week in Panama. To see the joy in their eyes, experience their engagement, and be a part of their journey to grow to be the best leaders for their country was incredible.

Throughout the healthcare community, individuals transformed, their self-confidence increased, and they were motivated to achieve beyond what they believed was possible. During one of my speaking engagements, I was approached by a nurse who had been following me for some time. She was going through difficult times, as she had been diagnosed with brain cancer. She heard my story of my grandpa and my mission to help others: "Listen with your eyes." She had shared that with her team and with the clinical team that were treating her. Her goal, like mine, was to make a difference.

My mentees began to mentor others. They empowered their team members to take ownership of their work and make meaningful contributions. The cultivated learning and growth culture became the cornerstone of their focus. A culture of innovation, collaboration and shared vision ultimately drove positive change in achieving their goals. It wasn't just about passing on clinical skills; it was about passing on the torch of servant leadership.

I am making a difference one person at a time, as a life coach, speaker, mentor, and trainer. The secret is empowering them to be the best they can be and to never give up on their dreams. It doesn't matter what others think; it matters what you think and what you put your mind to doing. My tagline for my business is "Coaching that Empowers You." My slogan is "Take one day at a time, never stop growing, never stop trying, keep your strength, and live your dream."

Out of challenges comes resilience. It helps to develop and strengthen essential traits. I faced a challenge that put my leadership skills to the test. I was engaged with the executive team as they were servant leaders like me. I was able to mentor others and encourage growth within the organisation. There were significant adjustments, and the values were changing. Instead of mentoring teams, I was put on assignments that kept me on the road five days a week, every week. The one person I looked up to began to change as he was receiving more responsibilities than hours in the day.

During this time, I took the opportunity to seek support and guidance from mentors. I enrolled in a Healthcare Leadership Certification program to continue my growth and enhance my leadership capabilities. I looked outside the organisation for a change, taking myself out of a place of discontent and realising I still had so much to give. I wasn't going to stop empowering others or stop empowering myself. Resilience is closely linked to emotional intelligence, and this emotional awareness has helped me enhance my interpersonal skills and leadership abilities, contributing to my success in team environments. The goal of empowerment is not just short-term success, but long-term growth and self-sufficiency. It is helping me and other individuals to develop the resilience and adaptability needed to navigate various challenges throughout our journey.

Collaboration and empathy are pivotal in many aspects of life, including relationships, work, and leadership. My aim is to create inclusive environments where all voices are heard, and valued. This goal builds strong, supportive teams, and they learn to trust each other. As a servant leader, I believe this fosters a culture of cooperation, creativity and compassion, allowing for emotional and professional growth. It is about paying it forward and encouraging those you empower to empower others. It is a holistic approach that combines sharing knowledge, nurturing skills, providing support, and creating opportunities. It's a powerful way to foster personal and professional growth, make positive change, and contribute to a more inclusive and equitable world.

You are never too young or old to focus on your growth. Taking communication classes, leadership development courses, and listening to podcasts are just a few ways to increase your knowledge and self-awareness. Reading or participating in book clubs will give you another perspective and continue your growth.

Working with mentors and executive coaches has provided me with growth and empowered me to become the leader I am today. They understood my challenges and gave me the tools I needed to succeed. My experience led me to become a life coach and mentor myself. I wanted to pay it forward and ensure women could take on any task and be the best leader they could be.

It is okay to fail forward, as you will learn from the process. It can be easy to give up if things don't go right. If you do, you will always ask yourself, "What if?" When you allow yourself to fail forward, you will enable yourself to grow. You pick yourself up, dust yourself off, and keep moving forward. Your personal and professional growth from this will take you to new levels and allow you to experience new beginnings.

"Remember, empowered women don't fear failure;
they embrace it as a steppingstone
to success on their path to leadership."

*"I define a leader as anyone
who takes responsibility for finding
the potential in people and processes,
and who has the courage
to develop that potential."*

Brené Brown

American professor, social worker, author,
and podcast host, known for her work on
shame, vulnerability, and leadership

Great leaders understand that we are the sum of the people we surround ourselves with, and Christy embodies this principle perfectly. As a community leader and beacon of hope, she uses her position to inspire and uplift others. Learning about this luminary is a privilege, and as you delve into her story, you'll uncover the powerful drive behind her mission.

Christy's journey begins with her humble beginnings in Nigeria, a source of strength and inspiration that fuels her desire to grow and enrich the lives of those around her. As a nurse, her innate passion for caring for others has become a cornerstone of her work, allowing her to impact her community significantly. Her experiences have unlocked a wellspring of compassion, revealing the profound importance of this gift in her mission.

A true protagonist and trailblazer, Christy founded her own community interest company (CIC) to create a safe and supportive space for women, focusing on women's health issues. Her visionary leadership ensures women can access the resources and community they need to thrive.

As you read Christy's story, you'll resonate with a selfless woman who wears her leadership badge with honour. She encourages other women to step into their leadership roles, inviting them to join her on a transformative journey. Christy's narrative is a testament to the power of humility, compassion, and the relentless pursuit of influence and making an impact.

Brenda

Christy Amalu

"Ladies, always remember that the people you are surrounded by determines whom you become."

Christy Amalu

Empowering Through Leadership
A Journey of Female Empowerment and Influence

In a world where challenges often seem insurmountable and barriers to success can appear daunting, the story of a shy girl who blossomed into a confident and influential leader stands out as a beacon of hope and inspiration.

This is the story of a woman who defied the odds, embraced her potential, and emerged as a trailblazer in the realms of healthcare, literature, and community empowerment. Through her journey from a quiet, introspective young girl to a dynamic and visionary leader, she has not only transformed her own life, but also touched the lives of countless others around the globe.

This is a story of female leadership at its finest, a story that proves that with determination, perseverance, and a steadfast commitment to one's dreams, anything is possible.

Chapter 1: The Journey Begins

Born into a modest family of six children and raised by a widowed mum in a small town, Ehime Mbano in Imo

State, Nigeria, our protagonist was a shy and reserved girl who often preferred the solace of books to the company of others. Despite her introverted nature, she harboured a deep-seated desire to make a difference in the world, a desire that would eventually shape the trajectory of her life in ways she could never have imagined. As she navigated through the challenges of adolescence and early adulthood, she discovered her passion for nursing – a field that not only allowed her to care for others, but also provided a platform for her to express her innate compassion and empathy.

After years of hard work and dedication, she earned her degree and embarked on a fulfilling career as a registered nurse. She pursued and gained qualifications in other areas of nursing, such as midwifery and mental health. Through her work in hospitals and healthcare facilities, she witnessed first-hand the struggles and triumphs of patients from all walks of life. It was in these moments of connection and empathy that she realised the true power of compassion and the profound impact that a single individual could have on the lives of others. Armed with this new-found understanding, she set out to expand her horizons and explore new avenues for personal and professional growth.

Chapter 2: The Power of Words

Driven by a thirst for knowledge and a relentless pursuit of self-improvement, our protagonist delved into the world of literature and writing. Drawing inspiration from her own experiences and the stories of those she encountered along the way, she began to pen her thoughts, ideas, and reflections on paper. What started as a personal catharsis soon evolved into a powerful medium for self-expression and advocacy. Through her books and articles, she sought to amplify the voices of the marginalised, shed light on pressing social issues, and inspire others to embrace their inner strength and resilience.

Her writings resonated with readers around the world, sparking conversations, igniting passions, and fostering a sense of community among those who shared her vision of a more inclusive and compassionate society. With each word she penned, she empowered others to speak their truth, challenge the status quo, and strive for a better tomorrow. Her books became beacons of hope for those grappling with adversity, symbols of resilience for those facing insurmountable odds, and testaments to the transformative power of storytelling.

Chapter 3: Leading with Purpose

As her influence grew and her reach expanded, our protagonist felt a calling to do more – to take her advocacy and activism to the next level and affect change on a larger scale. With unwavering determination and a clear sense of purpose, she founded an organisation dedicated to empowering individuals from all walks of life to reach their full potential and become agents of positive change in their communities. Through a combination of mentorship programs, educational initiatives and advocacy campaigns, her organisation provided individuals with the tools, resources and support they needed to overcome obstacles, unlock their inner potential, and pursue their dreams with confidence and conviction.

At the helm of this burgeoning organisation, our protagonist embraced her role as a leader with grace, humility, and a deep sense of responsibility. Drawing upon her experiences in nursing, literature, and community service, she led by example, inspiring others to follow in her footsteps and make a difference in the world around them. She understood that true leadership was not about wielding power or authority, but about serving others, lifting them, and enabling them to shine brightly in their own right.

Under her guidance, the organisation flourished, expanding its reach to communities far and wide, touching the lives of individuals from diverse backgrounds and cultures. Through a combination of innovative programs and strategic partnerships, she spearheaded initiatives that addressed pressing social issues, promoted gender equality, and fostered a culture of inclusivity and respect. Her leadership style was characterised by empathy, compassion, and a deep commitment to social justice, values that resonated with those who crossed her path and inspired them to join her in the pursuit of a more just and equitable world.

Chapter 4: Navigating the Challenges

Despite her many accomplishments and successes, our protagonist's journey was not without its share of challenges and setbacks. As a woman in leadership, she often found herself facing gender biases, stereotypes, and double standards that sought to diminish her contributions and undermine her authority. In moments of doubt and uncertainty, she drew strength from her inner resolve, her unwavering faith, and the support of her mentors and allies who believed in her vision and championed her cause.

Through perseverance, courage, and a steadfast belief in her abilities, she overcame these obstacles with grace and resilience, emerging stronger and more determined than ever before. She refused to be defined by society's expectations or limited by its constraints, choosing instead to chart her own course and blaze a trail for others to follow. Her journey was a testament to the power of perseverance, the strength of the human spirit, and the transformative impact of unwavering belief in oneself.

Chapter 5: Inspiring the Next Generation

As our protagonist reflected on her journey from a shy girl to a confident leader, she realised the profound impact that her story could have on younger women and girls who were navigating their paths to greatness. Determined to pay it forward and inspire the next generation of female leaders, she dedicated herself to mentoring, coaching, and empowering young women to dream big, work hard, and never give up on their aspirations.

Through her work in the church and her local community, she created opportunities for young women to develop their leadership skills, cultivate their talents, and step into positions of influence and authority with confidence and conviction. She believed that true empowerment came not from seeking power for its own sake but from using one's influence to uplift others, champion causes that mattered, and create a more equitable and just society for all.

Chapter 6: A Legacy of Empowerment

Today, our protagonist's legacy is a testament to the transformative power of female leadership and the enduring impact of one woman's determination to make a difference in the world. From her humble beginnings to her current role as a global influencer and change-maker, she has blazed a trail of empowerment and inspiration that continues to illuminate the path for others to follow. Through her tireless efforts, unwavering commitment, and steadfast belief in the potential of every individual to effect positive change, she has inspired a new generation of leaders to rise up, speak out, and lead with courage and compassion.

As she continues to mentor, coach, and empower young women through her organisation and community initiatives, she remains committed to fostering a culture of inclusivity, diversity, and equality where every individual has the opportunity to thrive and succeed on their own terms. She understands that true empowerment comes from lifting others, creating opportunities for growth and development, and building a community of support and encouragement that transcends boundaries and unites people for a common purpose.

Chapter 7: Embracing the Future

Looking ahead to the future, our protagonist is filled with hope, optimism, and a sense of purpose that propels her forward on her journey of empowerment and influence. She envisions a world where women and girls are no longer held back by societal norms or limited by cultural expectations, but are free to pursue their aspirations, fulfil their potential, and lead with authenticity and integrity.

With a renewed sense of purpose and a deepening commitment to her mission, she continues to push boundaries, challenge conventions, and advocate for change in the areas of healthcare, literature, and community empowerment. She remains a steadfast advocate for gender equality, social justice, and human rights, using her platform and influence to shine a light on issues that matter and inspire others to take action.

She is grateful for the opportunities, challenges, and experiences that have shaped her into the woman she is today. She remains humble in the face of her accomplishments, grateful for the support of her family, friends and mentors who have stood by her side through thick and thin, and determined to continue making a positive impact in the world for years to come.

Conclusion: A Call to Action

In conclusion, the story of our protagonist is a testament to the transformative power of female leadership, the enduring impact of resilience and determination, and the profound influence that one individual can have on the world around them. She serves as a source of inspiration and empowerment for women and girls everywhere, reminding them that greatness lies within and that with courage, determination and a steadfast commitment to dreams, anything is possible.

As she continues to empower, inspire, and lead with purpose, she invites others to join her in the quest for a more just, equitable and compassionate world where every individual has the opportunity to thrive and succeed. She calls on women and girls to embrace their potential, stand tall in the face of adversity, and use their voices to effect positive change in their communities and beyond.

"Empowerment is not a destination but a journey – a journey of self-discovery, growth, and transformation. Let us walk this path together, hand in hand, as we embrace our power, uplift one another, and create a world where every voice is heard, every dream is valued, and every individual is empowered to reach their full potential."

To the young women who are just beginning their journey, she offers these words of encouragement: "Believe in yourself, trust in your abilities, and never underestimate the impact you can have on the world around you. Your unique perspective, your voice, and your passion have the power to change lives, inspire others, and create a better future for all. Don't be afraid to take risks, challenge the status quo, and step into your greatness with confidence and grace. The world is waiting for your light to shine bright – don't hold back, for the world needs your leadership now more than ever."

As our protagonist's story continues to unfold and her influence continues to grow, she remains steadfast in her commitment to empowering others, inspiring change, and leaving a lasting legacy of compassion, courage, and leadership. Her story is a testament to the transformative power of perseverance, resilience, and a deep-seated belief in the potential of every individual to make a difference in the world.

Through her example, she challenges us all to rise above our fears, embrace our strengths, and lead with purpose and passion. She reminds us that leadership is not about the titles we hold or the positions we occupy, but about the lives we touch, the hearts we inspire, and the impact we leave behind. She shows us that greatness is not defined by external accolades or material success, but by the depth of our character, the strength of our convictions, and the legacy of love and service we leave for future generations to inherit.

In closing, let us heed the call to action that our protagonist embodies: to lead with courage, to empower with compassion, and to inspire with authenticity. Let us stand together as a united force for positive change, working tirelessly to create a world where all individuals – regardless of gender, background, or circumstance – have the opportunity to thrive, succeed, and lead lives of purpose and fulfilment.

As we embark on this collective journey of empowerment and transformation, may we draw strength from the example set forth by our protagonist and countless other women who have blazed trails, shattered glass ceilings, and paved the way for future generations to follow. Let us honour their legacies, amplify their voices, and continue their work with a renewed sense of purpose, passion, and commitment to building a more just, equitable, and inclusive world for all.

Together, let us rise, let us lead, and let us inspire, empowering one another to achieve greatness, affect change, and leave a lasting legacy of love, hope, and empowerment for generations to come. The future is ours to shape, the possibilities are endless, and the time for action is now. Let us march forward with courage, unity and determination, knowing that together, we can truly make a difference in the world and leave a lasting impact that will reverberate through the ages.

In closing, honour is given to whom honour is due. I will give glory to God Almighty who made this possible and many thanks to the lead author in this project, Brenda Dempsey, who extended an arm of fellowship to me and invited me to this project. I had many limitations ranging from lack of resources and time constraints, but due to her perseverance and belief in me, Brenda has brought me to intellectuals and forward-moving women from all works of life.

This is the power of female leadership. As Brenda said, "Remember the people you are surrounded by determine who you become."

This is the legacy we can create. Let us seize the moment, embrace the challenge, and together, let us change the world for the better.

Sometimes, you encounter a woman who inspires you to reach greater heights. Julie is one such woman, a true action figure on a global mission. Her litany of accomplishments over just 20 years will leave you in awe of what one person can achieve. Prepare to be amazed by this woman who embraces adventure at every turn.

Julie is a remarkable leader with an indomitable spirit, attracting others to join her journey. Like many renowned leaders, she has faced her share of challenges. Julie's spirituality immersion, commitment to a healthy lifestyle, and appreciation of the world's most incredible resource – water – reveal her belief in life's elixirs.

She surrounds herself with like-minded individuals who inspire her to become a better version of herself. What truly sets her apart is her unwavering ability to say YES. As you turn the pages of her story, you'll discover why this philosophy drives her and how it fuels her extraordinary life.

Julie invites you to dive head first and be inspired by a woman who grasps life with both hands and lives it to the fullest. Join me in walking alongside Julie for many years to come. Be inspired, seize your chance to uncover the secrets behind her incredible journey, and be motivated to embrace your own adventures.

Brenda

Julie Lewis

"Dream big, lead by example, flow like water and say YES to the adventure of life."

Julie Lewis

The Power of Stepping Up and Showing Up

My name is Julie Lewis and I am a pioneer rebel dedicated to a compelling cause: empowering individuals to become the most unique, resilient, and healthiest versions of themselves. This mission is critical in navigating the unpredictable waves of challenge and change. Through keynote speaking, running masterclasses, retreats and expeditions around the globe, I leverage the raw and honest beauty of nature as our classroom. I'm thrilled to have published my second book, *Uncharted Waters*, with Book Brilliance Publishing; it's a metaphorical journey through water, exploring how *'being more like water'* can help us in business and life.

Power of Authorship
Launching Ideas Into the World

I chose the Abu Dhabi International Book Fair to launch *Uncharted Waters* in the UAE as a high-profile platform for authorship in the Emirates. The timing was impeccable and allowed me to align with one of the UAE's most significant events for authors.

It is vital to act strategically once you have your book and I urge aspiring authors to explore what's happening in the book world where you live locally, regionally, and then internationally.

It was a blessing that the Abu Dhabi International Book Fair timed perfectly for *Uncharted Waters*. In the UAE, there are many other great book fairs and festivals to promote authors, such as the Sharjah Book Fair and the Emirates Literature Festival. These allow authors to gain visibility, network with peers, and create a lasting impact. It's essential to leverage market exposure and mix and mingle with other authors, journalists, and the media. Each connection is a stepping stone towards amplifying your authority and credibility.

Once you've attended a book fair, I highly recommend reaching out to the organisers to be a speaker, a moderator, or on a panel next time. Leverage each connection you make. It's so important to lead by example and keep building your brand, sharing your stories and insights over several media channels, and following up on every single call, email and request to show your professionalism.

Stepping Into Leadership
A Journey of Discovery

Leadership is not a title, it is a by-product of following your passion. When you do what you love and it is value and purpose-driven, that's when the magic happens; leadership becomes a way of being, living, and serving. Reflecting on more than two decades of leading multinational teams of women and men on global expeditions to more than 20 countries, including 10 to the Arctic and three to Antarctica, I can say, hand on heart, I love stepping into and expanding my leadership role. Every experience in business, life and adventure has shaped the journey of who I have become due to actively seeking challenging environments and situations to build resilience, courage, confidence, and leadership qualities.

It All Begins With Resilience

Transforming Challenges Into Strength and Opportunities

Resilience is at the very heart of leadership. It's often seen as a soft skill,; however, it is clear that without resilience, it is easy to fall apart and burn out. The fastest way to build resilience is to have more experiences; the more experiences we have, be they good, not so-good, or downright heart-breaking, the more resilient we become. The more resilient we become, the better we are at managing stress and anxiety.

I have observed three key transformations in those who journey with me:

1. Heightened self-awareness

2. Discovering one's strengths and playing to them

3. Acting, asking for help, and having a 'can-do' attitude

Resilient leaders are optimists; they hold themselves accountable, focus on solutions, have an open and flexible mind, and learn how to manage stress and anxiety.

Socrates advocated for us to "know thyself" and I agree with him! Self-awareness, awareness of others, and awareness of your environment are critical to success and growth. I love creating opportunities for people to challenge themselves physically, mentally, spiritually, and emotionally as part of their personal and professional development. It is only when we step out of our comfort zones that we can truly access our hidden strengths and depths. It's amazing how creative and resourceful we can be when we find ourselves in stormy waters!

Motivational speaker Jim Rohn said, "You become the average of the five people you spend the most time with," and from personal experience, I agree with him.

It's important to surround yourself with open-minded doers, dreamers and cheerleaders who will rally around, connect you with people and resources, mentor, and coach you. I make a point of hanging out with people who are 10 steps ahead of me, and have different skill sets and perspectives on business and life so that I can expand and grow. Punch above your weight and seek out opportunities to join mastermind groups that you know will take you to the next level.

Even if you don't think you're ready, say yes. Believe me, you will find a way or find someone to help you find a way. When I had the opportunity to speak at a TEDx event and then at a Million Dollar Round Table conference in Los

Angeles, I said yes and then found someone to help me with my presentations. I was brave and I know you can be brave too!

By saying yes, you let the universe know that you are serious and that alone attracts help from sources and resources beyond your imagination. I have a "crawl, walk, run" mantra that I use at the beginning of any new venture. This helps me take those first baby steps (saying yes!) that then progresses to quantum leaps along the way. The only way to learn something new is to do it until you know how to do it! Simple yet true.

Saying yes to leadership is about trust, energy, mind state, communication, decision-making, perseverance, connection, and collaboration. When all these skills are honed and developed, you can apply them in all areas of your life, not just in business.

I am a huge advocate for self-care. For me (and I highly recommend for you too), this is non-negotiable. To perform at your peak consistently means *putting your own oxygen mask on first*. That means thinking, eating, moving, sleeping, and hydrating like a champion athlete. It means getting the balance right between the time you spend in solitude and the time you are surrounded by people and being sociable. It means saying yes to you and no to others. It means setting healthy boundaries – yes, even with your family! It means quality recovery time, fun, travel, adventure, learning and development time – not only work, work work!

The sooner we learn this, the better. You cannot pour from an empty cup, so make sure your cup is full before pouring and remember to refill your cup by taking 'me time'. Being a wife, mother, employee, entrepreneur, business owner, caregiver, friend and 'all-rounder' takes a huge amount of energy and strength. It doesn't serve anyone for you to burn out and collapse because of giving too much of yourself.

Be your best and closest friend – you and your health, joy and freedom are top priority.

Embracing the Fusion of Male and Female Leadership Traits

Leadership transcends gender. It blends the best of both masculine and feminine traits. I have never felt or advocated a *'us and them'* approach; I prefer a leadership style that integrates both, to create a balanced approach that is adaptive, thoughtful, diverse, and inclusive.

There are many similarities and differences between male and female leaders. I have worked with women who are very much in their masculine energy and, for the most part, I am one of them! I have also worked with men who are very much in their feminine energy. Much depends on the roles and responsibilities of the position and the task at hand. The question is, does it require more of a left-brain analytical, logical, rational approach, or does it need more of a right-brain creative, free-flow, intuitive approach? Once you know that, find out who is best suited to the task – be they male or female.

One thing for sure I believe is that the 'command and control' leadership model of yesteryear is outdated and no longer works in today's business environment. I see more of a Socratic-leadership style these days, where individuals are encouraged to speak up and share their thoughts and ideas, and for women and men to work collectively to run a successful business. I don't think it matters whether you are male or female – what matters is your values, strengths, skill set, passion and your 'Why', as these will see you through both the calm and stormy waters.

Now, I know that this is a huge generalisation, but… I think women tend to be more intuitive. They will tap into each of their three brains before making big decisions – that is their head, their heart and their gut. They will explain what the situation is and ask for solutions from each team member rather than feeling they have to fix it alone.

I love the four archetypes in the creative approach to solving problems; the explorer who goes out and gets lots of new ideas from different places; the artist who draws, writes or explains how each of these ideas will look; the judge who assesses which ideas are good to go and which ones need to be let go; and finally, the warrior who makes the idea a reality. We each have a primary archetype and there is a little bit of each of these archetypes within us, so the goal is to focus on what you do best and find team members that complement you rather than replicate you! Focus on each other's strengths, combine them, and then you will be amazed at the results and outcomes possible.

In short, be true to yourself. Instead of trying to be more like a man, be more like the truest empowered version of yourself. There is nothing worse than trying to be something or somebody else or, worse still, comparing yourself to others. Be YOU and keep taking action; perfectionism and procrastination are the enemies of success and will rob you of joy, peace and creative freedom.

Voices of Women
Amplifying Female Leadership

Voices of Women is a testament to the power of female leadership, emphasising collaboration over competition. It is about creating a supportive network where women uplift each other, and share insights and experiences that span cultures and generations. *Voices of Women* is not simply about raising voices; it is about changing the narrative and demonstrating that women are pivotal in leadership roles.

There is something unique about being part of a value-aligned group of women. I talk a lot about values, as I believe they are the driving force of all our decisions. They determine who you are, how you spend your time and with whom, how you earn and spend your money, the conversations you have, the books you read, the movies you watch, the food you eat, the places you travel ... basically, everything! When you connect with value-aligned people, in this instance in *Voices of Women*, something very magical and alchemical happens.

When I first heard about the *Voices of Women* project, I thought it was an incredible way to reach a wider audience of women around the globe. It is important to encourage more women, no matter what age and stage they are on their journey, to STEP UP, SHOW UP AND SPEAK UP!

This book offers readers a unique opportunity to learn from each of the women participating in the project and explore the universal yet diverse lessons each of us has to share.

Coming together via this anthology creates collaboration within a solid ecosystem of women who support other women. Remember, "A rising tide lifts all boats," and this anthology is set to create a tidal wave of success to lift every reader.

Just imagine every single woman in this book linking arms with you. Just imagine each of the women taking your hand and walking beside you as you discover a new path ahead and then letting you go, so you can step into your very own personal power, knowing that someone has your back. See it as a rite of passage, a modern-day 'sheroes' journey where you have the courage and confidence to leave the comfort of everything you know, to explore new territories beyond your imagination.

I envisage *Voices of Women* as an essential resource and an anchor for other women to know that supporting each other is paramount wherever they are on their journey. When people come together and start talking, they soon realise they are facing the same issues, struggles, highs, lows, and plateaux on the journey. Periods of doubt are normal, especially when we are making big changes in the way we live and work. Knowing that you have an ecosystem of support to tap into makes a huge difference and can turn your doubt into inspired action.

Julie Lewis

Emerging Female Leadership in the Middle East

I left the UK aged 26 to work in the Middle East. Everyone thought I was crazy!

I left friends, family, and everything I knew behind to take the road less travelled. I was the first female sport and recreation manager in Kuwait back in 1989. I was there when Iraq invaded in 1990 and managed to escape across the desert into Saudi and get to the British Embassy to arrange a safe passage back to the UK. I returned to Kuwait in 1994, then moved on to Dubai in 1997.

Years later, at the tender age of 62, I am still thriving, learning and growing as a female expat and business owner in what is often and still perceived as a male-dominated country. I often comment that I am an 'Emarita' rather than an Emirati because I have lived in three of the seven Emirates that make up the United Arab Emirates! I moved from Kuwait to Dubai, then to Hong Kong, then back to Abu Dhabi, back to Dubai and more recently to Ras Al Khaimah in the northern Emirates. I love the UAE and consider it my home.

When people find out that I live, work and play in the Middle East, they immediately ask, "Oh, my gosh, what is it like working there? How did you adapt and adjust?" For this reason alone, it's important to share my story.

Having lived in the Middle East for more than a third of my life, I have witnessed transformative shifts for women. The region is buzzing with opportunities to lead, innovate, inspire, learn, and grow. From leadership summits to business councils to start-up initiatives and funding, the Middle East is a dynamic platform for women to excel. Women have always played a significant role here, despite what the media portrays. I have always felt safe and supported as a woman here, and it was easy to set up my business in the Freezone and get up and running very quickly.

Moving Forward With Voices of Women
The Global Impact

Looking ahead, *Voices of Women* will be a positive catalyst for global change. By sharing our stories and insights, we can inspire and encourage more women to take charge of their lives, put themselves in the driving seat and carve out a fulfilling and successful path for themselves and the communities they serve.

Moving forward with the changing role of women in business and entrepreneurship, I see *Voices of Women* as a positive anchor and resource. It has the potential to create a global ripple effect because of the women within the book you now hold in your hands. Women from different backgrounds, countries, professions and cultures, all united as a powerful force for good.

A Final Reflection

Back to the Beginning

Reflecting on the launch of *Uncharted Waters* at the Abu Dhabi International Book Fair, I am reminded of the powerful community that literature creates – a community that supports, uplifts and unites, irrespective of gender.

At my book launch, it was a male journalist, Nabil, who was my cheerleader and advocate. He kept bringing people over to the table where I signed books and ensured we had a successful event. Nabil brought men and women over to the table with enough enthusiasm and energy to light up the UAE! He introduced me to fellow authors, journalists and people who love poetry, reading, learning, and supporting each other. This beautiful experience reinforced the essential role that both men and women play in supporting and enriching our journeys.

Here's to many new adventures that include lessons to be learnt, uncharted waters to be explored, and the Voices of Women (and men) to be heard.

Together, we can navigate even the stormiest of seas and enjoy sailing the calm ones with a heart filled with love, joy and gratitude.

Natalie proudly calls herself a tech nerd, but she's much more – she's a female leader learning to embrace her inner strength. On her journey, she absorbs lessons that ignite her desire to become the best version of herself, both as a woman and a leader.

Stepping into your authentic self can be daunting, but it's also incredibly liberating. No longer bound by the need to please others or engage in unfulfilling activities, Natalie understands the importance of living authentically for true success and happiness. She knows many women face similar struggles and champions the idea that embracing your true self is the key to a fulfilling life.

Natalie believes that life's greatest lessons come from everyday experiences – relationships, choices, and the complexities we create for ourselves. Her mission is to simplify life, and a medical diagnosis propelled her to take decisive action and lead by example.

The most impactful leaders lead by example, openly discuss their failures, and share the lessons they've learnt. Natalie embodies this ethos. I encourage you to delve into her story, absorb her wisdom, and make the necessary changes in your life. Natalie's journey is a testament to the power of authenticity and the transformative impact of living true to oneself.

Brenda

Natalie Alsop

"As part of my journey, I have learnt that being a leader teaches you more about yourself and shows you who you need to become."

Natalie Alsop

Reflections on Stepping Into Leadership

My favourite module at university was human-computer interaction. I was fascinated with the psychology behind intuitive interfaces, which ensured humans and software could coexist and, more importantly, translated tech into something humans would understand. This set me on the road to web design. Little did I know that 20 years later, I would be enabling businesses to appreciate the relationship between human-computer interaction and their websites to successfully promote their businesses.

The Early Years
Change, Determination and Gumption

Not one 'Eureka!' moment defined me as a leader. It was more about stepping into my true self and believing what I knew I needed to share. No doubt you, too, have experienced not living your life your way. I want to share with you that this is okay because I learnt that this takes time.

For as long as I can remember, I have wanted to help people. This was partly because being brought up as a Jehovah's Witness, I was encouraged to help others learn the Bible's teachings. Growing up in a single-parent family, there were significant changes in my early life, so I accepted that change was normal. Is there something in your childhood that also allowed you to accept change, or perhaps you find change challenging? However, change has taught me resilience, which has served me well over the years.

#1 Technical and creative flair

Growing up, education appeared unimportant in my family, but if truth be told, my mother struggled financially. Like me, young people often fall into situations beyond their control, which still happens today. Finding themselves in bewildering situations often stifles their opportunities to follow their dream. This uncertainty led me to leave school at 16 with a handful of GCSEs. Without further qualifications, I fell into office admin roles.

In one early job, I taught myself how to use a computer to avoid making typewritten mistakes and having to use Tipp-Ex to make corrections. Although I didn't consider myself a leader at this tender age, I had unknowingly stepped into leadership. I took control by being proactive and made this innovative decision to use technology to make life easier. My once sceptical colleague was now on board with my ideas, illustrating that people followed my lead.

In another job, my creative flair and eye for layout revealed themselves. Once again, my proactive spirit took over, and I showed initiative by turning the dry sales PowerPoint presentations into something creative and engaging.

#2 Wanting more

Despite leaving school without any A levels, which stopped me from progressing in my educational life, I realised this lack of qualifications was limiting my career opportunities over time. At that time, all I seemed to hear was, "You need a degree, you need a degree, you need a degree". I left a secure job to become a mature student at 24, as well as having previously turned my back on my faith a few years before, causing great turmoil and distress. Additionally, no one in my family had done anything like this! Looking back, both momentous decisions showed my continued determination and gumption. On reflection, these decisions showed that I was unafraid to follow my own path. I realised I was prepared to stand out and not fit in.

#3 Challenged

Soon after my course started, a lecturer publicly undermined me, questioning my ability to complete the degree because I hadn't done A levels. I reasoned that I was accepted on the course because of my eight years of work experience, which I had described in great depth in my application. The admissions department supported my application, but the whole affair intensified my self-doubt, something that reoccurred over the years. It took a lot of strength to overcome this negative and unpleasant experience.

After much hard work, I proudly collected my 2:1 degree three years later. I fantasised about walking up to the disapproving lecturer, asking if he remembered our conversation, and presenting him with my award! I also fantasised about adding, "And before you say it, I did the work DESPITE your attempts to play a psychological game, and not to prove you wrong. Be careful of what you say; this stuff sticks." Have you ever wanted to put someone right but, in the end, didn't? That is okay.

#4 Triumph

After graduation, I worked as a web designer in the corporate world. Buried within me was an entrepreneurial spirit, and as a leader, I had to find a way to fulfil my dream of running my own business. I ran my boutique website agency for 17 years. One of the most vital things I have learnt is that business is all about connection because I believe that 'people buy people'. Today, I enable service businesses to learn the ropes of tech and the human side of their websites to successfully promote their businesses and connect with their audiences. And the irony of my favourite module all those years ago isn't lost on me.

A Leading Failure

#1 Building a team to grow

A few years into running my business, I was burnt out from doing everything myself. The business was growing, and the next logical step was to build and run a team. I naively did this whilst taking on additional costs and responsibilities.

#2 Swapping one set of problems for another

As your business grows, you soon learn that you swap one set of problems for another. I realised that having people work for you was challenging in a different way. My perfectionism was disabling, as I didn't trust my staff to do the job as well as I did. More importantly, my people-pleasing behaviour stopped me from leading my team and delegating and trusting them to do the work to my high standard. My restrictive traits created a barrier to growing my business.

#3 Failure

Everyone handles failure differently. However, my experience of failure when trying to grow my business was an expensive disaster. I felt stupid for not listening to others who had tried to guide me. Looking back, this experience taught me that striving for excellence rather than perfection helps a business succeed.

I felt sorry for myself for a while, but then I brushed myself down and continued. My priority was to strip everything back and focus on my clients and projects. It was yet more change, but my earlier experiences taught me that change is a part of life. If you have ever failed in something related to your career, perhaps you felt the same as I did.

#4 Reframing and learning from failure

Leaders need to understand that failure is part of learning and growth. All successful people have taken risks and failed at some point.

Female founder Christina Wallace is vice president of growth at Bionic. This growth solution company installs start-up cultures in large companies known for encouraging young girls and women into STEM. She soon discovered that everything doesn't always go to plan. She speaks openly about her failures and reinforces that "it's about learning from failure that is important."

I can relate to Christina Wallace's reframe. Today, I am careful to listen to others who are more successful, play devil's advocate, and take my time to make decisions. This has helped me become more confident and a better leader.

Marriage, Motherhood and Simplicity

#1 Motherhood and natural leadership

Becoming a mother taught me about natural leadership. My maternal side kicked in, and I instinctively knew what to do for my daughter's well-being. Some women struggle with motherhood for several reasons, including post-natal depression, feeling isolated, and losing their identity. However, losing my identity and confidence and trying to run a business soon took its toll. Like many new parents, the pressure of parenthood shows the cracks in relationships.

#2 Going it alone

Like many successful women, I, too, have a failed marriage. No doubt you know someone from a failed marriage, and this could be you. Becoming a single mum with a four-year-old daughter was tough and a significant life change. But I focused on making the right decisions for my daughter; keeping things simple and stable was key.

#3 Simple is best

"Life is really simple but we insist on making it complicated."

Confucius
Chinese philosopher

Humans often choose complexity over simplicity because they do not believe that simple things are intelligent. We all experience complexity bias at some point in our lives. My experiences have made me a realist, and I now believe that for something to be simple, it must first be complex.

"Simple can be better than complex. You have to work hard to get your thinking clean to make it simple, but it's worth it."

Steve Jobs
American businessman, inventor, and investor

The previous failure with the business and the breakdown of my marriage were a huge wake-up call. I had to admit that I was good at making things more complex than they had to be. This led me to realise a core value: SIMPLICITY. I now prioritise simplicity to guide my personal life, home, and work. If things start to feel complex, I stop, look at the triggers, and take stock.

#4 Trusting the process

All my business experience was useful, and I had to remind myself that it was a journey, not a destination. It was vital to look at my knowledge, skills, and experience as a process to get to where I am today. This underpins the need to trust the process, even if things seem uncomfortable and out of control. I share this with my clients and members when they feel the same about their website transformations. Perhaps you too have experienced the need to trust the process regarding your career.

Leadership and Health Issues

#1 Diagnosis

It takes all kinds of people to be a leader. Like many middle-aged women with more information in the world, we are finding out more about neurodivergence and people are questioning who they are.

In 2019, I was chatting to a close friend about her daughter and the potential that she may have ADHD. After reading about some of the symptoms, I recognised them in me. I started to question many aspects of my life, and after reflecting and seeing my GP, I went on a six-year waiting list and journey to get a diagnosis.

In September 2023, my appointment with a psychiatrist came through, and as suspected, I was formally diagnosed with a neurodivergent condition.

#2 The power of awareness

Discovering I was ADHD combined with impulsivity was bittersweet. So much made sense, but I also felt sad about what life might have been like had I recognised it sooner. But I accepted that my brain worked differently from others and that I wasn't stupid! I vowed to learn as much as possible. That's not to say everyone can be as accepting as I was; perhaps you can relate. But as a youngster, I realised I was a glass-half-full person, which I see as a blessing.

Self-awareness is a powerful part of emotional intelligence, a trait aligned with today's leadership, so I started researching and learning more about ADHD. Something interesting stood out: I had unknowingly created many coping strategies over the years. Instead of looking at the negativity, I reframed this to mean I am a natural problem solver. My differently wired brain allowed me to find solutions where others only saw problems.

Awareness and education have helped me to be more productive, successful and accepting of who I am – this, in turn, has made me a better leader.

I need structure and accountability to make sense of my scatter-brained approach and put things into the right 'categories'. The diagnosis has helped me access other support and medication, which works alongside the implemented coping strategies from my new-found awareness. If you are in this situation, then I appreciate that whilst medication has worked for me, it might not work for you.

#3 Making sense of it, coping and tying it all together

Recently, a peer I greatly respect said she did not see me as scatter-brained or disorganised and that my work is organised and methodical. I explained how this is because I have 'done the work'; I have reflected, been honest, and educated myself about how to cope better with ADHD and productivity. This journey has made me a better leader because I am happy to be vulnerable and share my experience, hoping it may help others to relate.

Emma Watson, the actress who plays Hermione in the *Harry Potter* film franchise, also has ADHD. And her experience is relatable:

"Becoming yourself is really hard and confusing, and it's a process. If you truly pour your heart into what you believe in —even if it makes you vulnerable — amazing things can and will happen."

The Pivotal Moment

For many years, I unconsciously exemplified leadership traits. However, it wasn't until 13 years after starting my business and during lockdown that I began to consider myself a leader.

#1 Connecting on a deeper level

Many people work with coaches without ensuring that they truly connect to the outcome and the coaching style delivered. Perhaps, like me, you have experienced this. It wasn't until I started working with a particular coach that things clicked into place. I joined their group programme to help simplify and streamline my offer. I was finally working with someone who was not only extremely successful and a role model, but also approached their work in a way that aligned with how I approached mine. Finding the right role model in your business is key to your success.

Furthermore, as I worked through the programme, my peers 'got' me and believed in me. Have you ever found yourself in the presence of others more experienced than you, yet they see you at the same level as themselves? That was key to transforming my confidence and finally seeing myself as a leader.

I realised that the more I did the same things consistently, the more it would compound and provide successful outcomes. The compound effect, whether negative or positive, provides a compounded outcome. For example, the more visible you become, the more success you will have. Similarly, your business will not grow if you do not show up where your ideal clients hang out.

#2 Getting comfortable with being uncomfortable

As my confidence grew, I started challenging myself to get comfortable with being uncomfortable, as I realised this is when growth takes place. When was the last time you found yourself feeling uncomfortable? When I get that horrible, sinking feeling, I stop, take stock, and ask myself why I feel uncomfortable. I encourage you to try this too. It is often because I am doing something new that I feel unsure of. However, I know I am in the right place because I am stretching myself. Soon, I will be comfortable, and there will be new things to get uncomfortable about!

An opportunity presented itself to speak at an event about online visibility. Having never done this before, I was both terrified and excited! I had been running a campaign about 'online visibility'; to illustrate this, I used a high-vis jacket in my marketing ideas. Bringing this to life on stage felt ridiculous and outrageous. Yet, I was on stage in my sunglasses and oversized high-vis jacket! Ironically, this costume allowed me to hide behind it, to share my vulnerability, and to be playful and tongue-in-cheek.

When you step outside your comfort zone, embrace your inner child and have fun; triumph awaits you. This new-found spirit enabled me to present and fully engage with the audience. Many came up to me afterwards to say how much they enjoyed my talk, how it resonated with them, and how it made them realise they needed to be more visible online. Raising my physical visibility improved my brand awareness and reinforced my leadership abilities and power to influence others to make positive changes.

#3 Interdependence

I always thought being independent was powerful, but I now realise you can only go so far. Interdependence, on the other hand, is vital. Interdependence is the relationship between two or more parties that depend on each other to survive. Each party has to offer something different to the other party that complements them and enables growth.

When you understand the significance of this aspect of emotional intelligence as a leader, you understand the importance of a team and begin to delegate like a boss, freeing you up to work in your zone of genius.

#4 The 'messy middle': trust the process

To reach your zone of genius, you must go through the 'messy middle'. That is where there is a lack of clarity, uncertainty, and confusion. Clarity appears only when you begin working through the messy middle, allowing you to strengthen your beliefs and trust the process.

I have found it helpful to learn the mantra, "I am exactly where I need to be", even in the messy middle and in my zone of genius. I urge you to try it the next time you feel uncomfortable.

#5 Simplicity and me

As a leader, I am comfortable in my own skin. My business is now stripped back and simple. Having raised my self-awareness and consciousness of my gifts and talents, I confidently help businesses to flourish. At the same time, I avoid getting burnt out, am a good mum, make a decent living, and feel fulfilled in my work.

Conclusion

As part of my journey, I have learnt that being a leader teaches you more about yourself and shows you who you need to become.

These days, I am true to myself by being unapologetic about who I am. Even though I am still a bit scatty, daft and clumsy, that is me. Everyone benefits from my other qualities of patience, empathy, compassion, and kindness.

Alongside simplicity, I also value stability, something I had to create for myself. Using these core values to steer and live my life has helped me become a better leader.

Three Takeaways To Empower Women and Develop Future Female Leaders

I certainly haven't got it all figured out. But here are three vital aspects of being a successful leader that I have learnt along the way:

#1 Get comfortable with being uncomfortable

If you feel uncomfortable, you are in the right place for growth. You know you are making progress when you begin to embrace feeling uncomfortable.

#2 The messy middle: trust the process and trust yourself

No one has got it all figured out. Be guided by experts, trust yourself, and listen to your gut; you have the answers within you. There is always a 'messy middle', but trust the process. Sometimes, it's a case of 'action over perfection; it's good enough for now.'

#3 Your core values and the compound effect

Know your core values to help you determine your direction. Allow these to keep you focused and moving forward. It is important to stay in your lane. The compound effect of self-belief and confidence will gather pace, so buckle up and enjoy the ride!

"Some people only ask others to do something. I believe that, why should I wait for someone else? Why don't I take a step and move forward?"

Malala Yousafzai

Pakistani female education activist and the youngest Nobel Prize laureate in history, the second Pakistani and the only Pashtun to receive a Nobel Prize

Dr Shama emphasises the importance of education and leadership for women to overcome societal challenges and create a better future. She shares her passion for the significance of a vision-driven life, humanised education, and female leadership.

Focusing on women's challenges in leadership positions, Dr Shama reveals the need for resilience, accountability, and ethics. Furthermore, when embracing leadership opportunities, there is an emphasis on the importance of accountability and responsibility.

Dr Shama stresses the importance of empowering women's voices through education and leadership to create a more equitable society.

Brenda

Dr Shama Hussain

"Pain is growth;
embrace it and affirm yourself
to be your best version."

Dr Shama Hussain

Be a Woman of Substance embracing the DNA of Your "U" FACTOR

The Power of Sisterhood

Being part of a group of like-minded women inspires you to share your stories and lessons, creating a feeling of belonging. While working with men, women and children is highly rewarding, there is a unique alliance when you join a sisterhood. When you step into your leadership, part of your vision is to create community, and the *Voices of Women* is an incredible effort to bring women from different parts of the world together to raise their voices.

A Vision of Connection and Inspiration

It is truly inspiring to see the emotions once hidden in women's hearts and minds being shared for the good of humankind. The evidence within these pages spreads positivity from heart to heart and mind to mind, allowing other women to connect with these stories and find inspiration. It's a beautiful initiative that deserves immense recognition.

Life's Fleeting Moments

I have always believed that life is short and fleeting. Within this brief span, we must strive to make a difference and create positive and infectious ripples that resonate worldwide. It would be best if you lived in a way that brings everlasting meaning and purpose to the life that belongs to you. Even on the last day of our lives, you should have no regrets, knowing you spent every minute with empowerment and vision. A life without a vision is like a body without a soul. This guiding philosophy drives me to foster a culture of happiness.

Spreading Happiness Worldwide

I aim to spread happiness worldwide because I believe every person is tirelessly working to achieve it. Often, we equate happiness with material success, but true happiness comes from recognising and utilising our resources wisely. When people are aware, educated and humanised, they can find balance and purpose in life.

Humanised Education: The Key to Happiness

Education is crucial in this journey but must be humanised, not purely materialistic. Humanised education fosters happiness, which spreads to others, and creates joy and fulfilment.

The current generation faces challenges that hinder this vision, often absorbed by gadgets and disconnected from real-life experiences and values. Some lack resilience and the ability to handle criticism, which is essential for personal growth and happiness.

Creating a Culture of Happiness

Our efforts are the catalyst that creates a world where happiness is prioritised, and education is humanised. By doing so, we can ensure that future generations inherit a world where they can live as beautiful, fulfilled creatures. We must shift our focus from mere material success to a balanced life enriched with joy, purpose and resilience. This way, we will not regret our lives and will leave behind a legacy of happiness for the generations to come.

Building Global Platforms for Positive Change

Through my vision and mission, I am honoured to have created three global platforms focusing on the Humanization of Education. My passion fuels my work as a creative visionary.

The first platform I created was the International Institute of Influencers, followed by the International Life Skills Technologies Private Limited and last but not least, Gulf Skill Pioneers, recently established in Oman.

United in Mission

These platforms are gateways to skill sustainability and are now present in 11 countries. With the support of over 40 global leaders, we unite in a joint mission to humanise education worldwide, influencing leadership across all demographics – women, children, and men alike. Our organisation is not limited to any single category of people, recognising that we are all part of a vital ecosystem. Each individual is a crucial link in the chain, and removing any link disrupts the harmony and balance we strive to achieve.

Celebrating Inspirational Partnerships

Our partnerships extend to numerous organisations globally, including the remarkable work of Book Brilliance Publishing's Brenda Dempsey, a beacon of brilliance and selflessness whose efforts I deeply respect and admire. She creates waves of positive change, and her unwavering commitment to her mission inspires me daily.

If I were to write an autobiography, Miss Brenda's name would undoubtedly grace its pages. She embodies the very essence of genuine, unmanipulated influence, much like a pencil that lets its graphite shine without alteration. Her authenticity and dedication are qualities the world desperately needs to see and emulate.

The Importance of Positive Influences

In our quest to amplify the voices of women, it is essential to surround ourselves with individuals who possess vibrant and empowering qualities. What we focus on profoundly affects our perception and outlook on life. Negative influences, even when unintended, can seep into our consciousness. Therefore, it is crucial to be discerning about the company we keep and the environments we engage with. We fortify our vision and strengthen our resolve by seeing and associating with positive, influential individuals.

Innovation and Inspiration

The organisations I connect with do more than just inspire; they innovate. They challenge me to push boundaries and think creatively about how we can further our mission. This synergy between inspiration and innovation propels us forward, ensuring our efforts are impactful and transformative. By fostering an environment of continuous growth and positive influence, we can create lasting change.

A Journey of Collective Empowerment

The journey we are on is one of collective empowerment and shared vision. By leveraging our platforms and partnerships, we are creating a ripple effect of positivity and progress. Each of us has a role to play in this ecosystem, and by working together, we can achieve a harmonious balance that benefits all. I envisage a world where we continue to inspire, innovate and influence, ensuring that the legacy we leave behind is one of profound impact and enduring happiness for future generations.

The Fulcrum of Leadership

Leadership is one of the most crucial concepts in our lives. Think of it as the fulcrum in a see-saw, the pivotal point without which balance and movement are impossible. Imagine a pair of scissors; the fulcrum is the central point that binds the two blades together, allowing them to function.

Without this central point, the scissors would be useless. Similarly, leadership serves as the fulcrum in any organisation or endeavour. The binding force brings together diverse elements, driving progress and achieving goals. Leadership, to me, is synonymous with influence.

Authentic Leadership: Creating Leaders

Authentic leadership is not about amassing followers, but about creating more leaders. In today's society, there's a misguided notion that the number of followers equates to effective leadership. Leaders boast about their follower counts, but this misses the essence of true leadership. It is not a popularity contest; it's about your impact and influence on others. A natural leader inspires and empowers others to become leaders themselves. This ripple effect of influence is the hallmark of genuine leadership.

Vision: The Core of Leadership

At the core of leadership is vision. Leaders must have a clear, compelling vision to guide their actions and decisions. Vision is what sets great leaders apart from the rest. It provides direction and purpose. Leaders such as Abraham Lincoln and Mother Teresa had profound visions that transcended their lifetimes. Lincoln's vision of a united nation, and Teresa's vision of compassion and service to the poorest of the poor, continue to inspire us today.

Proactiveness and Accountability

Proactiveness and accountability are two essential traits that define great leaders.

Proactiveness means taking initiative, anticipating challenges, and acting decisively. Accountability means taking responsibility for one's actions and decisions. An accountable leader builds trust and respect among their team and followers.

Exemplary Leadership: Mother Teresa

Mother Teresa exemplified these traits. Her vision drove her to leave her homeland of Italy and live among the poorest in India. Her proactive approach meant she didn't wait for others to join her mission; she took the first step and inspired others to follow. Her accountability was evident in her unwavering commitment to her cause.

Creating a Lasting Legacy

Leadership is about influence, vision, proactiveness, and accountability. True leaders do not just gather followers; they inspire others to become leaders.

By embodying these traits and continually striving to improve, we can create a world where leadership empowers others, fosters innovation, and drives positive change. Let us all aspire to be leaders who influence, inspire, and leave a lasting legacy.

Vision and Proactivity

Leadership begins with a vision. A leader's ability to foresee and plan for the future sets them apart. Vision is the first step, followed by proactive action. Great leaders don't wait for circumstances to dictate their actions; they lead purposefully and intentionally. They don't stop and ponder before acting – they act, reflect, and finally pause to evaluate. This approach ensures they stay ahead, making timely decisions that keep systems and processes from falling apart.

The Pitfalls of Hesitation

Hesitation can be detrimental to effective leadership. When leaders overthink before acting, they miss opportunities and allow situations to deteriorate. When they decide to act, it may already be too late. The critical difference between average leaders and great leaders is the ability to take initiative without unnecessary delay. This proactive mindset is crucial in maintaining momentum and preventing systemic failure.

The Power of Small Acts

Leadership is also about understanding the impact of small actions. Let me share a story with you.

A boy in a coffee shop wanted to buy a sundae and asked for the price of the 'everything' sundae, which was $10, and the regular ice cream, which was $6. He discussed the price difference and asked the server for the $6 ice cream. The waitress was not amused at the amount of time it took for him to decide which ice cream he would order.

Misjudgements and Assumptions

The waitress misjudged the boy, thinking he was wasting her time with his questions. Her reaction was dismissive and impatient. However, she realised her mistake when discovering that he had left a tip. The boy only had $10 and felt compelled to tip the server. His need to show appreciation was why he chose the $6 ice cream. This scenario underscores the importance of understanding and patience in leadership. Leaders should avoid jumping to conclusions and instead strive to understand the motives and perspectives of others.

Learning From Every Interaction

Every interaction offers a learning opportunity for leaders. The boy's behaviour taught a valuable lesson about empathy and foresight. He demonstrated that being proactive also involves anticipating the needs of others and acting accordingly. This level of awareness is what distinguishes visionary leaders from mere managers. Leaders must learn to see beyond the immediate and consider the broader impact of their actions.

Vision-Driven Leadership

Effective leadership is inherently tied to having a vision. Visionary leaders inspire and guide others towards a shared goal. They do more than manage – they lead by example and create environments where others can thrive. Female leadership, in particular, emphasises creating other leaders rather than just followers. This nurturing aspect is crucial for sustainable leadership development.

The Importance of Female Leadership

Female leadership brings unique strengths to the table. Female leaders often focus on empowerment and development, fostering an inclusive culture where everyone can contribute and grow. As the saying goes, leaders create leaders, not followers. This approach ensures that leadership qualities are cultivated at all levels, resulting in a more dynamic and resilient organisation.

Visionary and proactive leadership is essential for success. Great leaders create lasting positive change by acting decisively, understanding the impact of small actions, learning from interactions, and fostering other leaders. Female leadership, with its focus on empowerment, plays a critical role in this process, ensuring that leadership qualities are nurtured and passed on to future generations.

The Vital Role of Women in Leadership

In the vast tapestry of life, women play an indispensable role in shaping leaders. To understand this, consider the composition of our bodies: approximately 75% water, with the remaining 25% consisting of red blood cells, white blood cells, plasma, and platelets. This analogy extends to our society, where women form a significant portion of the population and are integral to the ecosystem. Their influence is akin to water – vital and pervasive – and their contributions are foundational to the fabric of our communities.

The Unique Qualities of Female Leaders

Women possess unique qualities that make them natural leaders. Among these qualities, resilience stands out as a defining trait.

A mother, for instance, embodies resilience in her unwavering commitment to her family. She will face any challenge, no matter how daunting, with a strength that seems almost superhuman. This inherent resilience is a gift bestowed upon women, empowering them to overcome life's peaks and troughs with grace and fortitude.

The Power of Female Leadership in Society

Imagine a society where female leadership is not only acknowledged but celebrated. Women's resilience can drive significant change across all sectors – be it in companies, schools or industries. Female leaders, with their indomitable spirit, are less likely to give up in the face of adversity. Their voices resonate, creating ripples of change that influence minds and hearts alike. They impact the conscious and subconscious minds of those around them, leaving a lasting imprint.

Transforming Ideas Into Actions

Take Miss Brenda, for example. As a leader, she speaks and is a visible example of resilience and determination. Her ability to transform information into action is remarkable. Unlike lecturers who offer ideas without execution, Brenda embodies the principle that implementation is vital to transformation. Her proactive approach and ability to turn concepts into reality set her apart as a true leader.

The Transformational Power in Households

In households, this transformational power is evident. Women often take on responsibilities with a sense of urgency and commitment that ensures the completion of tasks. They don't defer or delegate indefinitely, but execute with precision and care. This proactive nature is a hallmark of effective leadership and is abundantly found in women.

Overcoming Societal Barriers

Despite these inherent strengths, societal barriers often hinder women from fully exercising their leadership potential. You create an environment where women can thrive by addressing some pitfalls and exaggerations. However, often women's resilience and proactive nature can overcome these obstacles, driving them to lead with empathy and strength.

Leading by Example

Consider the story of a mother and child, where the mother remains calm and composed despite the child's outbursts. This scenario illustrates the essence of female leadership – thinking before acting, providing a steady and reassuring presence, and leading by example. The mother's ability to absorb the child's frustrations without reacting impulsively showcases her leadership qualities.

The qualities that make women exceptional leaders are deeply ingrained and divinely bestowed. Their resilience, proactivity, and ability to transform ideas into actions are invaluable. Society can benefit immensely from women's unique leadership in recognising and nurturing these qualities. By creating environments that support and elevate female leadership, we can harness the true potential of these remarkable qualities, leading to a more resilient, proactive, and compassionate world.

Embracing Challenges From the Beginning

There was a certain period in my life when every obstacle became a challenge to conquer. From a young age, I was inspired to see every difficulty as an opportunity for growth and leadership. This mindset shaped who I am today and drove me to influence others. As a student, a woman, and a leader, I have faced extreme challenges that have tested my resilience and determination. These experiences have taught me invaluable lessons about perseverance, responsibility, and the power of influence.

The Student Leadership Journey

Growing up in a middle-class family, I learnt the importance of hard work and leadership early on. My school played a crucial role in shaping these qualities. I was often chosen to represent the school, speak at events, and influence my peers. This responsibility instilled a sense of discipline and focus that would become the foundation of my leadership journey. Being a model student meant I had to embody the values I spoke about, influencing others through my actions.

Overcoming Academic Challenges

Transitioning from school to university was a significant challenge, especially from a middle-class background where financial constraints were a reality. Gaining admission to a prestigious university was not just a goal but a necessity. Only a few seats were available, and I knew my future would be drastically different if I failed. Failure was not an option. With relentless dedication over 45 days, I studied day and night, driven by the desire to make my family proud and to fulfil my vision.

The Power of Responsibility

Leadership is more than personal success; it's about taking responsibility for others. I felt a profound responsibility to prove my parents' efforts were not in vain and to make them proud. This sense of accountability fuelled my determination. My father once compared my efforts to a farmer's toil. Just as a farmer feels disappointed if his crop fails, I didn't want my mother and father to feel disheartened by my failure. This responsibility drove me to excel, and I emerged as the top student in my university entrance exam, outshining thousands without external coaching.

Transitioning into Adulthood

Entering adulthood and marriage brought new challenges. My leadership qualities, which were celebrated in my student life, were not always understood or appreciated by those in my new family. They sometimes perceived my assertiveness as dominance, not recognising it as leadership, discipline, and a commitment to values and ethics. This misunderstanding highlighted a societal issue where women's leadership qualities are often misinterpreted.

Finding a Voice

When women find and use their voices, it can be overwhelming for those not accustomed to such energy. However, leaders must shine brightly and not diminish their light. Education, especially the humanised and therapeutic kind, is about more than academic achievement; it's about empowering individuals to speak out, share their stories, and influence others.

My journey in education and leadership is about creating platforms for others to find and use their voices, promoting proactive and responsible leadership.

Inspiring Others Through Action

We can influence those around us by continuously speaking out and demonstrating proactive leadership. Over time, people begin to understand and appreciate the importance of these qualities. They see the positive impact of resilience, discipline, and responsibility. As leaders, we must inspire others to look within, recognise their potential, and embark on their journeys of influence. Doing so creates a ripple effect that transforms individuals and the larger society.

Overcoming Ignorance
A Journey of Leadership and Resilience

"Ignorance is the greatest hurdle to leadership." This profound truth has shaped my journey, as I have encountered ignorance in many forms, creating setbacks that tested my resolve and values. The journey was filled with extreme challenges, especially from my in-laws' family, pushing me to my limits. These were do-or-die situations, but the values instilled in me by my parents carried me through.

Lessons From My Parents

From a young age, my mother and father taught me the importance of ethics, values, resilience, responsibility, respect, and accountability. They emphasised never disrespecting anyone, no matter the circumstances, and always upholding my responsibilities. These teachings formed the bedrock of my character, giving me the strength to face and overcome life's obstacles.

"Never give up," they would say, and those words became my mantra.

The Crucible of Challenges

The challenges I faced from my in-laws were intense. They tested every aspect of my being, but instead of breaking me, these trials forged me into a stronger, more resilient person.

Pursuing my PhD over five years was one of my life's most challenging yet rewarding experiences. It not only provided me with knowledge but also reinforced my confidence. My husband stood by me as my backbone throughout this journey, offering unwavering support.

The Power of Experiential Education

If not for the leadership qualities and values instilled in me, I might not have emerged as the person I am today. I might have diminished under the pressure.

This realisation underscores the importance of a humanised approach to education. Education should not merely be about obtaining degrees, but about experiencing and internalising values such as resilience, adaptability, and responsibility. Life's challenges are unpredictable; without these qualities, one can easily be overwhelmed.

The Fuel of Adversity

Interestingly, the very challenges imposed by my in-laws acted as fuel for my growth. Like Newton's second law of motion, where more force results in more acceleration, the greater the challenges I faced, the more exponentially I grew – emotionally and intellectually. Each setback became a stepping stone, propelling me forward with incredible momentum.

Embracing Leadership in Adversity

Leadership is not just about leading others; it's about leading oneself through adversity. It's about using the challenges and ignorance of others as fuel for personal and professional growth.

This journey has taught me that resilience and perseverance are essential tools for survival and success.

The Call for a Humanized Education

My story is a testament to the power of experiential education and the need for a humanised approach to learning. Education should equip individuals with the skills and values to navigate life's inevitable challenges. It should foster resilience, adaptability, and a sense of responsibility. Only then can we create leaders prepared to face the world with strength and confidence.

In every challenge lies an opportunity for growth. By embracing the values taught by my parents and the lessons learnt through adversity, I have emerged more potent and more determined.

This journey has shaped me and reinforced the importance of nurturing these qualities in others. Leadership, after all, begins with leading oneself through the darkest times and emerging into the light, ready to inspire and lead others.

Embracing Leadership
A Guide for Young Women

1. Never compromise your happiness

When stepping into the realm of leadership, it's crucial to hold onto your happiness. Never compromise. Once you start compromising, it becomes a slippery slope. Your life's value should be set so high that negativity can't afford a place in it. Remember, your happiness is non-negotiable.

2. Value yourself like a priceless gem

Your values and ethics are your graphite – the core that strengthens you. If you compromise on these, you lose your essence. Just as a pencil without graphite is useless, you, without your values, are just a shell. Your subconscious mind knows this and will reflect it in your life.

3. The power of a smile

Carry your smile everywhere. It's a sign of life, distinguishing you from the rest of the world. Never give your smile a vacation. It's a testament to your resilience and reflects your inner joy.

4. Believe in yourself and God

In a society obsessed with technology, remember to stay spiritually strong. Trust in God's plan for you. You are unique, just like every fingerprint. This uniqueness makes you special. Believe in yourself and never underestimate your potential.

5. Success begins with You

The second letter in "success" is U. Focus on building yourself. By doing so, you contribute positively to society. Understand that your uniqueness is your strength.

6. The formula for personal growth

E + R = O

Events in life (E) are out of your control. Your Response (R) to these events is what determines the Outcome (O). If you face rejection, see it as an opportunity for something better. Remember, one closed door means another is waiting to open.

7. Embrace pain as growth

Pain and pressure are growth indicators, much like a pencil being sharpened. When you face challenges, embrace them as growth accelerators. Be patient and persistent; the rewards will follow.

8. *The Law of Attraction*

What you think reflects to you. The universe works in alignment with your thoughts. Affirm daily: "I am the best version of myself. I respond positively to challenges. I do not compromise on my values." This mindset will attract positivity and success into your life.

Final Thoughts on Leadership

Your journey in leadership is about staying true to yourself, valuing your happiness, and embracing challenges as growth opportunities. Remember, you are unique and special. Believe in your potential; the universe will align to help you achieve greatness.

From the first moment I met Caroline six years ago during an expedition to Malawi, I recognised her as the embodiment of a woman on a mission. Right from the outset of this brief but impactful trip, her determination to spread her work in Africa was evident. She can be proud that over 4,000 children and 20 trainers continue her initiatives in Malawi.

Caroline is a true leader; her education, expertise and experiences vividly illustrate this role. She understands the importance of reflection and using the lessons learnt to advance her vision and mission.

Caroline possesses many commendable leadership traits and deeply understands what it's like to face naysayers, criticisms from family, and mockery for her steadfast determination. Despite these challenges, she remains unwavering in her belief in herself and her impact on the world.

This story undeniably showcases a woman of substance, driven by purpose and passion. She never takes no for an answer and constantly pushes herself to the limits, practising what she preaches. Even in her advancing years, her boundless energy is evident – she has run the London Marathon two years in a row, thanks to the Total Release Experience™.

Prepare to be amazed…

Brenda

Caroline Purvey

"A true leader carries unwavering faith and belief in themselves, inspires others through love and passion, and consistently delivers results with integrity."

Caroline Purvey

The TIGHTROPE of Leadership

Becoming the founder of TRE UK® and creator of the unique Total Release Experience® programme came about from a chance opportunity that led me to discover my life purpose. It took my ability to lead to new levels. The invitation from Brenda to write a chapter on leadership for *Voices of Women* prompted a deep reflection of my own journey.

Throughout my former career as an A Level Business Studies teacher, I time and again revisited academic debates about leadership, its definitions, expectations, and evolving styles. A key question that continues to be asked is, "Are leaders born or made?" I believe that, much like those born with a talent for music, languages, singing or art, some people also have an innate capacity for leadership. Yet, there are also crucial aspects of leadership that we acquire through learned experience or the influence of others. I feel blessed that I was born with some of those talents, enhanced by learned experiences. Let me share:

> *"A leader is one who knows the way,*
> *goes the way and shows the way."*

John C. Maxwell
American speaker, pastor and author of
The 21 Irrefutable Laws of Leadership

I resonate deeply with Maxwell's words, which I shared in the concluding chapter of my book, *Feel It to Heal It.*

I wrote:

> *If you are a leader, then you have such an influence on those you lead. Be they children or adults, they will look to you for support and inspiration. They look at how you behave, your language, and as an influencer on their life, they may choose you as their role model. That comes with incredible responsibility.*

I still fully embody this stance on leadership today.

My life journey has encompassed many roles, including being a mother, grandmother, youth worker, business owner, entrepreneur, teacher, department manager, and more. Reflecting now comes the realisation I had been leading all along without labelling myself as a leader. Whether it was guiding my children or those of others, teaching students, serving or selling to clients, I had a responsibility to them all and was continually laying down a path for others to follow, providing support and inspiration even more than I recognised. Furthermore, to this day, I am consciously aware that my behaviour and language reflect who I am.

While writing, it occurred to me that my responsibility to all, consciously or unconsciously led, is like walking a tightrope. Laying down a path for others to follow was, and continues to be, a balancing act as I walk my TIGHTROPE.

Trust is a fundamental trait of my leadership. Life has taught me through personal betrayals that once trust is broken, it is difficult to mend. Trust is at the heart of my work. Clients place their trust in me to know that when they start their healing journey, they are going to be safe. If clients ever lost trust in me, it would for sure cast long shadows of doubt across all aspects of my business.

Closely aligned to trust is **integrity** – being honest in word and deed. It was rooted in me from childhood. My parents taught me kindness, compassion and honesty, highlighting the significant influence of parental leadership. From my early years, it was in my nature to be strong-willed, principled and driven. This has underscored the integral role that trust and integrity have in my professional and personal life. Knowing that clients coming to me were naturally in a place of fear of the unknown, our relationship has to start with trust – they have to trust me. Integrity, a lifelong principle of mine, is the root value of my business.

Inspiration and motivation come from leading by example. Having maintained a regular personal practice of releasing since 2011, I have first-hand experience of the journey it can take you on. My conviction grew as I delved deeper into the practice, witnessing in myself the powerful impact it was having on my physical, mental and emotional health and well-being, but even more so for our clients. The transformational healing from past wounds and a new-found resilience fuelled my courage to keep going. Experience and feedback over the years have more than confirmed my ability to be inspirational and motivational.

Growth for me, personally and in business, is my responsibility as a leader and reached a new level in 2011. On the final day of a transformative training in South Africa on how to release trauma trapped in our bodies, I found myself declaring to an international audience that I would champion this cause in the UK. That moment was pivotal; destiny led me there and the experience resonated with me in a way I cannot describe. I felt an overwhelming drive to lead and share what I had learnt with others.

Returning to the UK, I was a woman with a vision on a mission. Deep inside, I felt an indescribable feeling that I was taking hold of something very special. My intention to lead the way was profound, yet at that time, I had no idea to what extent or the impact I would have on others.

After relinquishing my position as Head of Business Studies at a military boarding school, I became free to embrace my 20-year passion for yoga. I transformed it from a sideline business to a full-time pursuit, with the opening of my yoga studio in early 2012. This new venture was not only about yoga but also my mission to introduce a groundbreaking practice that enables our body to release tension stored from our past stress and trauma. My studio became a sanctuary where individuals could explore well-being in a safe and supportive space, including this new methodology under my guidance. I was experiencing new growth not only in myself but also in my business.

Health is at the heart of my business. My mission as a leader is focused on health. Walking the talk is what I do. For 13 years, I have been doing for myself what I encourage others to do through me. It is true that health is our greatest wealth, for when it is gone, especially as a leader – what's left? Some leaders do not understand the impact that stress, overwhelm and trauma can have not just on their health, but their business, too. This also impacts the workforce and clients, as well as family and friends. Neglecting health comes at a high price.

From the outset, it became increasingly evident that lives were being positively transformed as a result of what I was sharing. Each person who learnt my process taught me more about the body's innate ability to heal itself. I realised it was experiential, and I started learning far more than I was ever taught. The impact on physical, mental and emotional levels was unique to each individual.

The Total Release Experience® evolved from the holistic impact it was having for those who connected with it. As I continuously observed myself and those I supported, listened to and learnt from, the health transformations were far beyond what I could imagine. My commitment was clear: I had a duty to spread awareness about this empowering, innate, self-healing capability we humans have to recover holistically from the impact of our past stress and trauma.

My mindset, words and actions strengthened and supported my journey through transition, stemming from my own transformative experiences. Always determined, the practice I taught others also enriched me, revealing unprecedented levels of strength. This personal evolution turned me into a formidable presence, a force to be reckoned with.

My conviction constantly grows as I continue to delve deeper into the impact of my programme and the powerful effect it has on the health of others. The profound changes I witnessed in myself, healing from past wounds and a new-found resilience, fuelled my courage to keep going.

These personal milestones shape my thoughts, language and actions, propelling me forward in my mission. Like myself, those on the programme discover holistic benefits in their health and well-being, including more energy, improved focus, memory, concentration, creativity, and so much more. Effortlessly, as a result, we all notice the positive impact on our business, work and daily life. Paying attention to our health serves to enhance our business's health and has paid dividends for me. From the outset, I became not just a participant in this field but a trailblazer, driven by a passion that continuously serves to renew my strength and resolve.

Tenacity has been a driver for my journey that has been far from easy; the challenges faced have only deepened my dedication. The path has been rugged, the sailing anything but smooth, but each step has been a testament to the power of embracing change and leading with conviction.

From the outset, after completing my training, I faced a stark realisation: I was on my own. There was no organisational support or leadership structure to guide me. This isolation, coupled with the initial criticism my enthusiasm received, posed my first significant challenge. I had a clear choice: to step up or give up. I chose to stand firm, to be true to myself and to pursue my passion, regardless of others' reactions. This decision to tenaciously go it alone has defined my path for over a decade, never once wavering from my chosen direction. I chose to lead the way, my way, no matter what.

The challenges I encountered were not typical of providing a well-being service. My transformative offering includes education, knowledge, guidance, and ongoing support. This gives clients a life tool that helps them to discover their 'SUPERPOWER' as they embrace a new freedom from the physical, mental and emotional issues caused by tension from their past stress, overwhelm or trauma. Despite the unmatched benefits of this process, the journey has been anything but smooth.

Over the years, I have faced scepticism and criticism, not only from therapeutic competitors but also from friends, family and complete strangers! Negative comments and outright avoidance were part of my reality. Yet, it was my deep-seated belief in the value of what I offer that fortified my resilience. I understand that much of the resistance I encounter is driven either by ignorance or fear – a universal response to stress. It was and still is exciting that every client was teaching me more; something very powerful was entrusted into my hands.

Given the early challenges I faced, I consciously chose to drive the practice forward in a way I knew deep down would have to be in contradiction to the way it was originally shared with me. Being true to what I believed was important to me and those I would work with.

Another significant challenge and learning opportunity presented itself when my son, Daniel, joined my business in 2015 when he returned to the UK after living in Germany for some time. Having used the practice I taught to navigate his own life challenges post-divorce, he brought his MBA skills and passion for my work to help grow my business. However, our leadership expectations initially clashed. Whilst Daniel was full of creative ideas, he expected more directive leadership from me. I favoured a more hands-off approach, trusting him to use his creativity knowing the vision and mission. This mismatch led us to have a heart-to-heart conversation. In so doing, we were able to forge a new understanding and a more effective collaboration.

Experience taught me that working with a family member introduces unique challenges. It necessitates a balance between personal and professional relationships, and requires clear communication from the outset. Flexibility is essential; I have learnt to switch between mother mode and business leader mode seamlessly. Daniel's growth, both personal and professional, has since aligned with the business, strengthening our partnership. We now drive the business forward together, though I retain the final say in key decisions.

My unwavering passion is as potent today as it was when I first embarked on this path. The realisation that what I had initially learnt was not something I simply stumbled upon – indeed, it found me – but I knew this was my life's purpose and it was exhilarating. The knowledge that I am fulfilling my calling gives me the tenacious strength to continue, despite the ongoing challenges.

Responsibility for others is integral to my role as a leader. It is essential as I lead the way for those whose lives I touch. The feedback I receive continues to be a constant source of inspiration and education, enhancing my knowledge. Every email, message and call that shares a story of a personal breakthrough, of miraculous healing, reaffirms my commitment. These testimonials are not just affirmations of their progress; they are reminders of my role as a leader in their lives.

The responsibility that comes with this role is immense, surpassing levels of past expectations, because those who put their trust in me, start the most powerful healing journey they will ever experience. Yet, it is this very responsibility, knowing my deeds and actions will impact others, that compels me to get out of bed each day and continue my work.

Opportunity presents itself when we least expect and I grab every single one that comes my way. For example, the choice I made to travel to Brighton, to work with a lady going through an acrimonious divorce, led to an article in *The Daily Mail*. The consequence of not taking action from this one-off opportunity to start sharing via workshops around the UK does not bear thinking about!

Daniel took his opportunity to step up with support. It provided me with an opportunity that if not taken, would have been regrettable. Daniel's growth, both personal and professional, has seen new levels that I am proud to observe as his mother, as well as a friend and a leader in the process.

As the potential of what we share continues to grow, I love the journey we have taken and our ability to Release, Recover and continue to Discover new levels of ourselves.

Perseverance for both of us was tested with Covid-19, as it challenged all of us globally. For me personally, one thing I never saw coming was the day we could not travel around the country to deliver our sought-after workshops. Overnight with lockdown came the realisation that there was NO business as usual.

Some years previously, Daniel had suggested creating an online programme. My response at the time was that it could never be done. Faced with no other alternative, we worked tirelessly; Daniel drove the technology as I invested financially and created the content from my vast experience and expertise.

The whole process required us both to step up and step out of our comfort zone, changing our thinking and approach. Yet, despite the setbacks and technical hitches, we persevered. Finally, within a few weeks, our four-module online programme was launched. We felt proud to think that clients would now be able to heal in their own home, whilst knowing they would feel safe and secure.

As a leader, I had to dig deep to ensure that the programme included everything from start to finish to give clients an experience as good, if not better, than they would have received in one of our workshops.

My responsibility to those who invested in the online programme was a big one. Both Daniel and I infused our love, passion and integrity into every step. The first launch was perhaps not the best, but it worked.

The sheer delight that brought a tear to my eye was when I received the very first session journal from a lady who shared, "I cried and felt scared, but with the sound of your voice, I knew I was safe so I continued. I felt so calm and peaceful at the end. Thank you!"

However, we did not stop there. Perseverance was necessary as we learnt and tweaked and learnt and tweaked some more.

To this day, we continue to improve the client's experience with us.

Evolving personally and as a business is essential. Reflecting on where I was over a decade ago and how we have evolved on all levels, I feel extremely proud. Where I am today has come from my many vast life and career experiences and the rich lessons learnt on the way. Early in my educational career, I aspired to reach headship, recognising that the success of a school heavily relies on its leadership. My first role as a department head was more by chance than choice, but it taught me that I thrive when given autonomy – trusted to deliver excellent results, which I did. Being told what to do was stifling for me. I would never have been able to enrich my students nor evolve to be who I am today if I had been suffocated. After 17 years in education, destiny took me out of the school system in 2010. My transferable skills in education and teaching would serve me well in what was to follow.

Despite initial doubts about the scope of my mission and how it would ever unfold, the universe seemed to align with my purpose. A chance encounter with a client who healed from her grief after losing her father led to a breakthrough. She introduced me to a friend going through an acrimonious divorce. As a journalist, she shared her story, which, as previously mentioned, was featured in *The Daily Mail*. Suddenly, my work was national news, and inquiries flooded in from across the country.

My journey to share in the UK was about to begin. Setting up workshops far and wide, word started to spread. This validation only strengthened my resolve and confirmed without doubt that my role was as a leader of something very special. At the time, I could not begin to imagine the journey it would take me on, but every situation had me evolving in a way I never thought possible.

I hope that the messages from my personal journey of walking the TIGHTROPE – Trust, Inspiration, Growth, Health, Tenacity, Responsibility, Opportunity, Perseverance Evolving – will serve to support aspiring leaders in a way that it has supported me.

The three tips I would give to my younger self to develop leadership skills for today's world are:

- Love what you do or find something else.

- Believe in what you do and, despite the challenges, never give up.

- Be truthful, kind and work with love.

'To be a true leader, have unwavering faith and belief in yourself, inspire others through the love and passion of your work, and consistently deliver results with integrity.'

Caroline Purvey

Brenda Dempsey has an unparalleled vision of wanting to change the world. Her mission is to make a difference to as many people as possible. Despite setbacks, Brenda has grown from humble beginnings in Clydebank to becoming a bestselling author, educator, coach and publisher.

Brenda is deeply committed to a holistic approach to everything she does and lives by her values of integrity, truth and collaboration. As she often says, she is "raw and real"! From leaving school with no qualifications to studying for her teacher training degree with four young children, Brenda has constantly shown drive, resilience and courage. She has also received many international awards for her leadership qualities. However, she is not someone who rests on her laurels and is always looking to push herself further.

As you read this final chapter of *Voices of Women*, you will see why Brenda's commitment, perseverance and energy has inspired many women to join the anthology and have their voices heard, loud and clear.

Brenda is the absolute embodiment of Voices of Women.

Olivia
Editor

Brenda Dempsey

*"When women link arms,
work together and raise their voices,
they can achieve anything
and everything they want.
Their potential is limitless."*

Brenda Dempsey

Unveiling the DNA of Female Leadership
Anecdotes Illuminating the Essence

The DNA of Leadership

Your DNA is inherently within you from birth to death. It is **you**. With this in mind, it ignites curiosity about whether you were born a leader or developed into one. Coming from the belief that we have everything we need within us, I consider that we are all leaders. The difference is that some courageously step into their leadership shoes and show the way. They illuminate their path so that others may also walk in their footsteps until they are strong enough to forge their own paths.

I love to reflect and thank my teacher training in the 1990s for teaching me to become a reflective practitioner. It has become a part of me, and I use it daily to improve myself, my circumstances, and my outcomes. With this belief in my heart, I can now look back at my childhood and how my leadership journey began.

I came from a modest background, born in a tenement building in Clydebank, Scotland. We had very little money, but as a six-year-old, I used to give my pocket money to the poor children of Africa each morning in class. Being brought up as a Catholic, we were encouraged by the missionaries to give to African babies so they could experience a better life and education. Donating gave me a great feeling inside; it spurred me on to give more, along with receiving beautiful certificates every time I filled out the card. In some ways, I demonstrated that I led by example, as not many other children gave their money.

Between the years of six and ten, I used to love playing the game 'Follow the Leader'. In the 1960s, my understanding was childlike, and I loved being out in front. I suppose it was paving a path for later in life. However, it was not until, as a ten-year-old, that I stepped out of my comfort zone and put on my leadership shoes.

As mentioned, I came from a poor yet rich family. Poor financially, but rich in love, care and protection. I was a daddy's girl and dared not go against my mother's wishes. She was a strong lady.

One day, just around teatime, I was watching the news, and to my horror, it showed images of scantily dressed Black children with pot bellies from Biafra, Africa. They were the victims of a war and consequently were starving and lacking medical care. At just ten years of age, I felt empathy. Tears rolled down my face, and something inside of me stirred. How can this be? I experienced my first compelling urge to do something, but what?

Herein lies a lesson learnt from being poor. My clothes were bought from jumble sales, often held by the church and Salvation Army. It was the only way I knew how to raise money.

I thought about this for days then I finally piped up to my mother, "Mum, I'm going to raise money for those poor starving children in Biafra!"

"What?"

"I'm going to raise money for those poor starving children in Biafra by having a jumble sale."

"No, you are not!" she retorted in a tone of voice that I had heard before and dared not go against.

Usually a very obedient child, something within made me go against my mother's instructions. I pushed her voice to one side and decided to go ahead, despite my usual behaviour of obedience.

I knocked on neighbours' doors, asking if they had anything for a jumble sale. A jumble sale usually included unwanted clothes, bric-a-brac, toys, books, and games. I soon had many items for my jumble sale as I had explained why I wanted their stuff and why I was doing it.

My mother's words still echo: "I told you not to do this jumble sale." But she mellowed, because my mother was also a kind and generous woman, and she reluctantly agreed to help me.

That Saturday, early in the morning, we put everything into different categories. I had no table, just the ground to showcase all I had collected. Thank God it wasn't raining! In fact, the sun shone. After a few hours of selling my wares, it was time to pack up. I had made the handsome sum of £8 12/6 shillings (about £8.50).

I believe this event marked the unleashing of my innate leader.

Many young children step up when they feel a stirring within; it compels them into action. Consider Malala Yousafzai, who was shot in the face by the Taliban in Afghanistan for daring to go to school. To Malala, education is everything. Her story echoed worldwide, and her experience only strengthened her. Inspired by her father, she established the Malala Fund, a charity dedicated to giving every girl an opportunity to achieve her desired future and a right to education. In recognition of her work, she received the Nobel Peace Prize in December 2014, becoming the youngest-ever Nobel laureate.

Life continued for me; ironically, I left school at 16 with no qualifications. I will explain the irony later on.

My next significant experience of leadership revealed itself as a young mother. I had moved from the town I grew up in, Clydebank, to Alexandria, some 16 miles apart. With two small children, there were few facilities for mothers and their children. Life was changing, and young mothers looked to each other for support.

When my firstborn was three years old, it was time for her to go to nursery. Fortunately, it was just across the road from my house. I loved it. Children have always been a big part of my life, as illustrated by that six-year-old and ten-year-old girl.

It wasn't long before the headteacher took me under her wing. We discussed facilities and a place for those under three years of age to learn social skills with other babies and toddlers. Before I knew it, I had agreed to form part of the first-ever working party that included education, social work, medical, psychologists, local councils and a layperson – me! This new situation unleashed the whole essence of collaboration and filled me with a sense of knowing that this opportunity led the way to reveal a value within me.

I continued to find myself steeped in education by supporting my children at school. By this stage, I was now a mother of four. I found myself in the Parent Teacher Association linked to the school, leading a musical group in the church and taking on teaching netball in my children's school. The immersion in education stirred my lifelong yearning to become a teacher. But how could I? I left school without a single qualification. Herein lies the irony mentioned previously. The young headteacher took me aside, said I would make a great teacher, and pointed me in the right direction to become one in my thirties.

Leadership kept rising within me throughout my life, and my teaching journey was no different.

I have learnt never to take life for granted. It can throw you curveballs. It presents opportunities that take you outside your comfort zone and situations where decisions are made you never thought possible. I left Scotland in 2005 after the death of my mother (who was English) and moved to Surrey, England. In 2016, I left my beloved education role to venture into coaching, entrepreneurship and business. What did I know? Yet, there was a calling within that I had to answer. Like that ten-year-old, I never questioned myself but followed my heart and soul.

Consciously, you do not go about thinking, "I am a leader"; you do what you do and be you. In my world, I call this being "raw and real", having authenticity running through your veins like a stick of Blackpool rock. I have also learnt that great leaders 'walk their talk'. They do not dictate what you should or should not do. They lead by example.

My upbringing taught me that belief. We never lied. My mother hated lies. My father never lied, and so integrity subliminally evolved. It, too, is part of my DNA. Many great leaders are also driven by integrity. They are the ones who say something and then take action. They make a difference, an impact. My purpose is infused with making a difference and an impact in our world too. The teacher in me is innate, so sharing stories, knowledge and wisdom is a way to illuminate paths for others to seek and follow before finding and carving their own.

Leadership as a Lifestyle

In 2020, life was not simply about dealing with Covid-19 and all its issues. I looked this situation in the eye, and despite its destruction worldwide, I discovered my mission. One that would propel my leadership into a new realm, providing me with a platform to truly embrace everything an effective and meaningful leader undertakes despite risk, challenges and self-doubt.

In June 2020, a new publishing house, Book Brilliance Publishing, emerged and was formed by three women based on client demands, opportunities and their experiences. It was no accident that we had met and worked together two years previously. I know this was our time to develop solid relationships based on integrity, reliability and collaboration.

Behind the scenes of running a business is a will to be the best version of yourself, to do the best job for your clients, and to build a formidable team that all pull in the same direction. A team with no 'I'. Here was a team where each one took the lead depending upon our strengths. It was my opportunity to give a voice to all of us.

The word 'voice' became my mantra. It is my purpose and has a special meaning. Voice means truth. Being silenced many times as a child and throughout an abusive marriage ignited a determination that all women, in particular, should be free to express their voices for themselves and the betterment of society.

However, this personal truth about life envelopes love and compassion. With a passion that fuelled my mission, I have since compiled five anthologies, including this one – *Voices of Women* – to provide a platform for men and women from all backgrounds, ages and cultures to find the courage to share their stories, knowing that there are lessons for the reader to learn. More than that, these stories are inspirational and illustrate that from adversity grows strength, power and light that creates ripples of brilliance.

I consider leadership as deep personal development where individuals take it to new heights. They embark on being the best version of themselves to serve and be a better leader. Leaders pay much attention to their holistic development, including emotionally, physically and psychologically. They create purposeful habits and routines that improve their mental health and well-being. They not only speak wisely but take action on what they say. They show up consistently and make no excuses for their mistake. They own them. They enjoy heightened awareness and use this as a superpower.

Here are three examples of modern women who have embraced female leadership traits.

Michelle Obama

Michelle Obama is widely admired for her leadership style, which emphasises personal development and authenticity. Throughout her tenure as First Lady of the United States, she championed initiatives focused on health and wellness, including the Let's Move! campaign aimed at combating childhood obesity. Michelle's commitment to holistic development is evident in her advocacy for mental health awareness and her emphasis on leading by example through healthy habits and routines. Beyond her words, Michelle takes concrete actions to effect change, such as launching the Reach Higher initiative to encourage young people to pursue higher education. She demonstrates consistency and accountability by owning her mistakes and learning from them, while her heightened awareness of social issues allows her to leverage her platform for positive impact.

Brené Brown

As a research professor and bestselling author, Brené Brown has become a leading voice on topics such as vulnerability, courage and resilience. Through her work, she encourages individuals to embrace vulnerability as a strength and to prioritise their emotional well-being. Brené's leadership is rooted in personal development, as she advocates for practices that foster emotional resilience and psychological growth. Her commitment to authenticity and accountability is evident in her vulnerability and willingness to share her struggles and imperfections. Her actions speak volumes as she translates her research findings into practical tools and strategies for personal growth and transformation. By consistently showing up and owning her mistakes, Brené inspires others to cultivate self-awareness and lead from a place of authenticity.

Angela Merkel

Angela Merkel, the former Chancellor of Germany, is known for her steady leadership and pragmatic approach to governance. Throughout her tenure, she navigated complex challenges with resilience and resolve, earning her domestic and international respect. A strong emphasis on personal development and self-mastery characterises Merkel's leadership style. She is known for her disciplined approach to decision-making and ability to stay grounded amidst uncertainty. Merkel's actions speak louder than words, demonstrating a steadfast commitment to her principles and values, even in the face of criticism or opposition. By owning her decisions and taking responsibility for their consequences, Merkel exemplifies the qualities of a true leader who leads by example and inspires others to strive for excellence.

The Genesis of Female Leadership

In the annals of history, the leadership narrative has often been dominated by tales of male prowess and authority. However, the emergence of female leadership has brought forth a paradigm shift, challenging conventional notions and reshaping the landscape of influence. At the heart of this transformation lies the unique DNA of female leadership, characterised by resilience, empathy and visionary insight.

The Rise of Greta Thunberg

A young female leader similar to Malala Yousafzai is Greta Thunberg. Greta gained international recognition for her activism in raising awareness about climate change. Like Malala, Greta began her advocacy at a young age, staging solo protests outside the Swedish parliament to demand more decisive action on climate change. Her determination and unwavering commitment to her cause quickly captured global attention, leading to the spread of the Fridays for Future movement, which inspired millions of young people around the world to join her in striking for climate action.

Greta's courage and resilience in the face of criticism and adversity mirror Malala's journey, demonstrating the transformative power of youth leadership in effecting positive change on a global scale.

The Power of Empathy and Collaboration

One of the hallmarks of female leadership is its emphasis on empathy and collaboration, fostering inclusive environments where diverse voices are heard and valued. Unlike traditional hierarchical models, female leaders often prioritise consensus-building and collective decision-making, recognising the strength that lies in unity.

The Sisterhood of the Supreme Court

The United States Supreme Court provides a compelling example of the power of female leadership in action. Justices Ruth Bader Ginsburg, Sonia Sotomayor, and Elena Kagan – often dubbed the "three amigos" or "sisterhood" – forged strong bonds based on mutual respect and collaboration. Despite their differing ideologies, these trailblazing women demonstrated that constructive dialogue and cooperation can transcend ideological divides, leading to more nuanced and equitable judicial outcomes.

Nurturing Future Generations

Female leaders can uniquely nurture and empower future generations, serving as role models and mentors for aspiring leaders. Through mentorship and advocacy, they pave the way for the next wave of trailblazers, instilling values of integrity, compassion and resilience.

Oprah Winfrey's Legacy of Empowerment

Oprah Winfrey, the iconic media mogul, epitomises the transformative impact of female leadership on future generations. Through her talk show and philanthropic endeavours, Oprah has uplifted countless individuals, particularly women and girls, empowering them to pursue their dreams and effect positive change in their communities. Her commitment to education and empowerment continues to inspire a new generation of leaders, embodying the essence of female leadership.

Breaking Barriers and Shattering Stereotypes

Female leaders defy stereotypes and break barriers, challenging ingrained biases and paving the way for greater gender equality and inclusivity. By transcending societal expectations and redefining notions of success, they inspire others to embrace their authentic selves and pursue their aspirations with courage and conviction.

Serena Williams: Champion On and Off the Court

Serena Williams, the legendary tennis champion, has redefined the game of tennis and shattered stereotypes and barriers with her trailblazing career. As one of the greatest athletes of all time, Serena has faced discrimination and adversity on and off the court, yet she has remained undaunted in her pursuit of excellence. Through her resilience and determination, Serena has become a symbol of empowerment for women of all backgrounds, proving that strength knows no gender.

The Legacy of Female Leadership

The legacy of female leadership extends far beyond individual achievements, shaping societies and inspiring positive change on a global scale. From boardrooms to battlegrounds, women leaders drive progress and catalyse transformation, leaving an indelible mark on the world and paving the way for a more equitable and inclusive future.

Jacinda Ardern: Leading with Compassion

Jacinda Ardern, the former Prime Minister of New Zealand, exemplifies the transformative potential of female leadership in times of crisis. During the aftermath of the Christchurch mosque shootings and the Covid-19 pandemic, Ardern's compassionate and decisive leadership garnered international acclaim, earning her widespread praise for her empathy and effectiveness. Her approach underscores the vital role of empathy and inclusivity in leadership, offering a blueprint for future generations of leaders to follow.

The DNA of female leadership is a complex and multifaceted phenomenon, encompassing traits such as resilience, empathy, collaboration and inclusivity. Through the lens of anecdotal stories, we gain a deeper understanding of the transformative power of female leadership and its profound impact on individuals, communities and societies at large. As we continue to celebrate and elevate female leaders worldwide, we can draw inspiration from their stories and strive to cultivate a more equitable and inclusive world for future generations.

I see the full circle of my life: my leadership ignited after witnessing those pot bellied, starving Biafran children; the phoenix rising as I left my abusive marriage to stand alone with four children and take my teaching degree; and the risk I took when leaving Scotland at a very fragile stage of my life, losing my mother, to undertaking a new adventure in England. I understand my purpose in life is to lead others by showing the way. That transition is just another opportunity to rise further, do better and make a more significant impression in the universe.

To the young women who dream of leading, remember you are that leader. You simply have to step up, show up, and speak up, because when you are fuelled with purpose and passion, the world listens.

I offer you three ideas to embrace in your life:

1. Be you, always – everyone else is taken, and you are as unique as each star in the universe.

2. Follow your dream – you are here for a purpose. Reflect, meditate and discover it, for it is within you right now.

3. Embrace lifelong learning – you are limitless; grow and learn every day, teach, study, and love the life you have been given.

It's time to be the creator and carve your own path, walk towards your destiny, and leave a legacy that makes this beautiful world a better place for having you grace it with your energy and soul.

"You are never too small to make a difference."

Greta Thunberg

Swedish Environmental Activist

Meet the
Voices of Women

Bailey Merlin – USA

Author | Bi+ Advocate

Bailey Merlin is the author of *A Lot of People Live in This House*, the co-host of the podcast Bisexual Killjoy, and a bi+ activist with a background in media and medicine. She holds an MFA from Butler University and an MS from Harvard Medical School. Her writing and her activism investigate the intersection of community and health.

Based in Boston, Bailey lives in an intentional community with a dynamic cast of humans, a dog, a cat, and a friendly ghost.

www.baileymerlin.com
www.instagram.com/bamaram_merlin
www.tiktok.com/@bamaram_merlin
www.linkedin.com/in/bailey-merlin

Layla Begum Ali – UK

Bay of Bengal Village to Leadership

Layla was born in Sylhet in North Bangladesh and came to the UK aged eight. She is a former youth worker in Tower Hamlets, East London, and teaches emotional intelligence and resilience to young people, empowering them to become leaders. She is also a life coach and a public speaker. Layla promotes Haji and Umrah on social media and became a Bangladeshi Diaspora Leader in 2021.

Layla has a degree in Criminology, a Post-Graduate Diploma in Healthcare and is an NHS leader in development. She won the Emerging Leader Award in 2014. After an investment scam, she was featured in a special investigation on BBC's *Panorama*. She is a location host for production companies and has some features coming up in 2024.

Layla writes to express positivity and empowerment with spirituality and healing.

www.x.com/Layla_Begum_Ali

Rosa Lopez Antonini – USA

Author | Software Engineer
Founder of Wonders of My World

Rosa is a self-development author, software engineer, and entrepreneur whose insights into the parallels between human behaviour and software engineering fuel her passion for helping others. Her debut book, *The Zero-Sum Game of You*, is a manual for personal transformation.

Rosa's lifelong fascination with science and metaphysics has profoundly shaped her empathetic approach and commitment to reducing human suffering. In her book, she equates personal growth with reprogramming one's mental software, advocating a 63-day challenge to replace negative habits with positive, sustainable behaviours. Rosa donates most of the proceeds from her book to sponsor educational programs for young adults in financial need.

www.rosaantonini.com
www.instagram.com/rosa.l.antonini
www.linkedin.com/in/rosaantonini
www.facebook.com/Author.LopezAnton21

Judith Ratcliffe – UK

Privacy Professional | Data Protection Officer
Hospital Radio Presenter | Conference Speaker | Author

Judith has been championing individuals' rights and helping organisations and government departments get privacy and data protection compliance *Right* for over a decade. She was called to the bar in 2010, although is not a fully-qualified barrister, as she has not done pupillage. She has advised many organisations on compliance, rights request handling, and other related matters.

Judith has also worked in financial crime prevention.

Judith's first privacy and data protection book, *Privacy and Data Protection in Your Pocket: Personal Data Breaches*, is out now. Her second privacy and data protection book will be on *Your Privacy and Data Protection Rights*.

www.linkedin.com/in/judith-r-6659452b

Dr Christi A Campbell (PhD, FNP) – USA

CEO & Founder of Contemporary Healthcare
and Christi Campbell Healing

Christi is a unique entrepreneur and healing energy conduit. Her deeply intuitive connection with the spiritual realm supports access to divine gifts which she utilises in her work. Following a challenging childhood, she answered the call to healing, becoming a nurse practitioner and culminating in a PhD. Nursing was the physical healing base needed to support her higher level of intuitively focused healing. Christi's own trajectory of soul awakening and enlightenment prepared her for the soul journey discovery and life transformation.

As a soul journey guide, Christi has created a sacred space with clarity of intention, allowing for growth, expansion and life-purpose discovery of a life filled with knowledge, experience, joy and fulfilment.

www.christicampbellhealing.com
www.facebook.com/christicampbellNDN
www.instagram.com/inspire2bgreat121

Natalie Heilling – Barbados

Founder | Author | Certified Energy Healer
Mindvalley Life Coach | 6 Phase Meditation Trainer

Natalie has worked as a leader for over 20 years, and is dedicated to guiding individuals on their journey to self-discovery and empowerment. She is the mastermind behind The Energy Game, whose mission is about unlocking potential and fostering fulfilment.

Additionally, Natalie proudly serves as the co-founder of Research Partners, who support businesses with executive recruitment support, while advocating for diversity in hiring practices.

Inspired by traumatic events in her life, Natalie strives to help her clients go from feeling stuck and disconnected from their lives, to finding inner peace and fulfilment.

www.linkedin.com/in/natalieheilling
www.instagram.com/natalie.heilling
www.facebook.com/natalie.heilling
www.theenergygame.co

Lyndsay Dowd – USA

Chief Heartbeat Officer, Heartbeat for Hire
Author | Coach | Speaker | Podcast Host | Disruptor

Lyndsay is the author of *Top Down Culture* and a featured guest lecturer at Harvard University. She has managed large, high-performing sales teams over the last 25 years, including 23 years at IBM.

Lyndsay is a thriving coach focused on leadership and culture, and has featured in many publications. Her company, Heartbeat for Hire, transforms leaders through building irresistible culture and modern leadership practices to get the best results. Lyndsay also hosts the top 5% globally ranked podcast, Heartbeat for Hire.

www.linkedin.com/in/lyndsaydowdh4h
www.instagram.com/lyndsaydowdH4H
www.facebook.com/LyndsayDowdH4H
www.youtube.com/channel/UC9asGvE8Ks4XjR
2UNwNmKDw
heartbeatforhire.com
www.topdownculture.com

Tiba Al-Khalidy – UK

CEO and Founder of Her Business Oasis
Executive and Business Coach | Author

Tiba is executive and business coach, specialising in empowering, inspiring and nurturing women as leaders to reach six-figures profit and enhance their confidence to create a lasting impact.

She is highly qualified with an accountancy and business studies degree and PG Certificate in Executive Coaching, bringing more than 25 years of expertise and experience in accounting and entrepreneurship. Tiba's extensive background equips her with unique insights into the challenges and opportunities faced by women in business.

Tiba has recently published *I Can Make It Happen*, a guiding companion for success and personal growth. When Tiba is not coaching, she is climbing mountains such as Snowdon, or cycling in Surrey's parks.

www.tibaalkhalidy.com

Eve Stanway – UK

Break Up Divorce Coach | Psychotherapist
Author | Speaker | Elite Development Coach

Eve Stanway is on a mission to empower individuals through tough conversations, enabling all voices to be heard and understood. Growing up amidst hardship and abuse, Eve lacked formal education but refused to be defined by her circumstances. Drawing from her own journey, Eve shines a light on the challenges of speaking out in intimate relationships and teaches the value of speaking up.

From silenced child to advocate for freedom, Eve's transformational story resonates with anyone striving to overcome adversity. She inspires others to find their voice and reclaim their power through her work.

www.evestanway.co.uk
www.linkedin.com/in/evestanway
www.x.com/evestanway
www.youtube.com/user/Evestanway
www.instagram.com/evestanway

Mimi Bland – UK

CEO and Founder of New Life Academy 2020 Ltd
Spiritual Mindset Mentor | Author | Speaker

Mimi is a passionate advocate for self-empowerment & self-mastery. She is also the bestselling author of *The Answer is You: The Formula to Master Your Mind and Your Emotions.*

Mimi has the ability to identify and see the true inner qualities of people. This allows her to connect with people both spiritually and vibrationally, to realise their true potential and how to connect to the power within themselves, and achieve life-changing transformations

Mimi is a visionary and has a strong belief system that aids her in offering a service that leads, inspires, motivates and empowers everyone to master themselves and achieve fulfilment, happiness, wealth, success, health and love.

www.mimibland.london
www.instagram.com/Mimibland.london
www.linkedin.com/in/mimi-bland-127a414b
www.facebook.com/mimi.bland1

Andrea Malam BEM – UK

Founder and Trustee of Saving Dreams
Philanthropist | Author | Speaker

Dr Andrea Malam BEM, FRSA, is a multi-award-winning leader in diversity, a role model, and a charity and volunteer ambassador who has featured in many lifestyle magazines and books.

Andrea is both a published author and a keynote speaker and inspires others to achieve their goals with emotional support, connection and empowerment.

Andrea is also the proud founder and trustee of Saving Dreams, a charity inspiring others by sharing stories and experiences, helping people to succeed at any stage of their career or business.

www.andreamalam.com
www.linkedin.com/in/dr-andrea-malam-bem-frsa-b38aa313a
www.instagram.com/honourable_woman
www.x.com/andrea_malam

Tracy Ho – UK

Award-Winning Executive Presence Coach | Speaker
CEO and Founder of Frame & Fame
Personal Branding and Image Consultant

Tracy specialises in elevating senior executives' leadership communication and presence for heightened influence.

As a certified international business etiquette and multicultural communication specialist and Gallup CliftonStrengths coach, Tracy empowers leaders to navigate the complexities of the international workplace. Her strategic personal branding expertise has earned her accolades, solidifying her global reputation as a thought leader.

With 18 years of communications experience, spanning Fortune 500 companies, media and government consultant roles, Tracy is a seasoned expert uniquely equipped to shape impactful narratives and guide professionals to success.

www.facebook.com/frameandfame
www.linkedin.com/company/frameandfame
www.x.com/Frame_and_Fame

Amanda Frolich – UK

Award-Winning Children's Entertainer
CEO of Amanda's Action Club

Amanda is CEO of Amanda's Action Club, the world's most fun, physical development concept, teaching preschool children how to be healthy and active from an early age.

Having spent 33 years working in the early years sector, Amanda was invited by the Children's Activities Association to become the Children's First Champion in Parliament, encouraging policymakers to put children first at the heart of all decision-making.

Her global animation TV series featuring Coach Amanda and the ACTIMATES is going to take the world by storm in 2024, and this wonder woman is certainly one to watch. Amanda is ready to transition into her female leadership role and has recently founded THRIVE, a community to grow and collaborate for leaders.

www.amandasactionclub.co.uk
www.linkedin.com/in/amanda-frolich-592834b

Dr Leslie Davis – USA

Licensed Clinical Professional Counsellor
Relationship Expert| SHE Matters Podcaster| Speaker

Dr Leslie Davis was honoured as the Top Mental Health Counselor of the Year by the International Association of Top Professionals, and empowers women and youth with tools to improve their relationships while coping with anxiety and depression. As a professed Black single mother in America, her podcast, SHE Matters, empowers single mothers around the world to develop healthy attachments, with the goal of reducing depression and suicidal ideation.

Dr Davis holds a BA in Sociology from Wheaton College and an MA in Professional Counseling from McKendree University. She holds a PhD in Counseling and Psychological Studies from Regent University. As a 10th Planet Jiu Jitsu Blue Belt, she practices the gentle art as a form of therapy and self-care.

www.therealdrleslie.com
www.facebook.com/leslie.d.lcpc
www.linkedin.com/in/drlesliedavis

Laura Bosworth – Scotland

MD and Founder of Worket Inclusive Search Practice
Inclusion Consultant | Speaker | Author

Laura is the founder and MD of Worket, a UK-based executive search firm transforming recruitment. An accomplished talent acquisition professional, she founded Worket in 2020, driven by a passion for inclusive leadership and authentic diversity. Unlike others, they go beyond traditional methods, prioritising innovative inclusive hiring practices that foster long-term commitment and growth. Laura's transparent, straight-talking approach ensures clients receive tailored, retained executive search services, bridging talent gaps globally.

Laura is a wife, proud mum to a teenager, and has three dogs and a horse. She advocates for multiple sclerosis research; she has MS and is proof that resilience knows no bounds.

www.linkedin.com/in/laura-bosworth
www.x.com/Bosworth_Lau

Dr Carolyn M. Rubin – USA

Owner of Carolyn M. Rubin Consulting | Life Coach
Host of TV Show *EmpowerFuse* | Author | Speaker

Carolyn received an honorary doctorate in the field of Health Sciences in recognition of her contributions to healthcare over the past 32 years. Her business, Carolyn M. Rubin Consulting, "Coaching that Empowers You," motivates, empowers and encourages others to achieve success and believe in themselves.

She lives by this motto: "Every day you go to work, you walk through the door with the eyes of a patient; if you do that, you will always be successful."

Carolyn holds certifications as a life coach and meditation trainer. She is an author, national speaker, a recipient of multiple awards, and has appeared on the Nasdaq billboard in Times Square, NY.

www.carolynmrubinconsulting.com
www.linkedin.com/in/carolynrubin

Christy Amalu – UK

CEO and Founder | Author | Motivational Speaker
Mentor | Ordained Pastor

Christy is an NHS senior clinical nurse advisor, an ordained pastor, a motivational speaker, an author and co-author, a mentor, a JP and a philanthropist. Overcoming a health challenge, she formed A Well Woman Network UK CIC., an organisation of women whose mission is to empower people to enhance health, and overcome hunger, hardship and vulnerabilities. She envisions a world in which the most vulnerable people have the power to lift themselves out of poverty and create healthy lives for their families and communities, now and for the future. She positively impacts women's lives, one at a time!

Christy is happily married and blessed with precious and gifted children as well as a grandson.

christy@awellwomannetwork.com
www.facebook.com/awellwomanfoundation
www.awellwomannetwork.com

Julie Lewis – UAE

Speaker | Explorer | Author | Rebel with a Cause

Julie is passionate about helping teams and organisations be the most resilient and vibrantly healthy version of themselves so they can succeed in business and life.

She has led multinational teams on over 70 successful global expeditions, including the Arctic and Antarctica. She loves sharing her experience-based wisdom and insights with teams looking for a leading edge.

Julie is the author of *Moving Mountains* and *Uncharted Waters*. She is a sought-after speaker, award-winning retreat leader, and loves being in nature and exploring wild places.

www.julie-lewis.com
www.linkedin.com/in/julielewis4
www.facebook.com/julie.lewis.98892
www.instagram.com/juliemileslewis
www.youtube.com/channel/
UC6slPF3NvZkR0K4RfDWaRjA
www.x.com/mountainhighme

Natalie Alsop – UK

Founder of Engaging Content | Strategist
Consultant | Speaker

Natalie has been in digital marketing since 2001, when the internet was new. She is a website designer who ran an agency-style business for many years.

Natalie now enables coaches, consultants and service professionals to master SEO and content creation for themselves so that they can generate enquiries from their websites and rely less on social media marketing.

Natalie's approach is holistic. She blends her knowledge of website tech, content marketing, blogging tactics, messaging frameworks and search marketing to teach and enable you to create compelling, engaging content that attracts prospective clients and search engines.

www.engaging-content.com
www.linkedin.com/in/nataliealsop

Dr Shama Hussain – Oman

Founder and CEO | Speaker
Visionary Leader | Humanitarian

Dr Shama Hussain is a seasoned professional with 20 years of global leadership in education, management, and direction. She is the founder and CEO of the International Institute of Influencers, Dean of Student Affairs Crown University and an Influential Woman of India. She is also a gold medalist and has a doctorate in gene profile studies.

Her commitment to the humanisation of education has led to innovation and creativity, and has empowered others worldwide to live a life of happiness through a new curriculum focusing on aspects of life that uplift the human spirit and bring joy.

When she is not busy creating new platforms and travelling the world, she loves to spend time with her beloved husband and two rock star children, having fun and building a life of fun, happiness and fulfilment.

www.linkedin.com/in/dr-shama-hussain

Caroline Purvey – UK

CEO and Founder of TRE UK® | Author
Creator of the Total Release Experience®
International Speaker | Founder RRD CIC

Caroline Purvey has invested over a decade in crafting a distinctive, sustainable and cost-effective programme aimed at eradicating needless suffering stemming from stress, overwhelm and trauma. Founder and CEO of the trustworthy brand TRE UK®, her FHT internationally accredited transformative Total Release Experience® programme touches the lives of individuals worldwide.

An international speaker and award-winning #1 author of *Feel It To Heal It*, Caroline has also been honoured with an Honorary Doctorate in Natural Medicine. Her work is vouched for by professionals, including doctors, counsellors, therapists and psychologists. Caroline's expertise knows no equal, matched only by her unwavering drive and passion.

www.facebook.com/treuk
www.linkedin.com/in/caroline-purvey
www.instagram.com/tre.uk

Brenda Dempsey – UK

Publisher | Entrepreneur | Master Coach | Philanthropist

Brenda Dempsey is an award-winning entrepreneur and publisher. As a Master Coach, she enables people to accelerate their potential and achieve their goals and dreams.

Brenda is a bestselling author and a woman of influence, and was voted Woman Leader to Look Up To in 2022. She is also the Chief Strategic Officer (CSO) of the International Institute of Influencers, the Vice President of the International House of Speakers, and an Advisory Board Member of Africa and Asia Chamber of Commerce.

Having a prominent and highly successful career as a teacher and coach, Brenda has a unique and powerful skill set that has enabled her to consistently facilitate the success and growth of others in many industries and countries around the world.

brenda@bookbrilliancepublishing.com
www.linkedin.com/in/brendadempsey
www.bookbrilliancepublishing.com

Acknowledgements

Iextend my deepest gratitude to the remarkable women whose stories grace the pages of this anthology. Your courage, resilience and unwavering commitment to empowering women have inspired us all. I am immensely grateful for your willingness to share your experiences and insights, knowing that your voices will resonate far and wide, sparking hope and igniting change.

I also express my heartfelt appreciation to the dedicated team behind the scenes – Olivia Eisinger, Zara Thatcher and Edna Garcia – whose passion and hard work brought this project to fruition. Your creativity, dedication and attention to detail have transformed words into a powerful force for empowerment.

I extend my sincerest gratitude to Emma Burdett, a beacon of leadership and advocate for women's empowerment. As the founder and CEO of WILD: Women in Leadership Deliver, Emma has tirelessly championed the cause of female leadership, reshaping perceptions and breaking barriers. Her insightful foreword sets the tone for this anthology, inspiring us to embrace our potential and amplify our voices. Emma's unwavering dedication to fostering a culture of inclusion and empowerment inspires us all. I am honoured to have her invaluable contribution to this project, and I express my deepest appreciation for her leadership and vision.

To our readers, thank you for embarking on this journey with us. May the stories within these pages serve as a source of inspiration, encouragement and empowerment as we collectively strive for a world where every woman's voice is heard, valued and celebrated.

Lastly, I acknowledge with deep gratitude the countless women who have paved the way for us, whose struggles and triumphs have laid the foundation for the progress we continue to pursue. We honour their legacy and commit ourselves to carrying their torch forward with humility and reverence.

Let us continue to amplify the Voices of Women, champion equality, and build a brighter future for future generations.

Brenda Dempsey

Get in touch with Book Brilliance Publishing!

www.bookbrilliancepublishing.com

www.facebook.com/PublishingMadeEasy

www.x.com/book_brilliance

www.instagram.com/bookbrilliancepublishing

www.linkedin.com/in/brendadempsey

www.linkedin.com/company/book-brilliance-publishing

Made in the USA
Middletown, DE
22 August 2024